...guin Books

...nadian Writing Today

CANADIAN
WRITING
TODAY

EDITED BY
MORDECAI RICHLER

PENGUIN BOOKS

Penguin Books Ltd, Harmondsworth,
Middlesex, England
Penguin Books Inc., 7110 Ambassador Road,
Baltimore, Maryland 21207, U.S.A.
Penguin Books Australia Ltd,
Ringwood, Victoria, Australia

First published 1970
Copyright © Mordecai Richler, 1970

Made and printed in Great Britain by
Hazell Watson & Viney Ltd
Aylesbury, Bucks
Set in Linotype Juliana

For Morley Callaghan

Contents

8 *Contents*

Acknowledgements

For permission to publish or reproduce the material in this anthology, acknowledgement is made to the following copyright holders:

for HUBERT AQUIN: an extract from *Prochain Épisode*, translated by Penny Williams, to McClelland & Stewart Ltd, Toronto, and to the author. (Originally published in French by Le Cercle du Livre de France, Montreal);

for MARGARET ATTWOOD: 'The Landlady' from *The Animals In That Country*, to Oxford University Press, Toronto, and for 'Journey to the Interior', to the author;

for EARLE BIRNEY: 'Way to the West', to the author;

for MARIE-CLAIRE BLAIS: an extract from *A Season in the Life of Emmanuel*, Copyright © 1966 by Marie-Claire Blais, translated by Derek Coltman. Reprinted by permission of Farrar, Straus & Giroux Inc., New York. (This first appeared in the *Tamarack Review*);

for GEORGE BOWERING: '30 Below', to the author. (This first appeared in the *London Magazine*);

for AUSTIN C. CLARKE: 'A Wedding in Toronto', to the author. (This first appeared in the *Tamarack Review*);

for LEONARD COHEN: 'All There Is To Know About Adolph Eichmann' from *Flowers for Hitler*, and 'Story' from *Let Us Compare Mythologies*, to McClelland & Stewart Ltd, Toronto;

for JOHN ROBERT COLOMBO: 'Recipe for a Canadian Novel' from *Abracadabra*, to McClelland & Stewart Ltd, Toronto;

for NEIL COMPTON: 'Broadcasting and Canadian Culture', to the author. (This first appeared in *Commentary*);

for RÉJEAN DUCHARME: an extract from *The Swallower Swallowed*, Copyright © 1966 by Éditions Gallimard, Paris; for this translation by Barbara Bray, Copyright © by Hamish Hamilton, to Hamish Hamilton Ltd, London, and to Atheneum Publishers, New York;

for NORTHROP FRYE: an extract from *Literary History of Canada*, to the University of Toronto Press, and to the author;

for ROBERT FULFORD: 'Galbraith in Dutton' from *Crisis at the Victory Burlesk*, to Oxford University Press, Toronto, and to the author;

for J. K. GALBRAITH: an extract from *The Scotch* (*Made to Last* or *The Non-Potable Scotch* – alternative titles), Copyright © 1964 by J. K. Galbraith, to Houghton Mifflin Company, Boston, and to Hamish Hamilton Ltd, London;

for MAVIS GALLANT: 'The Accident', to the author. (This first appeared in the *New Yorker*);

for ROLAND GIGUÈRE: 'Polar Seasons', translation from *F. R. Scott: Selected Poems*, to F. R. Scott;

for JOHN GLASSCO: 'An Evening Out' from *Memoirs of Montparnasse*, to Oxford University Press, Toronto, and to the author. (This first appeared in the *Tamarack Review*);

for JACQUES GODBOUT: an extract from *Knife on the Table*, to Éditions du Seuil, Paris; for this translation by Penny Williams to McClelland & Stewart Ltd, Toronto;

for ANNE HÉBERT: 'Manor Life', translation from *F. R. Scott: Selected Poems*, to F. R. Scott;

for GILLES HÉNAULT: 'The Prodigal Son', translated by F. R. Scott, to the translator;

for JOHN HERBERT: an extract from Act One of *Fortune and Men's Eyes*, Copyright © 1967 by John Herbert. Reprinted by permission of Grove Press Inc., New York, and of the author;

for DARYL HINE: 'The Wasp' from *The Devil's Picture Book*, to Abelard-Schuman Ltd, London;

for HUGH HOOD: 'Recollections of the Toronto Works Department' from *Flying a Red Kite*, to the Ryerson Press, Toronto;

for NAIM KATTAN: 'A Literature of Interrogation', translated by Joyce Marshall, to the author. (This first appeared in the *Tamarack Review*);

for WILLIAM KILBOURN: 'The Quest for the Peaceable Kingdom' from *The Making of a Nation*, to McClelland & Stewart Ltd, Toronto;

for MARGARET LAURENCE: an extract from A *Jest of God*, Copyright © 1966 by Margaret Laurence. Reprinted by permission of McClelland & Stewart Ltd, Toronto, Macmillan & Co. Ltd, London, Alfred A. Knopf Inc., New York, and of the author;

for IRVING LAYTON: 'The Modern Poet', 'Keine Lazarovitch: 1870–1959' and 'O Say Can You See' from *Collected Poems*, to McClelland & Stewart Ltd, Toronto, and to the author;

for NORMAN LEVINE: 'Ottawa Lower Town' and 'Slaughterhouse' from *Canada Made Me*, to the author;

for JACK LUDWIG: 'Einstein and This Admirer', to the *London Magazine*;

for CLAIRE MARTIN: extracts from *In an Iron Glove*, translated by Philip Stratford, to the Ryerson Press, Toronto. (Originally published in French by Le Cercle du Livre de France, Montreal);

for JOHN METCALF: 'Keys and Watercress', to the author. (This first appeared in the *Tamarack Review*);

for BRIAN MOORE: 'Preliminary Pages for a Work of Revenge', to the author. (This first appeared in *Midstream*);

for ALICE MUNRO: 'Walker Brothers Cowboy' from *Dance of the Happy Shades*, to the Ryerson Press, Toronto;

for JOHN NEWLOVE: 'Indian Women' from *Black Night Window*, to McClelland & Stewart Ltd, Toronto, and to the author;

for ALDEN NOWLAN: 'For Jean Vincent D'Abbadie, Baron St-Castin' from *Bread, Wine and Salt*, Copyright © 1967 by Clarke, Irwin and Company Ltd, and reprinted by their permission;

for JEAN-GUY PILON: 'The Stranger Hereabouts', translation from F. R. Scott: *Selected Poems*, to F. R. Scott;

for ALFRED PURDY: 'The North West Passage', 'Trees at the Arctic Circle' and 'Eskimo Hunter' from *North of Summer*, to McClelland & Stewart Ltd, Toronto;

for JAMES REANEY: 'The Katzenjammer Kids' from *The Red Heart*, to the author and to his literary agent;

for MORDECAI RICHLER: 'Dinner with Ormsby-Fletcher' from *St*

Urbain's Horseman, to the author. (This first appeared in *New American Review*);

for FRANKLIN RUSSELL: 'The Devil's Driveway' from *The Secret Islands*, to the author;

for HECTOR DE SAINT-DENYS-GARNEAU: 'Notes on Nationalism' from *The Journal of Saint-Denys-Garneau*, translated by John Glassco, to the translator;

for PIERRE ELLIOTT TRUDEAU: 'The Sorry Tale of French-Canadian Nationalism' from *Federalism and the French Canadians*, translated by Patricia Claxton, to The Macmillan Company of Canada Ltd, Toronto;

for WILLIAM WEINTRAUB: 'Fluxation and Slurrage', to the author. (This first appeared in *New American Review*);

for DAVID WEVILL: 'The Sounding' and 'Death of a Salesman' from *A Christ of the Ice-Floes*, to Macmillan & Co. Ltd, London, and The Macmillan Company of Canada Ltd;

for GEORGE WHALLEY: an extract from *The Legend of John Hornby*, to the author. (Published in Great Britain by John Murray Ltd, London, and in Canada by The Macmillan Company of Canada Ltd, Toronto); for an extract from *Hornby's Caribou Notes* to the Canadian Government, Department of Indian Affairs and Northern Development, Ottawa;

for ADÈLE WISEMAN: an extract from *Crackpot*, to the author;

for GEORGE WOODCOCK: 'The Novels of Callaghan' from *Lost Eurydice*, to the author.

Every effort has been made to trace copyright holders, but the publishers would be interested to hear from any copyright holders not here acknowledged.

Introduction

Canadians represent, as it were, the least militant North American minority group. The white, Protestant, heterosexual ghetto of the north. In spite of the emergence of Pierre Elliott Trudeau, we remain the English-speaking world's elected squares. To the British, we are the nicest, whitest Americans. To Americans, we symbolize a nostalgia for the unhurried horse and buggy age. In his youth, Edmund Wilson wrote in *O Canada*, he tended to imagine our country as a vast hunting preserve, and even in 1965 he got the impression, in Canada, of less worry and more leisure. 'It is possible, in English Canada,' he wrote, 'to have reasonable conversations in which people pretty well speak their minds – they listen, I noted, to one another instead of "shooting off their faces" in competition, as we are likely to do . . .'

Canada, remember, is a two-headed culture. The French is cocooned by language, the English isn't. We English-speaking, but not necessarily Anglo-Saxon, Canadians make up in touchiness what we lack in militancy. We have, mind you, reason to be touchy. From the beginning, Canada's two founding races, the English and the French, outdid each other in scornfully disinheriting us. A few arpents of snow, Voltaire wrote contemptuously of Canada in *Candide*; and Dr Johnson described the dominion as 'a region of desolate sterility . . . a cold, uncomfortable, uninviting region, from which nothing but furs and fish were to be had.'

Dr Johnson's insult was compounded by Samuel Butler who, after a visit in 1878, wrote A *Psalm of Montreal*.

> Stowed away in a Montreal lumber room
> The Discobolus standeth and turneth his face to the wall;
> Dusty, cob-covered, maimed and set at naught,
> Beauty crieth, and no man regardeth –
> O God! O Montreal!

> The Discobolus is put here because he is vulgar –
> He has neither vest nor pants to cover his limbs;
> I, Sir, am a person of most respectable connexions –
> My brother is haberdasher to Mr Spurgeon –
> O God ! O Montreal !

Since then Canadians have endured the disdain of Oscar Wilde, Wyndham Lewis, and even J. B. Priestley. In 1963, W. H. Auden wrote, 'The dominions . . . are for me *tiefste Provinz*, places which have produced no art and are inhabited by the kind of person with whom I have least in common.'

Whilst only yesterday General de Gaulle, stirring the nationalistic pot, flirted with Quebec, sending Malraux as an emissary ('France needs you,' Malraux told the sapient aldermen of the Montreal City Council. 'We will build the next civilization together.'), the truth is French intellectuals have not always been so enamoured of Quebec, a province which was largely pro-Vichy in sentiment during the war. When Gomez, the Spanish republican in Jean-Paul Sartre's novel, *Iron In The Soul*, finds himself in New York on the day that Paris has fallen, he sees only grins and indifference on Seventh Avenue. Then, on 55th Street, he spots a French restaurant, 'A La Petite Coquette', and enters, hoping to find solace. 'Paris has fallen,' Gomez says to the bartender, but he only gets a melancholy grunt for a reply. Gomez tries again, 'Afraid France is a goner.' Finally the barman says, 'France is going to learn what it costs to abandon her natural allies.' Gomez is confused until the barman adds, 'In the reign of Louis-the-Well-Beloved, sir, France had already committed every fault there is to commit.'

> 'Ah,' said Gomez, 'you're a Canadian.'
> 'I'm from Montreal,' said the barman.
> 'Are you now ?'

And Gomez goes off in search of a real Frenchman.

I do not subscribe, *pace* too many embittered Canadian small talents, to the wildly self-flattering theory that there is an anti-Canadian cultural cabal common to London and New York. What

I do believe is even more depressing. The sour truth is just about everybody outside of Canada finds us boring. Immensely boring.

American critics, with the notable exceptions of Edmund Wilson and Leslie Fiedler, have been consistently patronizing about Canadian writing. Wilson, who wrote the foreword to Marie-Claire Blais's novel, A *Season in the Life of Emmanuel* (an excerpt from which is included in this anthology), believes her to be a writer of genius, and he has written of Morley Callaghan that he is 'the most unjustly neglected novelist in the English-speaking world', possibly, he ventures, because of 'a general incapacity – apparently shared by his compatriots – for believing that a writer whose work may be mentioned without absurdity in association with Chekhov's and Turgenev's can possibly exist in our day in Toronto.' Leslie Fiedler is an impassioned admirer of Leonard Cohen's novel, *Beautiful Losers,* and his poetry. More typical, however, is the case of Dwight Macdonald, who was sent a batch of Canadian literary magazines a few years ago and wrote, 'They (are), in short, provincial – that is dependent on the capital city (London or New York), and yet insistent on a local autonomy which there aren't the resources to sustain.' Then, to repeat a favourite story of mine, there is the editor of a major New York publishing house who told me that one afternoon he and his associates compiled a list of twelve deserving but ineffably dull books with which to start a publishing firm that was bound to fail. Leading the list of unreadables was *Canada: Our Good Neighbour to the North.*

And yet – and yet – since then, a Toronto academic, Marshall McLuhan, whose early, richly Canadian *Counterblast* we were regrettably unable to use in this anthology, has become a ubiquitous American cultural presence. Another Canadian, John Kenneth Galbraith, is possibly the most distinguished intellectual survivor of the Kennedy administration.

Actually, when it comes to knocking the Canadian cultural scene, nobody outdoes Canadians, myself included. We are veritable masters of self-deprecation. 'I hate to say it,' Morley Callaghan once told a reporter, 'but there's really nobody in Canada I want to impress.' Jack Ludwig, another Canadian novelist, has written: 'Just how significant is it to *be* or *sound* Canadian anyway? ... If I choose to stand in a tradition why not the one to which Tolstoy and Flaubert and Dickens belong, rather than the one that includes Leacock, de la Roche, and Buchan?'

Robert Fulford, the editor of *Saturday Night*, feels that, whilst Dwight Macdonald was discussing a handful of intellectual journals, he did put his finger on the most serious problem of Canadian culture: we try to live beyond our means. Observing that we now even have a critical quarterly, *Canadian Literature*, exclusively devoted to Canadian literature, he writes it 'may find itself short of literature to criticize', and goes on to say that in Canada,

We have a kind of artistic autonomy, and we have a sort of cultural apparatus; but the people who make the apparatus work – the fiction writers, the playwrights, the other creative artists – are often hard to find. From this angle Canada looks like a giant tomato cannery: dozens of canning machines, hundreds of workmen trained to run them, scores of trucks waiting to transport the finished product – but no tomatoes.

A. M. Lower, the historian, mindful of intellectual immigration to the United States and England, has gone even further. He has written, 'It has tended to be the more able and especially the spontaneous . . . who have gone. . . . Canada has retained the withdrawn, the sedate and those with the least energy and ability.'

Among them, Northrop Frye, Marshall McLuhan, and Morley Callaghan, if I take only Toronto as an example.

Which is not to deny that many others have left. In fact it is a disheartening characteristic of this anthology that so many of the writers represented have opted out.

Marie-Claire Blais is in Wellfleet, Massachusetts; Jack Ludwig teaches at the State University of New York, Stonybrook, Long Island; and Frank Russell lives on a farm in New Jersey. Mavis Gallant, our most talented short-story writer since Callaghan, has made her home in Paris for more than ten years. Brian Moore, though still a Canadian citizen, divides his time between California and Europe. Margaret Laurence, David Wevill and Norman Levine live in England. Daryl Hine, a wanderer, can usually be found anywhere but in Canada.

The truth is Canadian writers, curious about their real worth rather than their national trading-stamp value, have traditionally packed their bags, sometimes defiantly, looking homeward only with scorn, which has hardly endeared them to those who, during difficult years, elected to stay home, fighting a lonely battle against bad taste and indifference, for a Canada Council, literate book pages, and a publishing industry with standards more than picayune.

The blistering quarrel between stay-at-home and expatriate remains an ugly one. In years past, young writers who found Canada too bland and parochial for their taste left because they were bored and there were no more than farm-club opportunities for them at home. Those who stayed behind, they argued, only did so because they preferred being big fish in a small pond. Well, yes, certainly fair comment on a number of second-rate writers who are world-famous in Canada, but never true of Gabrielle Roy, Ethel Wilson, Hugh MacLennan and others who, whatever their ultimate merit, stayed in Canada out of deeply-felt conviction. 'Toronto,' Morley Callaghan has said, 'is my village,' and today many young writers feel just as strongly about Vancouver, Montreal, or even St John's, New Brunswick. The pond is now not quite so small and happily young writers no longer feel so compelled to leave. Instead, they send their stories and poems to *Tamarack Review*, our most reputable literary quarterly. They publish their books of poetry on elegant non-commercial presses in Vancouver, Toronto, and Ottawa. The Very Stone House, the Coach House Press, the House of Anansi. The latter outfit, run by two young writers, Dave Godfrey and Denis Lee, is easily the most stimulating non-commercial press in the country. Not only experimental, intrepid, and encouraging to the young, but, even more singular, with something more ambitious than mere good-enough-for-Canada standards.

Twenty years ago, all this activity – some of it, admittedly, still more energetic than talented – would have been impossible.

When I was a student in Montreal during the late forties, we actually had a course on Canadian writing at Sir George Williams University : it was a standing joke among those of us who cared about literature. The do-it-yourself mimeographed text attempted no more than to list the author, dimensions, number of pages and photographs, if any, of every book, however innocuous, that had ever been published in Canada. At the time, as we began to read *Partisan Review, Horizon* and the *New Statesman,* one or perhaps two of us dared to say out loud in a tavern, 'I'm going to be a writer,' to which the immediate rejoinder was, 'What? You're going to be a *Canadian* writer?'

There were, in those days, several Canadian 'little magazines', but we would have considered it a stigma to have our stories or poems printed in any of them, just as the most damaging criticism you could make of another man's work was to say that Ryerson, still our leading and most uncritical purveyors of Canadiana, were publishing it in Toronto.

Our best-known writers – Stephen Leacock, Robertson Davies – were clearly within a British tradition. Hugh MacLennan, who self-consciously set himself to forging a Canadian literary tradition, was a special case. Gabrielle Roy, Roger Lemelin, Ethel Wilson, and Morley Callaghan especially, were the older writers we read not dutifully, but with honest pleasure.

Today, I believe, it is no longer necessary to apologize for being a Canadian writer. There are more than a fistful who can be read with honest pleasure and most of them, I hope, are included in this anthology.

Canadian culture has entered into an era at once embarrassingly grandiose, yet charged with promise. It all began twelve years ago with the founding of the Canada Council, whose annual budget has since grown to 21·5 million dollars. Now we can claim real achievement as well as blush at continuing provincial absurdities. Suddenly we have our very own honours list, a real, if over-productive publishing industry in Toronto, and an inflated market in Canadian MSS. We are also smitten with an overriding, unseemly hasty tendency to count and codify, issuing definitive anthologies of 100 years of poetry and prose and fat literary histories, as if by cataloguing we can make it real, by puffing, meaningful, especially if mere publication is taken as a licence to enshrine the most ephemeral stuff, as witness the following entry in *The Oxford Companion to Canadian History and Literature*:

BERESFORD-HOWE, CONSTANCE ELIZABETH (1922–), born in
Montreal ... she is the author of several historical romances. These include ... *My Lady Greensleeves* (1955), based on an Elizabethan divorce
case, in which she shows a sound command of historical detail.

What characterizes Canadian culture today is not so much
vitality and talent – though it is there at last, this anthology being
offered as evidence – as an astonishing affluence and beneficence.
Happily, an enlightened beneficence. But as the British health plan,
in its formative years, could be sniped at by reactionaries for handing out toupées to all comers, so our culture plan is vulnerable to
the charge of staking just about all the alienated kids to commit-
ting their inchoate, but modish, complaints to paper or canvas. On
the other hand, betting on fragile promise is a built-in hazard of
art investment and the people who run the Canada Council could
hardly be more decent and imaginative. It's a pity, then, that the
Council's first twelve years could come to be noted for one con-
spicuous omission. Morley Callaghan has yet to be presented with
its highest award, the Molson Prize.*
    Which brings me to our ludicrous, newly-minted honours sys-
tem, an innovation that must be seen as the last snobbish gasp of
our eldest generation, the unselective, slavish Anglophiles. Really,
in these austerity-minded days, it's time the Queen dismissed her
Canadian second-floor maid, the Governor-General, who is of course
Chancellor of the Order of the Companions of Canada, the rotary
club *ne plus autre*, which now entitles many a bore to write the
initials C.C. after his name, a measure hitherto accorded only to
bottles of medicine. I'm not bitten by an anti-royalty bug, but the
Governor-General in Canada, unlike the Queen in England, is not
part of the indigenous tradition, a tradition struggling to emerge,
but a divisive reminder of colonial dependence, justifiably resented
by the new militant French-Canadian writers, say Hubert Aquin,
Jean-Guy Pilon, and Jaques Godbout, all of whom are represented
in this anthology.
    Writing about the Canadian scene some years back, I spoke of

* Morley Callaghan was awarded this prize in 1970, after the Introduction
to this volume went to press – Ed.

being raised in a country where there were only isolated voices of civilization, here a poet, there a professor, and, between, thousands of miles of wheat and indifference. To be fair, among the first to be made Companions were at least three such cherished voices: Gabrielle Roy, Hugh MacLennan, and F. R. Scott. But once more Morley Callaghan was overlooked. And then insulted. For, on second thought it seems, he was asked to accept the also-ran Medal of Canada.

Meanwhile, lesser writers are blowing the dust off early manuscripts and digging old letters out of the attic, mindful of the burgeoning market in raw Canadiana. Book-length critical studies of just about everybody in the house are threatened, operas are being commissioned, ballet companies subsidized, and townships sorely in need of tolerable restaurants and bars are being paid to erect theatres instead. If Canada was once loosely stitched together by railroads, such is the force of today's culture boom that it may be reknit by art palaces coast-to-coast, though there hardly be plays or players, not to mention audiences, to fill them.

If once the arts in Canada were neglected, today, such is our longing, they are being rushed into shouldering a significance not yet justified by fulfilment, which brings me to the importance of Northrop Frye.

Non-Canadian readers familiar with Professor Frye's larger body of work are perhaps unaware of his special Canadian office. Among so many uncritical celebrators, he is our keeper of true standards. In his 'Conclusion' to the *Literary History of Canada*, he writes, had the evaluative view, based on the conception of criticism as concerned mainly to define and canonize the genuine classics of literature, been the History's guiding principle, 'this book, would, if written at all, have been only a huge debunking project.' There is no Canadian writer, he reminds us, 'of whom we can say what we can say of the world's major writers, that their readers grow up inside their work without ever being aware of a circumference,' yet he allows that the evidence shows 'that the Canadian imagination has passed the stage of exploration and has embarked on settlement' and concludes the writers featured in the *History* 'have identified the habits and attitudes of the country, as Fraser and MacKenzie have identified its rivers. They have also left an imaginative legacy of dignity and high courage.'

This anthology, then, is of writers embarking on settlement. It is not meant to be historical or definitive. It entertains no over-large claims unless it be considered such to say (and this is a real measure of recent Canadian literary achievement) that I believe it to be sufficiently fresh and talented to engage the interest not only of dutiful buyers of Canadiana but of a broader, more exacting, audience appreciative of good new writing whatever its origins.

Finally, a note about my method of selection. With some notable exceptions (say Frye, Birney, Saint-Denys-Garneau, George Woodcock), I have sought out the younger writers, those who have made their mark within the last ten, fifteen, years. Some of them, and this too is indicative of recent Canadian literary progress, are already well known abroad. Say Brian Moore, Mavis Gallant, Marie-Claire Blais, Leonard Cohen, Margaret Laurence, and of course Pierre Elliott Trudeau. Others will soon be better known. I have also, though this was never the crucial criterion, tried to select writers who would give a picture of Canada region by region, for we are still a fragmentary nation, yet to be bound by a unifying principle, a distinctive voice, a mythology of our own.

Many critics, professors, editors, and other writers have helped me with advice and suggestions whilst I was compiling this anthology. I am especially grateful to Robert Weaver, Naim Kattan, and Robert Fulford. The final selection, it goes without saying, is my own responsibility. Put plainly, this is an anthology of the Canadian writing I like.

MORDECAI RICHLER
December 1968

Neil Compton

BROADCASTING AND CANADIAN CULTURE

Montreal may be the best place in the world in which to watch television. With the aid of a community cable or rooftop antennae, Montrealers can tune in to the programmes not only of three Canadian networks (two English and one French), but also of three American ones from stations in northern New England. The two English Canadian networks frequently feature programmes from the B.B.C. or I.T.V. in Britain; less frequently, the French network uses material produced in France.

The viewer's choice extends from the usual quizzes, panel games, and situation comedies to bold experiments in documentary and drama. There are productions of Molière, Sheridan, and Shakespeare – and of Albee, Pinter, and Beckett. (Nothing lights up network switchboards with indignant calls like a good sordid modern play.) On the late show recently there have been opportunities to see such films as *Rashomon*, *Hiroshima Mon Amour*, and *L'Avventura*, all uninterrupted and unabridged.

However, the cacophonous and kaleidoscopic airwaves of Montreal are more than a viewer's paradise: they are also an epitome of the conflicts and confusions of the country as a whole. Canada owes its very existence as a sovereign state to the triumph of communications policy over geography, economics, and cultural diversity, yet the same electronic media which make Canada possible are presently adding to the strains and tensions which endanger the confederation.

Canada, of course, is a geographical absurdity – a country of nearly 4,000,000 square miles, where eighty per cent of the population lives within a strip 3,000 miles long and 150 miles wide along the American border. The strip is not even continuous; the regions of Canada are cut off from one another by formidable natural barriers such as the Great Lakes, the Laurentian Shield, and the Rocky Mountains. By contrast, much of the boundary with the United States is purely arbitrary and theoretical. Like the rivers that rise in Canada and flow down across the border, Canadians themselves move north and south more easily and frequently than they move east and west. Far more Canadians have visited the United States than have visited any province other than the one in which they live. Surveys have shown that Canadians in the various regions often share more attitudes with their immediate neighbours to the south than they do with their fellow countrymen in other regions.

National unity under such circumstances can be achieved only at a price. The railways, telegraphs, highways, airways, and waterways that keep traffic and information moving from east to west have been expensive to build and maintain; often they duplicate services that might have been more cheaply and conveniently available in the United States. Wages in Canada tend to be lower and the cost of consumer goods higher than they are in the United States. But Canadians have been willing to pay this price for the maintenance of political identity, and an expanding economy has helped to make the burden tolerable.

The combination of immense capital costs and comparatively low returns has meant that government rather than private initiative dominates the communications field : through the characteristically Canadian institution of the crown corporation, the federal government owns a railway system, a major airline, a telecommunications organization, the Polymer Corporation, the National Film Board (which is now engaged in the production of full-length feature films as well as documentaries), and the Canadian Broadcasting Corporation. One of the best things about Canadian public life is the imagination and efficiency with which these enterprises have been run.

At this moment, cultural diversity is probably a greater problem to Canada than either geography or economics. If we apply to the Canadian population Karl Deutsch's definition of a 'people' which stresses 'complementary habits and facilities of communication' (including shared language, memories, customs, preferences, libraries, statues, signposts, and the like) we find English and French

Canadians lacking in many of the necessary common characteristics. The difference is more than a matter of mere language: as Deutsch says, the Swiss, with their four languages, are one people. The Canadians, with two, are not. Not quite, and not yet.

The French Canadians (they number about a third of the population) are descended from 60,000 original *habitants* whose roots in France were cut off by the Conquest of 1759. Their involvement with English-speaking Canadians has been less a matter of choice than of necessity. Though French communities may be found scattered from the Atlantic to the Pacific, the St Lawrence river valley is in the fullest sense the heartland of French Canada. The feeling of inwardness, of a shared (and tragic) history, of loyalty to a common faith and a geographical *patrie* or homeland is very strong among French Canadians. It has enabled them to maintain their unique identity in the face of the most formidable social and economic challenges.

In contrast to the fierce historicism of French-Canadian society, the English-speaking majority seems to lack any roots in the past. Though there is an epic quality to the early history of English Canada (matching the heroic tragedy of the French), somehow the links which connect this period with the present seem to have been severed, and few English Canadians feel much emotional identification with the explorers, fur traders, and administrators whose courage and imagination helped to open up the northern half of this continent. Canadian history has tended to have an unaccountable reputation for dullness among high-school students. This may be in part because so many of the early heroes were, and thought themselves, Englishmen or Scotsmen rather than Canadians. In fact, Canadian history, unlike American, has been largely made by outsiders: Canadians have no self-defining Declaration of Independence or Revolutionary War; they have not fought a civil conflict in defence of their national identity. The very constitution which gave them independence was an act, not of any Canadian body, but of the British Parliament.

The ancestors of most English-speaking Canadians emigrated to Canada fairly recently. They came at different times, from different places, and for different reasons. Their descendants' loyalty is not directed to one religion, one locality, or one set of values. For them, Canada is no warm, tight *patrie* to be loved or hated, but almost the reverse – an emptiness so vast that the image of the humans who live in it becomes dwarfed and blurred. Their myths tend to be geographical rather than social; the national motto is not *e pluribus unum* or even *e duobus unum*, but *a mari usque ad mare* (from sea to sea); visionary politicians wax eloquent not over 'the Canadian way of life' but over the untapped natural resources of the northern hinterland; until recently the bleakly and inhumanly beautiful landscape of the Laurentian Shield dominated both poetry and painting in English Canada. Hugh Kenner, the waspish expatriate who wrote scornfully of a 'pathological craving for identification with the subhuman', was being only slightly unfair.

The combination of French-Canadian introspection and English-Canadian ambiguity might seem enough to daunt even the most wildly optimistic planners of a bilingual northern Utopia, but the past few generations have added a further obstacle to the realization of the Canadian dream: the border offers no defence against the overflow of American popular culture. Far more Canadians regularly read American magazines than Canadian ones; of ninety-six periodicals that sell over 100,000 copies a month in Canada, ninety-two are American. Nearly forty per cent of the Canadian population lives close enough to a U.S. television station to enjoy good reception, and, even on Canadian stations, American programmes dominate the air during prime viewing hours. On commercial radio the American hit parade is as endemic as it is in the United States.

Canadian newspapers are local enough in character, but a high proportion of their foreign news comes from such American agencies as the Associated Press and United Press International. Ann Landers, Peanuts, and Walter Lippmann are as ubiquitous in Canada as across the border. In fact, apart from the wire service of the Canadian Press, virtually all nationally syndicated newspaper features originate in the United States.

No wonder Canadian nationalism (as distinct from local patriotism) tends to be 'cool'. The French feel no enthusiasm for a federal entity dominated by *les anglais*, and the English, through long exposure to American media, are likely to know as much, or more, about American history and politics as they do about their own. This marginality is a fundamental fact about Canadian society. A few years ago, nearly one in three Canadians felt so little identification with the political establishment that he said he was ready to scrap it: a survey conducted by *MacLean's* magazine in 1963 revealed that twenty-nine per cent of the population, French and English, favoured political union with the United States; sixty-five per cent were ready to contemplate economic union. The euphoria of Centennial Year and EXPO 67 probably fanned the flames of English-Canadian patriotism (at least temporarily) but, as the de Gaulle episode demonstrated, many *Québecois* think 1967 marks the anniversary of *cent ans d'injustice*.

Those who, for whatever reason, wish to resist the tendencies I have been describing must solve the problem of assisting Canadian media to flourish in competition with their wealthy and entrenched American rivals. How to do this without alienating votes or interfering with the free flow of ideas has baffled every Canadian government since the 1920s. No solution has ever been found which commands universal support in press and parliament: debates on broadcasting or publishing policy are invariably hot and ill-tempered.

For this reason, the publicly owned Canadian Broadcasting Corporation has been for over thirty years the most embattled of all federal agencies. The C.B.C. was founded in 1936 to provide a national and predominantly Canadian broadcasting service to as high a percentage of the population as was technically possible – an aim beyond the resources and outside the purpose of a private commercial system. Today the Corporation owns and operates six separate radio or television network services in two different languages. Ninety-eight per cent of the population, from the Atlantic to the Pacific, and from the forty-ninth parallel to above the Arctic Circle, lives within range of its radio service. The English television network uses the longest microwave relay system in the world to link St John's, Newfoundland, to Victoria, British Columbia, 4,000 miles and six time zones away. The C.B.C.'s Montreal studios are said to be the world's largest centre for the production of French-language T.V. programmes, while Toronto is beginning to rival

New York as the second city of North American English television. The C.B.C.'s annual budget amounted last year to nearly 150,000,000 dollars, of which under a third came from advertising and the remainder from public funds.

These operations are carried out on behalf of a total audience not much larger than that of the New York viewing area, scattered over a territory thirty times larger than Great Britain, and in the face of strong competition for audiences and sponsors from private commercial stations whose total annual income far exceeds that of the C.B.C.

The Canadian Broadcasting Corporation's mandate from Parliament involves four objectives which are set out in the preamble to the Broadcasting Act (1968):

1. It should offer a balanced fare of information, enlightenment and entertainment for people of all types and with all interests.
2. Its services should be extended to all parts of Canada.
3. It should broadcast in both French and English, and meet the special needs of the various geographical regions.
4. It should 'contribute to the development of national unity and provide for a continuing expression of Canadian identity.'

Three of these four are explicitly concerned with creating a sense of Canadian identity, and the fourth (the provision of a balanced service) is really a means to achieve the others. Evidently the C.B.C. is intended by the federal government to be an instrument for the forging and maintenance of a distinctive bilingual Canadian nationalism. So far as I know, no other broadcasting system in the Western world conceives of its function in quite these terms. The American networks certainly do not have any comparable ambition, and the various European agencies are the expressions of long-established national cultures. The closest parallel of which I am aware is the Australian Broadcasting Corporation, but the A.B.C. has neither to cope with two languages nor to compete with the combined blandishments of three wealthy American networks. (It is also supported entirely by public funds.)

Can a medium of mass communication in a free society really accomplish such a purpose? The Premier of Quebec, Daniel Johnson, has gone so far as to identify the C.B.C.'s concern for unity with fascism. There have always been attacks on the Corporation for its allegedly impractical, Utopian, and paternalistic policy. Critics usually claim to speak on behalf of the great majority of Canadians (though cynics might suspect them of representing more limited interests). However, the evidence is overwhelming that Canadians in general approve of the Corporation's objectives. In 1963, the C.B.C. commissioned an elaborate survey of 'what the Canadian public thinks of the C.B.C.'. It showed that well over ninety per cent of the population approves even the most high-minded statements of C.B.C. purpose, and that slightly smaller majorities think the Corporation fulfils these aims very well (the one exception being 'helping French and English Canadians to understand and learn about each other'; only fifty-seven per cent thought the C.B.C. did well here).

However, even the most starry-eyed C.B.C. executive knows that programme policy cannot be based on the expectations aroused by such a survey. The commercial rating systems may be very crude indicators of the real involvement between viewers and their T.V. sets, but they are accurate enough to indicate a depressing contrast between what viewers say and what they do. Most of us, whatever may be our theories about the immense potentialities of broadcasting, turn to television (as others turn to detective stories or science fiction) primarily for relaxation and amusement. Any realistic daily programme schedule must contain a very high proportion of light entertainment, and this necessity involves the C.B.C. in some extraordinary compromises with its own principles.

The bitter fact is that most Canadians have formed their taste in entertainment from the most popular American network shows. The only Canadian productions which attract an equal or greater audience are televised games of the National Hockey or Canadian Football Leagues. In order to hold on to its audience and prevent them from switching to rival channels, the C.B.C. must devote most of its time during prime viewing hours to American programmes. This great instrument of Canadian culture cannot plan its winter schedule until after the United States networks have announced theirs. Thanks to the C.B.C., the Canadian Sunday evening is dominated not by home-produced shows but by Walt Disney, *Green Acres*, Ed Sullivan and *Bonanza*. Of the four hours between six and ten p.m., only one half-hour is devoted to a Canadian production – a panel quiz show.

One does not have to subscribe to any exaggerated theory about the influence of the media to see that such a state of affairs can lead only to the slow Americanization of the Canadian audience. Opinions may differ as to the desirability of that development, but official Canada must view the tendency with concern and horror. The Board of Broadcast Governors, which regulated all broadcasting in Canada until 1968, decreed that television stations must maintain an average fifty-five per cent Canadian content in their programmed schedules. This ruling was ill-conceived: it made no distinction between, say, the *Beverly Hillbillies* and a programme like *Camera Three*; it raised the prospect of bad cheap Canadian programmes driving viewers to American channels; and the definition of Canadian content was so hedged with qualifications that the World Series and President Johnson's acceptance speech were considered Canadian, on the grounds of strong viewer interest. Even at best, as Alan Thomas, a shrewd and witty critic suggested, the ruling could lead to no more than a fifty-five per cent Canadian audience.

The only adequate answer to the challenge of American influence would be the development of a genuine indigenous Canadian popular art. There is, however, no successful Canadian equivalent to such classic American T.V. genres as the Western or the family situation comedy. Whatever may be their artistic limitations, such dramatic stereotypes enshrine profound (if sometimes inaccurate) popular intuitions about American life. For better or for worse, Canada seems to be a land without comparable myths of its own.

The C.B.C. has done its best to supply the lack, but with mixed success. An attempt to wean Canadian children away from such second-hand heroes as cowboys and Davy Crockett with a million-dollar series on the life of the explorer and adventurer Pierre Radisson was one of the most disastrous projects ever undertaken by the Corporation. Even the Mounties have been more successfully exploited in the American media than they have been at home. A

C.B.C. dramatic series about a Royal Canadian Mounted Police detachment was less painfully inadequate than *Radisson*, but failed to generate the mythic intensity of a second-rate Western. Two recent series – *Seaway* (a bad one about adventures up and down the St Lawrence Seaway) and *Wojeck* (a good one based on the lifestyle of a famous crusading Toronto coroner) – were so obviously (though unsuccessfully) designed for eventual sale to American networks that the action often seemed to be taking place in some mythical, undifferentiated North American republic. Clearly, even television has not yet succeeded in triumphing over wilderness, distance and climate to create an indigenous Canadian popular art. Not in English, at any rate.

On the French T.V. network, though, things are so very different that when Montrealers switch from Channel 6 to Canal 2, they seem to be transported to a different city. Radio Canada has all the energy, imaginative vitality, and rapport with its audience that English-speaking producers long for. The French-Canadian community might have been especially designed to support a popular television service: it is homogenous, large enough to provide a variety of audiences but not so large as to be formless, and it is protected from undue outside influence by the language barrier. Of the large number of popular artists to achieve fame on Radio Canada during the past ten years, perhaps the most impressive are an indigenous school of *chansonniers* – particularly Gilles Vigneault, Pauline Julien and Monique Leyrac who have won international followings. Since the French T.V. network began operation, French Canada has ceased to be frightened by the bogy of assimilation – which kept her for generations in a state of defensive isolation from the world – and has begun to take an ebullient and aggressive delight in her own unique identity. It is impossible to doubt that television has played a vital part in stimulating this renaissance.

Thus the C.B.C.'s attempt to serve Canada's two cultures equitably succeeds, insofar as it does, at the expense of national unity. The more effectively it serves either community, the more it will reinforce those characteristics which set them apart from one another. Naturally, the Corporation is aware of this paradox and has tried to resolve it. There have been a number of rather self-conscious and embarrassed bilingual variety shows which served to dramatize rather than bridge the gulf. Dozens of programmes on all four networks have undertaken the task of explaining the French and the English to one another. It is doubtful whether these have been very successful in influencing the mass of the population. There are, after all, many pitfalls in the way of mass communication. Even apart from the general tendency of the media to focus on and dramatize the conflict and violence in any situation, one is reminded of the experiment recently carried out by the B.B.C.: a radio programme of advice on travelling in France ended by discouraging more potential tourists than it encouraged because more listeners were frightened by the prospect of problems they had not expected (language, currency, etc.) than were reassured by the helpful hints. The Canadian confederation has rested for years on certain convenient mutual misunderstandings between English and French Canadians. Now that the new media are ensuring that they understand one another only too well, discord rather than harmony is the initial consequence.

For all this, however, the C.B.C. is one of the great forces for reason and civilization in Canada. Once we grant the fact that a native popular culture does not and probably cannot exist in English Canada, we are free to recognize that C.B.C. programme policy has been about as liberal and imaginative as one could reasonably expect. If the achievement seems at first glance less impressive than that of (say) the B.B.C., allowances must be made for the vast differences between the geographical, cultural and political circumstances of the two great organizations. In particular, the B.B.C. has had the advantage of serving a huge concentrated homogenous audience, with no need to depend upon either government grants or commercial revenue, or (during its crucial early years) to compete with either or both domestic or foreign rivals.

The new media have often been accused of battening parasitically upon the creative energy of real art, vulgarizing its themes, and seducing its practitioners with fame and money. This may be so in societies with a deeply rooted traditional culture, but it has not been so in Canada. With its small, dispersed population and puritan, philistine outlook, English Canada in particular had virtually no serious professional tradition of music or theatre at the time that the C.B.C. was established. Now, half a dozen cities have cadres of actors, musicians, and dancers who are able to earn a tolerable living by combining live performance with appearances on radio or T.V. The Corporation's budget for serious programming in the field of the arts may be small in relation to the whole, but it is enough to insure that composers, playwrights – even poets – can hope for at least occasional commissions which involve few or no concessions to popular taste, and sometimes not even to the medium.

It is usually on radio that such minority intellectual and artistic interests are now catered to. Almost deserted by commercial sponsors and banished from the living-room by the family T.V., C.B.C. network radio has become a kind of middle-brow Canadian magazine, at its best the electronic equivalent of the *Atlantic Monthly* or the *Saturday Review*. As one might deduce from its middle-class ambience, it was for years the most eloquent and influential instrument of enlightened nationalism in Canada. Recently, a sudden boom in book publishing and a greatly increased scale of cultural grants by the Canada Council have made the radio service less centrally important than it once was.

Canada's marginal culture – occupying a middle ground between British and American, English and French, civilization and wilderness – appears to favour the interpretative and critical, rather than the fiercely creative, intelligence. Life in Canada inculcates a respect for the brutal, objective thusness of nature and an awareness (sometimes a wry one) of the validity of opposition to it. The success of EXPO 67 was due less to the originality of individual buildings or exhibits than to the way in which an almost chaotic variety of forms was orchestrated by a brilliant team of planners and coordinators into a harmonious whole.

This is the ideal temperament for documentary, and the greatest triumphs of Canadian broadcasting, as of Canadian cinema, have been in this field. The C.B.C.'s audience has become accustomed to workmanlike documentary programmes (many of them produced by the National Film Board) as part of the regular weekly diet on both radio and television. Occasionally, these soberly factual productions come close to the heights of poetry and truth : among the most interesting have been *One More River*, a painfully vivid study of the Negro civil rights movement, and *Warrendale*, an example of *cinéma verité* in which long-distance microphones and hand-held cameras give so intimate and painful a glimpse of life in a home for disturbed children that the C.B.C. did not dare to broadcast it, releasing the film instead for cinema exhibition. During the 1967–8 season, three full-length features – *Notes for a Film about Donna and Gail* and *The Ernie Game*, by Don Owen; and *Waiting for Caroline* by Ron Kelly – applied similar techniques to fictional themes.

Recently, the documentary spirit has been tending toward irony, another mode encouraged by Canada's comparatively helpless proximity to stronger or wealthier neighbours. The basic technique is simple – to juxtapose pictures and commentary (often by the subject himself) in order to achieve almost Swiftian satiric intensities. Recent little masterpieces have included *Lonely Boy*, about the Canadian pop singer Paul Anka; *The Image Makers*, about the public relations industry; and *Lorne Greene's Bonanza*, about the one-time C.B.C. announcer and Stratford Festival actor who has struck it rich as Ben Cartright. But the *chef d'œuvre* of this genre so far is undoubtedly *One Time Around*, in which Hugh Hefner expounds the Playboy's philosophy against a shifting background of playmates, bunnies, and penthouse parties.

Irony and parody are also the mode of the T.V. comedians Wayne and Shuster. Their relentless spoofing of every sacred or profane cow – from biculturalism and the Stratford Festival to cool jazz and teenage fashions – is more obvious and less sophisticated than the documentary tradition I have described, but it probably comes closer to the expression of a native popular art than anything else on the C.B.C. English network. The conclusion seems to be that though Canadians may lack a strong sense of their own identity, they do not allow this to inhibit them in deflating fraud or pomposity, whether it be native or foreign. In developing this genre, the C.B.C. may, like Holden Caulfield, have found its own unique way of confronting the modern world.

John Robert Colombo

RECIPE FOR A CANADIAN NOVEL

after Cyprian Norwid

Ingredients : one Indian,
one Mountie, one Eskimo,
one Doukhobor.

Add : one small-town whore,
two thousand miles of wheat,
one farmer impotent and bent.

His fair-haired daughter too,
then a Laurentian mountain
and a Montreal Jew.

Include also, a young boy
with a dying pet,
and a mortgage unmet.

Should this sour, sweeten
with maple syrup –
French-Canadian even,

but dilute, if foreign
to the taste.
Stir, until beaten.

Drop in exotic and tangy
place names – Toronto,
Saskatoon, Hudson Bay.

For distinctive flavour :
garnish with maple leaves.
Mix, then leave.

Dice in one Confederation poet
complete with verse
(remove mould first).

To prepare the sauce:
paragraphs of bad prose
that never seem to stop.

Bring to a simmer,
but avoid a boil.
Pour, place in oven, bake.

Slice or leave whole.
Serves twenty million all told –
when cold.

Pierre Elliott Trudeau

THE SORRY TALE OF
FRENCH-CANADIAN NATIONALISM

We have expended a great deal of time and energy proclaiming the rights due our nationality, invoking our divine mission, trumpeting our virtues, bewailing our misfortunes, denouncing our enemies, and avowing our independence; and for all that not one of our workmen is the more skilled, nor a civil servant the more efficient, a financier the richer, a doctor the more advanced, a bishop the more learned, nor a single solitary politician the less ignorant. Now, except for a few stubborn eccentrics, there is probably not one French-Canadian intellectual who has not spent at least four hours a week over the last year discussing separatism. That makes how many thousand times two hundred hours spent just flapping our arms? And can any one of them honestly say he has heard a single argument not already expounded *ad nauseam* twenty, forty, and even sixty years ago? I am not even sure we have exorcized any of our original bogy men in sixty years. The Separatists of 1962 that I have met really are, in general, genuinely earnest and nice people; but the few times I have had the opportunity of talking with them at any length, I have almost always been astounded by the totalitarian outlook of some, the anti-Semitism of others, and the complete ignorance of basic economics of all of them.

This is what I call *la nouvelle trahison des clercs*: this self-deluding passion of a large segment of our thinking population for throwing themselves headlong – intellectually and spiritually – into purely escapist pursuits.

Several years ago I tried to show that the devotees of the nationalist school of thought among French Canadians, despite their good intentions and courage, were for all practical purposes trying to swim upstream against the course of progress. Over more than half a century 'they have laid down a pattern of social thinking impossible to realize and which, from all practical points of view, has left the people without any effective intellectual direction.'*

I have discovered that several people who thought as I did at that time are today talking separatism. Because their social thinking is to the left, because they are campaigning for secular schools, because they may be active in trade union movements, because they are open-minded culturally, they think that their nationalism is the path to progress. What they fail to see is that they have become reactionary *politically*.

Reactionary, in the first place, by reason of circumstances. A count, even a rough one, of institutions, organizations and individuals dedicated to nationalism, from the village notary to the Ordre de Jacques Cartier, from the small businessman to the Ligues du Sacré-Cœur, would show beyond question that an alliance between nationalists of the right and of the left would work in favour of the former, by sheer weight of numbers. And when the leftists say they will not make such an alliance until it is they who are in the majority, I venture to suggest once again† that they will never be so as long as they continue to waste their meagre resources as they do now. Any effort aimed at strengthening the nation must avoid dividing it; otherwise such an effort loses all effectiveness so far as social reform is concerned, and for that matter can only lead to consolidation of the *status quo*. In this sense the alliance is already working against the left, even before being concluded.

In the second place, the nationalists – even those of the left – are politically reactionary because, in attaching such importance to the idea of nation, they are surely led to a definition of the common good as a function of an ethnic group, rather than of all the people, regardless of characteristics. This is why a nationalistic government is by nature intolerant, discriminatory, and, when all is said and done, totalitarian.‡ A truly democratic government cannot be

* *La Grève de l'amiante*, p. 140.

† I have already tried to point out the strategic inanity of the nationalists of the left, in *Cité Libre*, March 1961, p. 4.

‡ As early as 1862, Lord Acton was already writing thus: 'The nation is here an ideal unit founded on the race. . . . It overrules the rights and wishes of the inhabitants, absorbing their divergent interests in a fictitious unity; sacrifices their several inclinations and duties to the higher claim of nation-

'nationalist', because it must pursue the good of all its citizens, without prejudice to ethnic origin. The democratic government, then, stands for and encourages good citizenship, never nationalism. Certainly, such a government will make laws by which ethnic groups will benefit, and the majority group will benefit proportionately to its number; but that follows naturally from the principle of equality for all, not from any right due the strongest. In this sense one may well say that educational policy in Quebec has always been democratic rather than nationalistic; I would not say the same for all the other provinces. If, on the other hand, Hydro-Quebec were to expropriate the province's hydro-electric industries for nationalistic rather than economic reasons, we would already be on the road to fascism. The right can nationalize; it is the left that socializes and controls for the common good.

In the third place, any thinking that calls for full sovereign powers for the nation is politically reactionary because it would put complete and perfect power in the hands of a community which is incapable of realizing a complete and perfect society. In 1962 it is unlikely that any nation-state – or for that matter any multinational state either – however strong, could realize a complete and perfect society;* economic, military, and cultural interdependence is a *sine qua non* for states of the twentieth century, to the extent that none is really self-sufficient. Treaties, trade alliances, common markets, free trade areas, cultural and scientific agreements, all these are as indispensable for the world's states as is interchange between citizens within them; and just as each citizen must recognize the submission of his own sovereignty to the laws of the state – by which, for example, he must fulfil the contracts he makes – so the states will know no real peace and prosperity until they accept the submission of their relations with each other to a higher order. In truth, the very concept of sovereignty must be surmounted, and

---

ality, and crushes all natural rights and all established liberties for the purpose of vindicating itself. Whenever a single definite object is made the supreme end of the State – the State becomes for the time being inevitably absolute.' John Dalberg-Acton, *Essays on Freedom and Power* (Glencoe, 1948), p. 184.

* See Jacques Maritain, *Man and the State* (Chicago, 1951), p. 210.

those who proclaim it for the nation of French Canada are not only reactionary, they are preposterous. French Canadians could no more constitute a perfect society than could the five million Sikhs of the Punjab. We are not well enough educated, nor rich enough, nor, above all, numerous enough to man and finance a government possessing all the necessary means for both war and peace. The fixed per-capita cost would ruin us. But I shall not try to explain all this to people who feel something other than dismay at seeing *La Laurentie* already opening embassies in various parts of the world, 'for the diffusion of our culture abroad'. Particularly when these same people, a year ago, seemed to be arguing that we were too poor to finance a second university – a Jesuit one – in Montreal.

In answer to this third contention, that sovereignty is unwork- able and contradictory, the Separatists will sometimes argue that once independent, Quebec could very well afford to give up part of her sovereignty on, for instance, re-entering a Canadian Confedera- tion, because then her choice would be her own, a free one. That abstraction covers a multitude of sins! It is a serious thing to ask French Canadians to embark on several decades of privation and sacrifice, just so that they can indulge themselves in the luxury of choosing 'freely' a destiny more or less identical to the one they have rejected. But the ultimate tragedy would be in not realizing that French Canada is too culturally anaemic, too economically destitute, too intellectually retarded, too spiritually paralysed, to be able to survive more than a couple of decades of stagnation, emptying herself of all her vitality into nothing but a cesspit, the mirror of her nationalistic vanity and 'dignity'.

Translated by Patricia Claxton

Anne Hébert

MANOR LIFE

Here is an ancestral manor
Without a table or fire
Or dust or carpets.

The perverse enchantment of these rooms
Lies wholly in their polished mirrors.

The only possible thing to do here
Is to look at oneself in the mirror day and night.

Cast your image into these brittle fountains
Your brittler image without shadow or colour.

See, these mirrors are deep
Like cupboards
There is always someone dead behind the quicksilver
Who soon covers your reflection
And clings to you like seaweed

Shapes himself to you, naked and thin,
And imitates love in a long bitter shiver.

Translated by F. R. Scott

James Reaney

THE KATZENJAMMER KIDS

With porcupine locks
And faces which, when
More closely examined,
Are composed of measle-pink specks,
These two dwarf imps,
The Katzenjammer Kids,
Flitter through their Desert Island world.
Sometimes they get so out of hand
That a blue Captain
With stiff whiskers of black wicker
And an orange Inspector
With a black telescope
Pursue them to spank them
All through that land
Where cannibals cut out of brown paper
In cardboard jungles feast and caper,
Where the sea's sharp waves continually
Waver against the shore faithfully
And the yellow sun above is thin and flat
With a collar of black spikes and spines
To tell the innocent childish heart that
It shines
And warms (see where she stands and stammers)
The dear fat mother of the Katzenjammers.
Oh, for years and years she has stood
At the window and kept fairly good
Guard over the fat pies that she bakes
For her two children, those dancing heartaches.
Oh, the blue skies of that funny-paper weather !
The distant birds like two eyebrows close together !

And the rustling paper roar
Of the waves
Against the paper sands of the paper shore !

William Kilbourn

THE QUEST FOR THE PEACEABLE KINGDOM

Canada is a different kind of American society, a North American alternative to the United States. Everywhere in the twentieth century man is becoming American, or to put it another way, is moving in some way towards a condition of high industrialization, affluence and leisure, instant communication, an urban man-made environment, and a mingling of cultures and traditions in a mobile, classless, global society. There is no country in the world, except the United States, which has gone farther in this direction than Canada; none that has done so in such an American way; or any that is so experienced in the art of living with, emulating and differing from the United States. If Canadians (and perhaps others) wish to explore the real freedoms open to them in such a society and to escape the blandness and boredom, the sameness and despair latent in such a brave new world, they could usefully examine the subtle but profound ways in which Canada differs from the United States.

For some purposes there are other countries with which Canada can be more profitably compared. Brazil and Australia are both, like Canada, middle power federations whose vast lands were taken from primitive peoples and partly settled and developed by Europeans. But the contrasts are also great. The tropical jungle or desert of the southern hemisphere, the white immigration policy and British racial stock of Australia, the huge Indian population, terrible poverty and wide class differences of Brazil, sets each of them apart from Canada, which in these respects is thoroughly American. Explorers of identity had best compare Canada with the United States.

When William Van Horne gave up his American citizenship after completing the C.P.R., he remarked, 'Building that railroad would have made a Canadian out of the German Emperor.' The inexorable land, like the Canadian climate, has always commanded the respect of those who have tried to master it. It is simply overwhelming. The voyager from Europe is not suddenly confronted by the rational outlines of a colossal liberty goddess; he is slowly swallowed, Jonah-like, by a twenty-two-hundred-mile-long river gulf and lake system. Coming in by air, he finds himself, scarcely past Ireland, flying above the shining blue-set islands of Bonavista-Twillingate, hours before he touches down in Toronto or Montreal. Further inland, islands come by the Thousand – or the Thirty Thousand; there are more lakes than people, and more forests than lakes. Except in small pastoral slices of southern Ontario and Quebec, the original wilderness of bush or prairie presses close to the suburban edge of every Canadian town. Even Toronto surprised a recent British visitor who called it 'a million people living in a forest'. In summer the boreal lights, a shaking skyful of LSD visions, can remind the most urban of Canadians that they are a northern people, that winter will bring again its hundred-degree drop in the weather, and that their wilderness stretches straight to the permafrost, the ice pack and the pole.

Nature dreadful and infinite has inhibited the growth of the higher amenities in Canada. The living has never been easy. The need to wrestle a livelihood from a cruel land has put a premium on some of the sterner virtues – frugality and caution, discipline and endurance. Geography even more than religion has made us puritans, although ours is a puritanism tempered by orgy. Outnumbered by the trees and unable to lick them, a lot of Canadians look as though they had joined them – having gone all faceless or a bit pulp-and-papery, and mournful as the evening jack-pine round the edges of the voice, as if (in Priestley's phrase) something long lost and dear were being endlessly regretted. Or there are those who run – by car, train or plane (flying more air miles per capita than any other people), lickety-split as if the spirit of the northern woods, the *Wendigo* himself, were on their trails. Nature has not always been an enemy, but she has rarely been something to be tamed either. At best we have exploited her quickly and moved on. No wonder the atmosphere of our towns still often suggests that of the mining camp or the logging drive, the trading post or the sleeping compound. If transportation has been crucial for Canada, and our main-street towns attest the worship of train and motor car, then communications (more telephone calls than anybody else), particularly radio and television (the world's longest networks), have been vital. It is no surprise when some of old Rawhide's Canadian characters become so addicted to the telegraph key that they can only talk in the dah-dah-dits of Morse code.

Survival itself is a virtue and a triumph. Images of survival abound in our popular mythologies: whooping cranes and Hutterites, dwarf ponies on the Sable Island sand dunes, the Eskimo in their howling prison of ice and snow. Ask the Nova Scotian or the French Canadian what he has done in this country of his these two or three centuries and more. 'I survived,' is the answer – though neither of them is satisfied with mere survival any longer.

But Canadians have also learned to live with nature and derive strength from her. It is not just the Group of Seven who came to terms with her terrible grandeur. From the first military surveyors and the C.P.R. artists down to the abstract expressionists of postmodern Toronto, our painters have been profoundly influenced by the Canadian landscape. 'Everything that is central in Canadian writing,' said our great critic, Northrop Frye, 'seems to be marked by the immanence of the natural world.' The American critic Edmund Wilson sees the most distinguishing feature of Hugh MacLennan's work to be the unique way the author places his characters in 'their geographical and even their meteorological setting'. Our historians do not argue about the amount but the kind of influence geography has had on our history – whether it has been the north–south pull of North American regionalism or the east–west thrust of the St Lawrence and Saskatchewan river systems and the Laurentian Shield. The fur trade of the Pre-Cambrian forest was not only crucial to Canada's economic life for two centuries, but by 1867 it had literally determined the basic outlines of our political boundaries.

Precisely because life has been so bleak and minimal for so long in so much of Canada, the frontiers, far more than in the United States, have been dependent on the metropolitan centres of Toronto and Montreal and Europe. A visitor to pioneer Saskatchewan in

1907 remarked at the strange sight of a sod hut with a big Canadian Bank of Commerce sign on it, open for business. The essence of the Canadian west is in that image. Organized society usually arrived with the settlers or ahead of them – not only the branch bank manager, but the mounted policeman and the railway agents, the priest and the Hudson's Bay factor. Dawson City at the height of the gold rush had its sins and shortcomings, but even here lawlessness was not one of them. Violence and terror do not yet stalk the subways or the streets of darkest Toronto. The posse and the desperado belong to the American wild west, the citizen vigilante to the American metropolis.

Among peoples as different as the Métis and the Doukhobors, the community and its custom was the dominating force in western settlement. Even the most self-reliant Protestant pioneer in Canada West or Alberta was never quite a Davy Crockett or a Daniel Boone. From the founding of the Hudson's Bay Company in 1670 to that of the C.P.R. and the dozens of modern crown corporations, the large, centrally planned enterprise, dominating its field and supported by government regulation, has been typical of Canadian development. As the historian William Morton says, Canada, in contrast to the United States, is founded on the principle of allegiance rather than social contract, on the organic growth of tradition rather than an explicit act of reason or assertion of the revolutionary will. The B.N.A. Act sets up the objectives of peace, order and good government rather than those of life, liberty and the pursuit of happiness. The fact and principle of authority is established prior to the fact and principle of freedom. In the British tradition of monarchy, parliament and law, specific liberties are carved out within the ordered structure of society. There is in Canadian political, business and social life a certain formality and conservatism that reflect this fact. This conservatism has its regrettable side, of course. The walking dead are out in numbers – the mediocrats, the antihothead vote. We are 'the elected squares' to one writer and 'the white baboos' to another; for our inefficiencies there is no excuse. A little talent will get you a long way in an uncompetitive society, protected by tariffs and government rewards. A Canadian has been defined as somebody who does not play for keeps. Even his anti-trust laws fail to enforce business competition as ruthlessly as the American ones.

For a Canadian, unlike a Frenchman, Britisher or American, there has not been one dominant metropolis. The English-speaking Canadian had New York and London as well as Toronto and Montreal, and for the French Canadian there has been Paris as well. This condition breeds a divided vision, sometimes paralysing, sometimes detached and ironic, always multiple, and useful for living in the electronic age's global village. It has meant that Canadians have been better interpreters and critics of culture than creators of it – great performing musicians and actors, for example, but few good composers or playwrights. In politics and diplomacy this has led to an extreme pragmatism. Our two major parties are even less the preserve of one class or doctrine than the American parties. Certainly there has been nothing like the Republicans' monopoly of the rich and the free enterprise creed. There are no strong ideological overtones about the Canadian approach to other people and world affairs.

When a distinguished American socialist advocate of free love and pacifism was turned back by Canadian immigration authorities in 1965, the liberal governor of Minnesota deplored this unexpected evidence of McCarthyism in Canada. It was of course nothing of the kind. In a sense, it was just the opposite – an almost touchingly stupid application of the letter of the law, born of respect for regulations. There was little real concern about doctrines. In Canada ideas abound and rebound with Hindu proliferation, and except among some French Canadians are not taken very seriously anyway.

There is a lingering aura of the European established church in Canada which is very different from the American separation of church and state and its consequence – the political religion of America that has prevailed so long in the United States. The Canadian churches' influence and status can be a strain on some people's liberties, but they are also a bastion against the more absolute dogma of an all-embracing spiritual patriotism. Canada is a land of no one ideology, no single vision; it is a cultural freeport, a way station for travellers (who often move on soon to the other America), a no-man's land even or at least no abiding city, a place not easily confused with paradise or the promised land. This 'indigestible Canada', this Marx Brothers' Freedonia, this Austro-Hungary of the new world, with its two official peoples and its multitudes of permitted ones, its ethnic islands and cultural archipelagos, its ghettos of the unpasteurized and unhomogenized, this harbour of old Adams unable or unwilling to be reborn or to burn just yet their old European clothes, but growing attached, many of them, as deeply as the Indian or the pioneer to the landscape of farm and city – this Canada has, alas, not even carried *this* characteristic as far as it might (perhaps lest it become a principle), since in practice it has been extremely difficult for Asians and West Indians to immigrate to Canada.(The first use of the newly acquired Canadian navy in 1914 was to escort an unwanted shipload of Sikhs out of Vancouver harbour.) By contrast, one conjures up a hopeful vision of the year 2067 in which the majority of Canadians will be of Chinese origin – though the ones that speak English, who will be called 'Anglo-Saxons' in Quebec, will undoubtedly have their quarrels with those who speak French, some of whom will be unable to get their children taught in French in British Columbia.

Canadians often apologize for or feel guilty about the lack of revolution or civil war in their history to stir up their phlegmatic souls. The poet James Reaney recalls someone at a cocktail party sneering at one of the Riel rebellions because so few people were killed. 'What on earth would he be satisfied with? Tamburlaine's pyramid of human skulls?' Many new nations, from the United States to Indonesia, have found it necessary to make war almost immediately on other people in order to prove their own virility. Canadians have gone to war chiefly because other people in distant parts of the earth have been invaded. They have not even held any imperial possessions, like those of Australia and New Zealand. Just a bit more easily than Englishmen or Americans, Canadians can imagine what it was like to be an Indian in Gandhi's day, a Chinese at the time of the Boxer Rebellion, or a Dominican rebel in 1965. We have been invaded by the forces of manifest destiny four times, and we have been a nation of defeated peoples, a refuge of exiles, from the beginning.

Most of us first came here merely to get away from something worse – tsarist pogroms or Soviet tanks, black slavery or Vietnam draft boards, Irish potato famine or Highland eviction, unemployment, scandal, revolutionary zeal or the dead hand of the past. Or else, hardest of all, we were a conquered people in our own land, and only now, after two hundred years of second-class citizenship, have begun to be *maîtres chez nous*.

Canadian history has been a passion rather than an action. It has been, as one writer put it, 'a stolid and phlegmatic struggle against heavy odds. Canadians dealt as a rule with forces beyond their control, in many cases the by-products of other lands. "Courage in Adversity", the motto of the old Nor'wester, remained a stark national necessity for the Canadian brigades that shot the rapids and toiled across the portages of their stormy history.'

The Canadian hero in the poetry of Ned Pratt is the anonymous representative of a beleaguered society, who has confronted and survived both the 'grey shape of the palaeolithic face', and the diabolic, shrill commands of the 'Great Panjandrum', Pratt's symbol for 'the mechanical power of the universe, who controls the stars, the movement of matter, the automatic instincts of living things, even of reason and consciousness', that Prince of Darkness who thinks he is God. The hero's real source of strength is his knowledge that the Panjandrum is not God, 'that for him there can be no God who has not also been a human being, suffered with the beleaguered society, yielded to the power of death and yet conquered it'.

To identify that which is most essentially Canadian in our literature, Northrop Frye recalls a painting, *The Peaceable Kingdom*, which depicts a treaty between Indians and Quakers, and a group of animals, lions, bears, oxen, illustrating the prophecy of Isaiah; it is a haunting and serene vision of the reconciliation of man with man and man with nature. Frye suggests the Canadian tradition as revealed in literature might well be called a quest for the peaceable kingdom.

In a world where independence often arrives with swift violence, it may be good to have one nation where it has matured slowly; in a world of fierce national prides, to have a state about which it is hard to be solemn and religious without being ridiculous, and impossible to be dogmatic. In a world with tendencies to political division and cultural homogeneity, Canada is a country which still stands for the alternative of political federation and cultural and regional variety. In a world that strives for absolute freedom and often gains only oppressive power, Canada presents a tradition that sees freedom in a subtle creative tension with authority; in a world of vast anonymous power élites. Canada is a society whose leaders number no more than Aristotle's five thousand and can know each other personally without being stifled or hopelessly parochial. In a world haunted by the fear of overpopulation, one is grateful for a place with room for more. In a world of striving for moral victories, it is good to have a country where a sort of moral disarmament is possible. ('You and your goddam moral victories,' says an Arthur Miller character who might well be a Canadian. 'We're killing one another with abstractions. Why can't we ever speak *below* the issues?') In a world of ideological battles, it is good to have a place where the quantity and quality of potential being in a person means more than what he believes; in a masculine world of the assertive will and the cutting edge of intellect, a certain Canadian tendency to the amorphous permissive feminine principle of openness and toleration and acceptance offers the possibility of healing.

The Fathers of Confederation chose the title 'Dominion' for the country they had made. Typically it was a second choice, after their British rulers rejected the title they wanted. It comes from the Hebrew scriptures, the seventy-second psalm, a few other words from which may serve as a loose-fitting epigraph to what we have been saying here, as well as some sort of ground from which the good hope of another hundred years may spring.

Let men flourish out of the city like grass upon the earth / Let there be an abundance of grain in the land / The mountains also shall bring peace, and the hills righteousness unto the people / He shall come down like rain upon the mown grass, even as the showers that water the earth / Let all nations call him happy, let his name continue as long as the sun / For he shall deliver the poor when he cries, the needy also and him that has no helper / Let his dominion also be from sea to sea, and from the river unto the world's end / And blessed be the name of his majesty forever. Amen and Amen.

John Glassco

AN EVENING OUT

Schooner was a great frequenter of brothels, and one evening when Bob was working on *The Politics of Existence* he suggested we accompany him to a place which he praised highly.

'It's very quiet, not at all *chi-chi* or expensive,' he said. 'Licensed and inspected, of course. It's even historical: Edward VII used to go there incog., or so they say – anyway there's an oil-painting of him over the bar. First we'll have dinner down by the Porte Saint-Denis. I know a restaurant there that serves the finest snails in the city.'

Graeme had won 100 francs that afternoon throwing dice at the Dingo, so we agreed at once.

The restaurant was very dark, with mouldering tapestries on the walls, gas chandeliers, and tarnished mirrors; it was half filled with elderly, respectable, mottle-faced men, all bent over their plates, many of them wearing infants' bibs to protect their shirts from the juices and sauces. Schooner ordered four dozen snails for us, to be followed by three broiled lobsters and a bottle of Chablis.

I had never tasted such snails; fat, tender and of marvellous flavour, they were swimming in a sauce of browned butter, parsley and garlic. Schooner ate more than half of them, and when the lobster came I was able to enjoy it too as it deserved.

Paris, Schooner told us, was full of restaurants like this, though they took a little finding. 'The one thing to watch out for in a restaurant,' he said, 'is a head-waiter or a maître-d'hôtel; as soon as you see one, turn round and walk out. Also, beware of chafing-dishes.'

'But how can you tell a good restaurant?' said Graeme.

'I've found that three good signs are a small menu, darned table-cloths, and an old dog on the premises. Mostly, however, you go by instinct.'

'How about the proprietor being dressed in a blue apron?' I asked.

'Why, that quaint garment is an indication the food may be good, or it may not, but the bill will certainly be far too high and probably added up wrong. No, the proprietor of a good restaurant wears shirt-sleeves in summer and a woollen coat-sweater in winter. Also, oddly enough, the food is always better when he is thin, bald and depressed-looking. You may think all this fantastic, but I assure you I have compiled all these features of a good restaurant by using the same process Lombroso did in arriving at his rules for the physiognomy of a criminal. Lombroso, of course, was a scientist. But the painter's eye, like the writer's, records all these things subconsciously.'

We had coffee at a small café facing the Porte Saint-Denis. It was now almost eleven o'clock, and the July night was soft and perfumed; the sky had still the lingering traces of the violet light of evening; crowds of shopgirls in their long dresses and clerks in little bowler hats and tight jackets were strolling slowly along; up over Montmartre Bébé Cadum displayed her infantile, indecent grin. We had St James rum with our coffee and smoked the last of our American cigarettes. At last we rose to go to the brothel; for Schooner said this was the best time – when the girls were wide awake and still fresh and before the drunks arrived.

'The place opens at six o'clock and closes sharp at four in the morning,' he said. 'By the way, have you got enough money?'

We had almost seven dollars left. 'More than enough,' said Schooner. 'This is no *de luxe* trap.'

It was clear, as soon as we entered the tall narrow-fronted building at 25 rue St Apolline over which a pink light shone modestly, that the place was no stuffy abode of wealth and tedium. A narrow dark corridor led directly into a large red-lighted and red-papered room filled with low tables and plush-covered benches like those of the first-class Canadian railway-carriages of my childhood; drinks were being served to mixed couples by an elderly waiter in the usual black alpaca waistcoat and floor-length white apron, and it took a few moments to realize that all the women were young and completely nude. At the door was a raised cash-desk presided over by a neat little old sharp-featured lady in black silk, with steel-rimmed spectacles and grey hair drawn back in a tidy bun; at the far end of the room, under a large and smiling portrait of Edward VII, behind a long table covered with glasses of beer, lounged a dozen other naked beauties smoking and chatting. The informality was enchanting. We sat down at a corner table and ordered a bottle of iced *mousseux*. The old lady nodded politely to Schooner, gave Graeme and me a single penetrating glance, and raised a finger to the table of the beauties. At the sign they all rose, ran forward, and fell before our table in a torrent of flesh, wriggling their haunches, shaking their breasts, chattering obscenities, and sticking out their tongues.

'Take your pick,' said Schooner. 'We have to buy three of them a drink anyway. If you don't like one, she'll take her drink back to the big table by herself.' He studied them with a jovial but judicious air. 'I rather like the big Norman girl in the middle,' he said, crooking a finger at a superb blonde with breasts like cantaloupes, who gave a cry of triumph and at once squeezed in beside him.

I had already made my choice: a jolly-looking little brunette with bobbed hair who had shaved in every strategic place and wore a rhinestone choker. She sat down and clasped my hand tightly. Graeme was undecided, and I believe his final choice was determined less by personal preference than by compassion: it was a beautiful but modest-looking mulattress who stood in the background, protruding a pair of superb pear-shaped breasts, with her hands clasped behind her head and eyes raised soulfully to the ceiling.

The girls ordered whatever harmless mixture they were supposed to drink: deep pink in colour, it was served in tall glasses and graced with a spoon.

'This stuff,' confided my brunette, 'is only *limonade* and grenadine. But what can you do? Now I, I like to flush my kidneys with something that has some heart in it. Darling, when Madame Hibou isn't looking sprinkle me a little *mousseux* in my glass for the love of God.'

This was not too easy. Madame Hibou seemed to have a dozen pairs of eyes in her head. However, when a solemn-looking client in rusty black rose from a bench and was led to the cash-desk by one of the girls, her attention was taken up by the business of making out a chit for the room and entering the transaction in a ledger. I took the opportunity of filling my friend's half-empty glass with the pink *mousseux*, which she drank off immediately.

The conversation was refreshing though far from intellectual. After a while it became little more than a boasting-contest between the Norman girl and the brunette as they vaunted their abilities in bed : it seemed there was nothing they could not do. Graeme's mulattress, who had recently arrived from Senegal and could speak no more than a few words of French, merely bared her magnificent teeth from time to time and rolled her eyes. 'She is just a child of nature,' said my brunette, 'but she has a heart of gold.'

'Well, I'm for bed,' said Schooner as we finished the bottle of wine. 'For your information the rooms cost fifteen francs and the girls twenty-five each, unless you're staying the night, when it's double – but that's only for businessmen from out of town who want to save on a hotel bill.'

At the cash-desk we all paid for our rooms in advance; the girls were to be paid afterwards. Having received our chits from Madame Hibou, all six of us mounted the stairs, arm in arm, and were shown to three adjoining rooms by an elderly chambermaid with a hare-lip who took the chits and then suggested that if we wanted the doors unlocked between our rooms she would do so for an additional fifteen francs. 'It will make for more variety,' she said, 'without any sacrifice of discretion.'

This seemed like a good idea. We paid the extra money and saw the rooms transformed into a suite.

'Mind now,' said the chambermaid, 'you must be out of here in an hour from now when your tickets expire. And Arlette, my girl,' she warned Schooner's companion, 'be sure you behave yourself. No unseemly noise ! Good evening, gentlemen.'

We were soon engaged in the business of the evening. To me, this first experience of a French prostitute was a revelation. I had, quite simply, never enjoyed myself so much in my life, and I soon understood the source of Jeanne du Barry's attraction for Louis XV and how well it was comprised in her own terse formula, '*Je l'ai traité en simple putain.*' After a short rest Graeme switched to Arlette and Schooner to the brunette, while I took the mulattress. When it came to my turn with Arlette, however, I was in no condition to continue, and while Graeme and Schooner were running their third course she perched on the bidet and entertained me with the story of her life on the farm in Normandy, 'where I hope to retire some day,' she said, 'and raise a big family and look after some nice geese. But for all this I need money, you know, so won't you give me a little tip? Then I won't tell your friends how *tired* you were.'

Having paid this piece of blackmail to the extent of five francs, for which she kissed me affectionately, I then brushed my hair and got dressed just as there was a loud rap on the hall-door accompanied by the chambermaid's voice hissing through her hare-lip: '*C'est l'heure, messieurs. S'il vous plaît!*'

Graeme and Schooner appeared a minute later and the six of us descended the stairs, once again arm in arm. Having settled our modest score with Madame Hibou, we all exchanged compliments with the girls, bade them good night, and sallied out into the velvety Paris night.

Hubert Aquin

FROM PROCHAIN ÉPISODE

Very little time passed between my solitary promenade on the shores of Lake Geneva and my arrest in midsummer Montreal. After reading K's message, everything rushed ahead in disorder: my departure from Lausanne, the firing of four Rolls Royce motors on the Swissair DC8, the flight over the Juras, the interminable, heavenly nothingness, then federal customs at Dorval Airport. All in all, nothing happened between that departure and my forced confinement, unless you count the jet-time from one city to another. In Montreal, I went first to 267 Sherbrooke St West. I found several open-necked Hathaway shirts, several books thrown here and there and a vivid sense of having returned home. All this time, K was somewhere in the Hanseatic fog of Antwerp or Bremen. She was not with me; I had become again a man alone, stripped of love. I scanned the newspapers; I found nothing about our 'interests'. I tried to telephone my contact: a recorded announcement told me over and over that the service at that number was discontinued. Fine. Now what? I walked a great deal, thinking this over and trying to adjust as quickly as possible. I could risk going ahead on my own, since I couldn't reach my contact by telephone. A risk worth taking; after all, I had to contact some member of the network. I decided to telephone M himself. Just then, I was wandering down Pine Avenue near the Mayfair Hospital: I took the Drummond St stairway and entered the Piccadilly for a King's Ransom. After that, I went to the row of telephone booths opposite the Québecair counter in the hotel hallway, and I dialled M's number. We talked abracadabra for the benefit of RCMP officers who listen in, though it has another meaning for us. And so I learned, in that super-coded language, that our network had been short-circuited by the antiterrorist squad and that several agents were in their twentieth day of detention in the Montreal Prison and, things go in threes, that the money brought in by our experts in fiscal levying was now part of the consolidated budget of the central government. Disaster, in conclusion, which M escaped only by a miracle. Troubled by these revelations, I drank another King's Ransom in the bar of the Piccadilly. The next day, I emptied my savings account at the Toronto Dominion Bank, 500 St James St West. I pocketed $123 in all, enough for one week's modest living. From the telephone booth outside, opposite the Nesbitt Thompson building, I called M again, as arranged. We made a rendezvous for exactly noon-hour in the aisle of Notre-Dame Church, close to the tomb of Jean-Jacques Olier; certainly, we didn't name either that illustrious abbey, or the ancient church whose presbytery adjoins the Montreal Stock Exchange.

It was exactly eleven when I left the booth. Since I had an hour to kill, I walked along Rue Saint-François-Xavier to Craig St, and I entered Mendellsohn's. I love that shop; when I enter it, I always have the feeling that I am going to find the pocket watch of General Colborne or the revolver with which Papineau ought to have committed suicide. First I admired the collection of swords and sabres on my left, including a Turkish scimitar which I would like to have hung above my bed. But I knew from experience that the price of their sidearms was usually inflated; moreover, I know the owner, you can't bargain with him. There is no sale to be found in his shop. I went to look at the helmets; I had already been struck by a Henry II model, a decrepit object of truly impressive proportions. They wanted $40 for it; of course, if I haggled a bit, I could have had it for less. But that would still have been an extravagance on my part, given what was left in my pocket. Anyway, what would I do with a helmet? Close by, there was a complete outfit for one arm: gauntlet, elbow-piece and brassard. It was sixteenth-century, rather hard to identify, but of an unusual style. That disjointed arm of tempered black iron had a tragic aura, like the amputated arm of a hero. If I were to hang it on the apartment wall, I wouldn't be able to look at it without shivering. To escape the pressure of the clerk, I returned to the front of the shop and looked at the window display of neat rows of watches and other types of clock. These old pocket watches have always fascinated me : I love their golden double-hinged cases, their scroll-work covers and the engraved initials of their former owners. I looked at several to pass time. Finally, I noticed a pocket watch whose gold had dulled with age, but which was finely chiselled with the cipher of some unknown dead person. My decision was made: I drew out a $10 bill. But the clerk reminded me that he must add the cost of the chain, and the total bill was $12·75. Oh well, it wasn't exorbitant; and I truly wanted to own a pocket watch to measure lost time. The case, made in England, contained a Swiss movement which turned with eternal regularity. I set the hands: it was exactly 11·45. It was time.

I went back on to Craig St, then along the steep incline of Rue Saint-Urbain toward Place d'Armes, which I crossed diagonally. Before entering the church, I bought a paper. As usual, I took care to retrace my steps, zigzagging a bit, to foil any attempt at following me. I entered the Alfred Buildings, at 707, and left it again by the door on Rue Notre-Dame. I crossed Rue Notre-Dame at a run and found myself, after several athletic leaps, in the obscurity of the church.

The silence inside was somehow terrifying: I was suddenly caught at the throat by the mystery of this obscure, magic forest. My steps echoed through the building. I reached the cross-aisle without seeing anyone in this deserted temple, and without hearing any other noise than the multiplied echo of my own feet. A shivering purity inhabited that sacred place. I was a few seconds ahead of M; while waiting, I sat down close to the side-chapel, lost in retreat and prayer. In an excess of fervour, I took care not to open my paper, though I burned to pull it out and see if they mentioned the preliminary inquiries. When M appeared, coming from the altar toward me (God knows how!), I stifled a surge of emotion. Everything happened so quickly. I felt a noise on my right: the door of the confessional was open. I saw a meticulously dressed man hurry toward me. Another, at the same moment, seemed to rise out of the transept. He too looked entirely respectable. M and I had time to exchange a glance of despair, but not a single word. They led us to the porch. We were taken out by the stairway on Rue Saint-Sulpice, handcuffs on our wrists. An unmarked car was waiting; we were put in the rear, according to the policeman's orders. The rest: a shapeless stretch of time that has now lasted three months, interrupted by the withering and the humiliation which led me to the abysmal depths of writing.

Prisoner in solitary, transferred sullenly to an institution, almost forgotten; I am alone. Time has fled and still flees, while I swim here in a plasma of words. I await a court case from which I expect nothing and a revolution which will return everything to me. . . . Oh, how eager I am to run free again in the disordered breadth of my country and see you again in the flesh, you my love, where now I see you disappearing into the white frailty of paper. Where are you? In Lausanne or in your apartment on Tottenham Court Road? . . .

Endless imprisonment is undoing me. How can I believe that I shall escape? I've tried a thousand times to leave: there is no way to do it. One link is still missing from my sequence of flight. In fact, this book has no logical ending-point. Armed violence is missing in my life, so is our wild triumph. And I am anxious to add that final chapter to my private story. I suffocate here, in the cross-grill of neurosis, while I smear myself with ink and, through the sealed window, stroke your legs. My memories haunt me. I walk again on the Quai d'Ouchy, between the phantom château and the Hôtel d'Angleterre. My failure comes back to me with the force of unfinished actions and motionless shreds of Alps. When I burst out of the château near Echandens, I had already spoiled everything.

'. . . I'll seat myself at a table very near the orchestra, anyway, he won't know me. When you have finished with him, you will join me there. . . . But you must understand. I'm exhausted, my love. This whole business is going very badly for me. I'm afraid; I'm afraid of the worst. I simply have to see you soon . . .'

The words of command freeze in his mouth and fill me with confusion and fear. Everything is mixed up; memory collapses. Gestures fall apart. On the point of leaping, I keep waiting for the right moment, my finger on the trigger. From one instant to the next, I am surely going to find the word I need to shoot H. de Heutz. Everything is movement; yet I remain fixed and I wait, for several seconds, to strike properly.

'. . . I'm afraid, I'm afraid of the worst. I simply have to see you soon. . . . Listen : above all, don't forget the colour of paper and the code, right? You'll find it all in the account of the battle of Uxellodunum by Stoffel, page 218. . . . Now, tell me: where are the children?'

At these words, I moved. And instead of carrying through, my coordination snapped : something in me flinched, and H. de Heutz was aware of my presence. Two bullets had struck the carvings of the Henry II sideboard before I was even ready to counter-attack. The intermittent gun-fire which followed broke the sacred ritual of the scenario I had planned : our combat took place in the most disgraceful confusion. I'm sure I struck H. de Heutz with at least one bullet; but I cannot be sure I killed him. In fact, I'm practically sure I didn't kill him; anyway, I don't even know where I wounded him, for I flew through the garage door without even turning around. And then I heard another detonation. He probably fell to the floor when he was hit, and from that position tried desperately to shoot me down. Unless he crouched behind a piece of furniture with the single aim of forcing me to uncover myself? I sped from the château at the wheel of the blue Opel. After failing in every effort except my final flight, I arrived, after a wild ride, in front of the Hôtel d'Angleterre. Then I realized that it wasn't H. de Heutz that I had missed, but that in nearly missing him, I had just missed my rendezvous and my entire life.

K had left and I had no way to get in touch with her. Broken by her absence, I was in despair as it is not permitted to be when one is involved in revolution. For a long time I wandered around the terrace of the Hôtel d'Angleterre, feeling I had ruined everything. At best, I had wounded H. de Heutz, but at what cost ! Here I am, defeated like our nation, more useless than any of my brothers : I am that obliterated man who circles the shores of Lake Geneva. I stretch myself on a page of mock-insanity, I lie flat on my belly to agonize in the blood of words. . . . I look for a logical end to all the things that have happened, but cannot find one ! I burn to be done with it and to put the final period to my indefinite past.

Translated by Penny Williams

Irving Layton

THE MODERN POET

Since Eliot set the fashion,
Our poets grow tame;
They are quite without passion,
They live without blame
Like a respectable dame.

Bountiful Lady, good Sir,
In search of a pet?
Would you therefore consider
A modern poet?
He's for purchase or to let.

His pedigree? Uncertain.
But come now agree
He's the one to entertain
Your guests after tea.
A wit and a scholar is he.

Poets are shocking, you say?
Villon, Baudelaire –
Ho ! They come gentler today;
Their language most fair . . .
Ah-ha, you'll order a pair?

KEINE LAZAROVITCH 1870–1959

When I saw my mother's head on the cold pillow,
Her white waterfalling hair in the cheeks' hollows,
I thought, quietly circling my grief, of how
She had loved God but cursed extravagantly his creatures.

For her final mouth was not water but a curse,
A small black hole, a black rent in the universe,
Which damned the green earth, stars and trees in its stillness
And the inescapable lousiness of growing old.

And I record she was comfortless, vituperative,
Ignorant, glad, and much else besides; I believe
She endlessly praised her black eyebrows, their thick weave,
Till plagiarizing Death leaned down and took them for his mould.

And spoiled a dignity I shall not again find,
And the fury of her stubborn limited mind;
Now none will shake her amber beads and call God blind,
Or wear them upon a breast so radiantly.

O fierce she was, mean and unaccommodating;
But I think now of the toss of her gold earrings,
Their proud carnal assertion, and her youngest sings
While all the rivers of her red veins move into the sea.

O SAY CAN YOU SEE

When I read somewhere
that Amerigo Vespucci
had been a pork butcher
and finance agent
in prosperous Florence,
I saw at once

the Muse of History
was a meticulous poet
with a fine sense
of the fitness of things.

Hugh Hood

RECOLLECTIONS OF THE TORONTO
WORKS DEPARTMENT

From *Flying A Red Kite*

In the spring of 1952, six weeks after I finished my M.A. courses and involved myself in further graduate studies, I decided that I'd have to find a better summer job.

I had been working for the English publisher, Thomas Nelson and Sons, as a stockroom boy. The pay was low, and the work remarkably hard. I had only been on the job ten days, but after an afternoon stacking cases of *The Highroads Dictionary* (familiar to every Ontario school child) ninety-six copies to the case, in piles ten cases high, I saw that this state of affairs could not go on. These packing cases were made of heavy cardboard, strongly stapled and bound; they weighed seventy-five pounds each and they had to be piled carefully in a complicated stacking system. You had to fling the top row of cases into the air, much as you'd launch a basketball. I started to look for something less strenuous.

At length an official of the National Employment Service who handled summer placements at Hart House, a Mr Halse, a man remembered by generations of Varsity types, suggested that I try to get on the city. I took an afternoon off from Thomas Nelson's and went up to the City Hall, to Room 302, a big room on the west side with a pleasant high ceiling. I was received with courtesy and attention, and after filling out some forms I got a job as a labourer in the Works Department, Roadways Division, payday on Wednesdays, hours eight to five, report to Foreman Brown at Number Two Yard on College Street tomorrow morning, thank you! I stood at the counter a little out of breath at the speed with which I'd got what I came for.

'You're not very big,' said the clerk at the counter. 'Are you sure you can handle a pick and shovel?' As the wages were twice what I'd been getting, I thought I'd try it and see.

'I can handle it,' I said. I've never seen anybody killing himself at the pick-and-shovel dodge. I asked the clerk for the address on College Street and, oddly enough, he didn't know it.

'But you can't miss it,' he said. 'It's next to the Fire Hall, three blocks west of Spadina. Ask to see Mr Brown. And you'd better get on the job on time, the first day at least.'

I thanked him and strolled back to Thomas Nelson's where I explained that I'd found something that paid better, and would they mind letting me go at the end of the day. They didn't seem surprised.

'You've got three days' money coming,' said the stockroom superintendent dolefully. He sighed. 'I don't know how it is. We can't keep anybody in that job.' I said nothing about the cases of dictionaries.

Although it was the middle of May, the next morning was brisk, a bright sunny day with the promise of warmth in the afternoon. I was glad that I'd worn a couple of sweaters as I came along College Street looking for Number Two Yard. It wasn't hard to find. It stood and still stands just west of the Fire Hall half-way between Spadina and Bathurst, on the south side of College. It's the main downtown service centre for roads and sidewalks, responsible for the area bounded by Bathurst, Jarvis, Bloor, and the waterfront. Any holes or cuts in the roadway, any broken sidewalks, or any new sidewalks not provided by contractors, are tended by workmen from this yard. It also serves as a reception desk for calls connected with trees, sewers, and drains from all over town. There's always a watchman on duty to attend to such matters, day or night.

I walked into the office and stood next to a washbasin in the corner, feeling a little nervous. Most of the other men on the crew were ten years older than I, although I spotted a couple my own age. None of them looked like students, even the young ones; they were all heavily tanned and they all discussed their mysterious affairs in hilarious shouts. There was a counter in front of me, and behind it some office space with three desks, a space heater, some bundles of engineers' plans of the streets hanging in rolls above the windows. It was the kind of room in which no woman had ever been, but it was very clean.

Outside a green International quarter-ton pickup with the Works Department plate on the door came smartly into the Yard. A one-armed man got out and began to shout abusively at the windows of the Fire Hall. This was the foreman, Charlie Brown, who conducted a running war against the firemen because they persisted in parking their cars, of which they had a great many, in his Yard. He bawled a few more curses at the face of the Fire Captain which was glued to a third-storey window, and came inside, immediately fixing his eyes, which were brown, small, and very sharp, on me.

'Goddam-college-kids-no-bloody-good,' he shouted irritably, running it all together into a single word; it was a stock phrase. He glared at me pityingly. 'Where the hell are your boots?' I was wearing a pair of low canvas shoes of the type then known disparagingly as 'fruit boots'.

'Cut 'em to bits in five minutes!' he exclaimed, quite rightly. I wore them to work one day later on, and the edge of the shovel took the soles off them in under five minutes.

'Go across the street to the Cut-Rate Store. Tell them Charlie sent you. Get them to give you sweat socks and boots. You can pay for them when you draw some money.' I tried to say something but he cut me off abruptly and as I went out I could hear him mumbling, 'Goddam-college-kids-no-bloody-good.'

I had a good look at him as he banged noisily around the office when I came back wearing my stiff new boots. He was a burly man, about five-eleven, with a weathered face, a short stump of a right arm – the crew called him 'One Punch Brown' – a pipe usually in his mouth. He was the kindest boss I ever had on one of those summer jobs; there was no reason for him to care about my shoes. The workmen cursed him behind his back but they knew that he didn't push them too hard. And yet he managed to get the necessary minimum of work out of them. I found out, purely by accident, that the way to make him like you was to say as little as possible. It was fear that made me answer him in monosyllables but it suited him.

Charlie had four men in the office with him and three gangs of labourers out on various jobs, widely separated in the midtown district he was responsible for. In the office were an assistant foreman named George – I can't remember his last name – and a clerk named Eddie Doucette who sometimes chauffeured Charlie around town. Usually Charlie drove himself, and how he could spin that little International, stump and all; he used the stump to help steer, along with the good arm.

Then there were two patrolmen who kept checking the streets and alleys in our district, reporting any damage to the roads and sidewalks, and the condition of any recently accomplished repairs. Johnny Pawlak was one of them, a slope-shouldered rangy guy of thirty-three or -four, a bowler and softball player, the organizer of all the baseball pools. The other was called Bill Tennyson, a lean, wiry, chronically dissatisfied griper, always in trouble over his non-support of his family, and half-disliked and suspected by the rest of the men in the office for vague reasons. Finally there were the three gangs out on the job : Wall's gang, Mitch's gang, and Harris's gang. Wall ran a taut ship, Harris an unhappy ship, and Mitch a happy one. I never worked for Wall, but I did the others, and the difference was wonderful.

When I got back from the Cut-Rate Store it was already half past eight. "What are we going to do with this kid?' I heard Charlie Brown ask rhetorically as I came into the office.

'Aimé's still off,' said George softly. 'You could send him out with Bill and Danny.' They stared at me together.

'Ever handled a shovel?'

'Yes.'

'Go and help with the coal-ass.'

'Coal-ass?'

'Do you see those men and that truck?' They pointed out the windows. Across the Yard beside a couple of piles of sand and gravel a stubby old guy and a man my own age were sitting, smoking idly, on the running-board of a city dump-truck.

'Go out with them today. And take it easy with the shovel or you'll hurt your hands.'

I left the office and walked over to tell the two men, Bill Eagleson and Danny Foster, that I was coming with them.

'What's your name?'

'Hood.'

'All right, Hoody,' said the older man, Bill, 'grab a shovel.' After a moment he and Danny stood off and studied my style.

'Do much shovelling?'

'Not a hell of a lot, no.'

'Swing it like this, look!' They taught me how, and there really was an easy way to do it, one of the most useful things I've ever learned, a natural arc through which to swing the weight without straining the muscles. It was the same with a pick or a sledge; the thing was to let the head of the instrument supply the power, just like a smooth golf swing.

When we had enough sand and gravel, we yanked two planks out of a pile and made a ramp up to the tailgate.

'We'll put on the coal-ass,' said Bill Eagleson.

'What's that?'

'Cold asphalt. It's liquid in the barrel and dries in the air. We use it for temporary patches.'

Danny and I rolled an oil-drum of this stuff around to the bottom of the ramp. Then we worked it up to the tailgate and into a wooden cradle so that one end of the drum was flush with the end of the truck. Bill screwed a spigot into the end of the drum and we were all set.

'You're the smallest, you sit in the middle,' they said flatly.

Apparently Danny and the absent Aimé fought over this every day. When we had squeezed into the front seat, Bill checked over the list of breaks in the roadway and we set out. It was already nine o'clock.

As we drove slowly along, the barrel bouncing and clanging in the back, they told me that our job was to apply temporary patches where damage had been reported by the patrolmen or a citizen, to save the city money on lawsuits. The idea was to get the patch down as soon as possible. They weren't meant to be permanent but they had to last for a while.

We stopped first behind some railway sidings on the Esplanade, next to the Saint Lawrence Market, to fix some shallow potholes. Bill filled a large tin watering-can with coal-ass and spread the black tarry liquid in the hole. Then Danny and I filled it with gravel. Then more coal-ass, then a layer of sand, and finally a third coat of the cold asphalt to top off.

'It dries in the air,' said Danny with satisfaction, 'and tomorrow you'll need a pick to get it out of there.' He was quite right. It was an amazingly good way to make quick repairs that would last indefinitely. From the Esplanade we headed uptown to Gerrard Street between Bay and Yonge where we filled a small cut in the sidewalk. Then Bill parked the truck in the lot behind the old Kresge's store on Yonge.

'Time for coffee,' we all said at once. We sat at the lunch counter in Kresge's for half an hour, kidding the waitresses, and I began to realize that we had no boss, that Charlie wasn't checking on us in any way and that Bill had only the nominal authority that went with his drivership. Nobody ever bothered you. Nobody seemed to care how long you spent over a given piece of work, and yet the work all got done, sooner or later, and not badly either. If you go to the corner of St Joseph and Bay, on the east side, you can see patches that we put in nine years ago, as sound as the day they were laid down. By and large, the taxpayers got their money's worth, although it certainly wasn't done with maximum expedition or efficiency.

When we'd finished our coffee it was obviously much too late to start anything before lunch, so Bill and I waited in the truck while Danny shopped around in Kresge's for a cap. He came back with something that looked like a cross between a railwayman's hat and a housepainter's, a cotton affair that oddly suited him. We drove back to the yard, arriving about eleven forty-five, in comfortable time for lunch. We were allowed an hour for lunch but it always ran into considerably more. The three big gangs didn't come into the Yard except on payday, unless they were working close by. It seemed to be a point of protocol to stay away from the Yard as long as possible. Each gang had a small portable shed on wheels, in which the tools, lamps, and so forth, could be locked overnight, and these sheds are to be seen all over the downtown area.

After lunch a few more holes. About two-thirty or three we parked the truck in the middle of Fleet Street with cars whizzing past on both sides. Danny handed me a red rag on a stick. 'Go back there and wave them around us,' he said. 'We'll fix the hole.'

I stood in the middle of Fleet Street, that heavily travelled artery, and innocently waved my flag, fascinated to see how obediently the cars coming at me divided and passed to either side of the truck. Now and then a driver spotted me late, and one man didn't see the flag at all until the last second. I had to leap out of his way, shouting, and he pulled way out to his left into the face of the oncoming traffic and went around the truck at sixty-five.

Pretty soon Bill and Danny were finished and we got into the truck and drove off. 'Payday tomorrow,' said Danny thoughtfully. 'You won't draw anything this week, Hoody. They pay on Wednesday up till the previous Saturday.'

'We'll buy you a beer,' said Bill generously. He began to tell me about himself. He was an old ballplayer who had bounced around the lower minors for years, without ever going above Class B. Afterwards he came back to Toronto and played Industrial League ball until the Depression killed it. Then he had come on the city, and had now been with the Roadways Division for fifteen years.

'Just stick with us, Hoody, and keep your mouth shut,' he said, repeating it with conviction several times.

'You'll be with us at least until Aimé gets back,' said Danny. I asked what had happened to Aimé. It appeared that he'd been found sitting in a car that didn't belong to him, in a place where the car wasn't supposed to be. He got thirty days and it was taken for granted that he'd be back on the job, same as ever, when he got out. Many of the men had had minor brushes with the law. A few weeks later Danny got caught, with two of his friends and a truck, loading lengths of drainpipe which they planned to sell for scrap, at a City Maintenance Station south of Adelaide Street. They just drove the truck into the station after supper and spent six hours loading pipe. They might have got twenty-five dollars for it, dividing that sum between them. It didn't seem very good pay for six hours' work; when I suggested this to Danny he shrugged it off. He hadn't figured out that his time was worth more than he could possibly have made on that job.

Bill Tennyson, the sulky patrolman, had often been charged with non-support by his wife, and with assault by his father-in-law. He passed his nights alternately at his nominal place of abode, where his wife and children lived, and a bachelor friend's apartment in the Warwick Hotel. An unsettled life, and an irregular, whose disagreeable circumstances he used to deplore to me in private lunch-hour chat. Charlie disliked him, and used to ride him quite a lot; he was the only man in the whole crew to whom Charlie was consistently unfair. He had that irritating goof-off manner which always infuriates the man who is trying to get the job done. Yet he had no vices, drank little, didn't gamble. No one knew how he spent his money and no one liked him.

He had his eyes on Eddie Doucette's desk job. But Eddie could type after a fashion, and had some sort of connexion at the Hall which everybody knew about and never mentioned – he might have been a nephew of the City Clerk or the Assistant Assessment Commissioner – I never found out for sure. But nobody was going to get his job away from him.

Eddie wore a cardigan and a tie, and rode around in the truck with Charlie and George, while Tennyson wore sports shirts and walked his beat. The rest of us wore work-clothes of an astonishing variety. My regular costume, after Aimé came back and I had to get off the coal-ass crew, was an old Fordham sweatshirt which my brother in New York had given me and which by protocol was never laundered, jeans, work-boots, and the same pair of sweat socks every day, and they too were never laundered; they were full of concrete dust at the end of the day and by September were nearly solid. I could stand them in the corner, and they never bothered my feet at all as long as I washed off the concrete as soon as I came home.

That first day we got back to the Yard about four. We walked into the office, clumping our boots loudly and officiously on the floor. Charlie and George had gone out somewhere in the truck and wouldn't be back that day. Apart from Eddie, the only person in the office was a man who was sitting in Charlie's swivel chair, bandaged to the eyes. He seemed to be suffering from broken ribs, collar-bone and arm, shock, cuts, abrasions, sprains, and perhaps other things. He was having trouble speaking clearly and his hands shook violently. He and Eddie were conspiring over a report to the Workmen's Compensation Board.

This man became a culture-hero in the Works Department because he was on Compensation longer than anyone had ever been before. Everyone felt obscurely that he had it made, that he had a claim against the city and the province for life. He would come back to work now and then, and after a day on the gang would be laid up six weeks more. They spoke of him at the Yard in awed lowered voices.

'How do you feel, Sambo?' asked Bill solicitously.

'Not good, Bill, not good.'

'You'll be all right,' said Bill.

The injured man turned back to Eddie who was licking the end of his pencil and puzzling over the complicated instructions on the report. 'It says "wife and dependants",' he said uncertainly. 'We'll put them down anyway. If it's wrong we'll hear about it.'

'I want to get my money,' said Sambo.

'You'll get it soon enough.'

I could not think where anybody could pick up that many lumps all at once. 'What happened to him?' I asked.

'He was Aimé's replacement till yesterday,' said Bill unconcernedly, 'but some guy on Fleet Street didn't see the red flag. He was our last safety-man before you.'

I thought this over most of the night, deciding finally that I would have to be luckier and more agile than Sambo. The next day was a payday, and in the press of events I forgot my fears and decided to stick with the job as long as I could. At lunchtime, the second day, most of the men expressed commiseration at the fact that I would draw no money until next week.

Bill Tennyson came out of the office with his cheque in his hand and an air of relief written all over him.

'Nobody got any of it this time,' he said, as nearly happy as he ever was; his salary was almost always diminished by the judgements of his creditors. 'How about you, Hood, you draw anything?'

I told him that I wouldn't get paid for a week and he stared at me dubiously for a minute, coming as near as he could to a spontaneous generous gesture. Then all at once he recollected himself and turned away.

Charlie Brown told me that if I was short he could let me have five dollars. I could have used it, but it seemed wiser to say 'no thanks' and stretch my credit at my rooming house for one more week. He seemed surprised at my refusal, though not annoyed.

'You're on the truck with Bill and Danny, aren't you?'

'Yes.'

'Stay out of trouble,' he said cryptically and went out and got into the quarter-ton, holding a roll of plans under his stump and stuffing tobacco into his pipe with his good hand. All over the Yard men were standing in clumps, sharing a peculiar air of expectancy. Some went off hastily, after eating their sandwiches, to the nearest bank. Danny Foster let his cheque fly out of his hand and had to climb over the roofs of several low buildings on College Street in order to retrieve it. A quiet hum of talk came from the tool-shed behind the office where the gang-bosses ate whenever they came into the Yard. There they sat in isolated state, old Wall, ulcerated Harris, and the cheerful Mitch, the best-liked man at the Yard, sharing their rank, its privileges and its loneliness.

The undertone of expectation sensibly intensified as the lunch-hour passed; payday was different from other days. The whole business of the gang-bosses on paydays was to ensure that their crews should be on a job proximate to a Beverage Room. One of the reasons that Harris was so unpopular was that he was a poor planner of work schedules; his men often had to walk six or even eight blocks from the job to the hotel. Mitch, on the other hand, seemed to have a positive flair for working into position Tuesday night or Wednesday morning, so that one of our favourite places, the Brunswick perhaps or the Babloor, was just up an alley from the job. I don't understand quite how he managed it, but if you worked on Mitch's gang you never had to appear on a public thoroughfare as you oozed off the job and into the hotel; there was always a convenient alley.

Bill and Danny and I left the Yard sharp at one o'clock bound for some pressing minor repairs on Huron Street behind the Borden's plant. When we got there we couldn't find anything that looked at all pressing, except possibly a small crack beside a drain. We filled it with coal-ass, Bill laughing all the while in a kind of sly way. I asked him what was so funny.

'Johnny must have reported this one,' he said. 'He knows where we go.'

'Go?'

'Oh, come on !' he said.

'Should we stick the truck up the alley?' asked Danny.

'Leave it where it is,' said Bill. 'Nobody's going to bother it.' He was perfectly right. The truck sat innocently beside the drain we'd been tinkering with for the rest of the afternoon, with CITY OF TORONTO WORKS DEPARTMENT written all over it in various places. A casual passer-by, unless he knew the customs of the Department, would assume that the truck's occupants were somewhere close by, hard at work. Everything looked – I don't quite know how to put this – sort of *official*. Danny leaned a shovel artistically against a rear wheel, giving the impression more force than ever.

We walked up Huron Street towards Willcocks.

'Where are we going?' I asked, although by now I had a pretty good idea. Anybody who knows the neighbourhood will have guessed our destination already. I'm talking about that little island of peace in the hustle and bustle of the great city, the Twentieth Battalion Club, Canadian Legion, at the corner of Huron and Willcocks. This was the first time that I was ever in one of the Legion halls. I had always innocently supposed that you had to have some kind of membership. Nothing could be further from the truth, and the knowledgeable drinkers of my time at the university would never be caught dead in a public place like the King Cole Room or Lundy's Lane.

It was a custom hallowed by years of usage that Charlie Brown, George, and Eddie Doucette should spend Wednesday afternoon in the Forty-Eighth Highlanders Legion Hall over on Church Street. It gave one a feeling of comfort and deep security to know this.

We went into the Twentieth and took a table by a big bay window. The houses on the four corners of Huron and Willcocks were then perhaps eighty-five years old, beautifully proportioned old brick houses with verandas at the front and side, and a lovely grey weathered tone to the walls. Like many of the original university buildings, these houses had originally been yellow brick, which the passage of nearly a century had turned to a soft sheen of grey. It was one of those beautiful days in the third week of May without a trace of a cloud in the sky, the trees on Willcocks Street a deep dusty green, and now that most of the students had left town the whole district seemed to be asleep. That was one of the finest afternoons of my life.

'Are we gonna go back to the Yard?' said Bill to Danny, really putting the question of whether they would take the truck home with them or not. They were deciding how much they meant to drink. And the nicest thing of all from my point of view was that they took completely for granted that they would take turns buying me beers. I was always glad that I had frequent opportunities to reciprocate.

There was an unspoken decision to make an afternoon of it.

Over in the opposite corner, fast asleep with a glass in front of him, sat the inevitable old Sapper who would revive later on to give us a detailed account of his exploits at Passchendaele. Next to him were two Contemptibles with identical drooping wet moustaches engaged in another of their interminable games of cribbage. All afternoon their soft murmur of 'fifteen-two, fifteen-four' droned away peacefully in the background. It was a place where a man could stretch out and take his time. In all the time I was in the Twentieth after that, though I saw plenty of men thoroughly drunk, I never saw one really troublesome or nasty.

At a big round table in the middle of the room, all by himself, shifting a pair of small eyes in a head of heroic proportions, drinking mightily, sat a young man whom I vaguely remembered having seen around the university. This was the tenor, Alan Crofoot, now a favourite of Toronto audiences but in those days dabbling in the graduate department of Psychology a block away. We grew to be good friends later on and I often reminded Al that this was the first place I'd seen him close to, though we didn't speak. Once or twice that afternoon he glanced across at our table, plainly wondering why I had FORDHAM lettered on the front of my sweatshirt. I let him work on it.

There wasn't a waiter; you had to go to the window. In a minute Danny came back with three ice-cold Molson's Blue and glasses on a tin tray. As a matter of fact we had had a fairly busy morning, we were sweaty, we had just had a heavy lunch – nothing ever tasted any better than a cold beer on a beautiful afternoon with nothing to look forward to but more of the same.

In those days I had a small local reputation as a better than fair beer drinker with plenty of early foot, though with nothing like the stamina or capacity of Al Crofoot, say, or any of half a dozen other redoubtable faculty members and graduate assistants of my time. But I couldn't even stay close to Bill and Danny, who drank two to my one, never appearing to feel it and never becoming obstreperous or downright disagreeable as I regularly did myself, and as my usual drinking companions often did. It was a great pleasure to pass the afternoon with them. And when five o'clock came they both pressed money on me, in the unspoken recognition that I would naturally go on to another Beverage Room after dinner. We parted on the best of terms.

Soon this comfortable alliance was dissolved by circumstance, when Aimé arrived back at the Yard after doing his thirty days. He flatly refused to go out with one of the gangs; he had earned his place on the coal-ass crew, he felt, and no goddam college kid was going to get it away from him. Bill and Danny were indifferent in the matter, as was natural, and at length, about a quarter to nine the first morning Aimé was back, Charlie called me in from where I was sitting smoking to ask me how I felt about it. You see, he respected the prescriptive right that I'd already acquired in the job. There was an unspoken but very strong sentiment at the Yard that once a man got his hands on a soft spot he acquired a kind of generally sanctioned right to it. Charlie peered at me sidewise as I came into the office and leaned casually, as I'd already learned to do, on the counter.

'What about this, Hood?' he asked sharply but, I sensed, half-apologetically. 'Aimé wants his job back.'

'Fine,' I said. He looked at me with relief, palpably surprised that I hadn't made more of a fuss.

'You'll have to go out with Harris,' he said warningly.

'Okay.'

Aimé looked at me. 'No hard feelings, kid, you understand.'

'No,' I said, smiling. He went outside and picked up a shovel. Soon I could hear him wrangling with Danny over who was to sit in the middle.

'Goddam French-Canadian bastard !'

'Shut your fat mouth, Foster !'

The three of them got in the truck and drove off.

Naim Kattan

A LITERATURE OF INTERROGATION

The relations of French-Canadian writers with their society have always been family relations. Whether he glorifies the past of his people, sings its praises and extols its way of life, or whether he chooses a return to the source, steeping himself in the literature of the mother country or in the marginal life of bohemia and non-conformity, he remains, quite independent of his will, a member of the family. He was faced always with a dilemma : would he accept being a provincial or would he seek vainly for a parent state to which to attach himself? France, his mother country, had betrayed him twice over, by abandoning him, an orphan, on American soil, and by breaking during the French Revolution with its own traditions. At last, though often in an ambiguous manner, the writer has conquered his spiritual territory. Divided between a Europe whose circumference he is in process of redrawing and an America he accepts only half-way and begrudgingly, he is identical with all the writers who are making their way, cautiously and despite themselves, into the age of technology – an age also of the specific, for one is no longer simply in North America when all the cultures have been melted down in a single crucible.

American literature is today an aggregate of regionalisms and particularists. Jews, Negroes, writers of the South or of the West, they express all the fractions of a complex if not finally elusive reality. So French-Canadian writers, those that accept their particularism and those that wish to be the standard-bearers of a newly found identity, are completely of their time. They are also of their continent.

The French-Canadian writer who gives expression to the life of his people no longer has a bad conscience about not belonging to the world. For him universalism takes its point of departure from the soil. This willingness to accept particularism has manifested itself in poetry as well as in the novel and the theatre. The poets were the first to examine and, in varying degrees, give utterance to the unstable equilibrium between the writer and his milieu. Since the end of the last world war, young French-Canadian poets have no longer been content merely to multiply pale imitations of French poets. True, the latter continued to exercise their influence, but now it was an indirect influence that supported an originality finally assumed.

Gilles Hénault, Roland Giguère, Paul-Marie Lapointe, and Jean-Guy Pilon voiced in low tones or with shouts the ills of the French Canadian. And while Anne Hébert murmured of the incomplete life and private agonies, these other poets, her juniors, were appealing with all their strength for a better future. It was a poetry of anticipation. In this time of transition, while a new society was emerging from the old, the poets were the harbingers of a new age. They did not try to escape from their native soil, nor did they idealize it. They were seeking a harmony with which to affirm a reconciliation still more wished for than achieved.

In his poem, 'Trees', Paul-Marie Lapointe sang of the beauty of a real country. His lyricism surged from the actual and the concrete. In dissimilar voices, such poets as Gilles Hénault, Fernand Ouellette, Roland Giguère, and Jean-Guy Pilon called for fraternity beyond the boundaries of the land of their roots. Gaston Miron (notably in 'La mort agonique') voices the pain and difficulty of achieving harmony. The poet's rediscovery and acceptance of his roots was not an immediate assumption. It had to be won by constantly renewed efforts. But Miron is too integrated with the soil for despair. His voice is angry.

The French-Canadian poet embodies the ambiguity of his people since he cannot survive without reconquering a language he sees as both endangered and curtailed. Would he possess his personal vocabulary had his language been diminished at the outset? This question presided over the birth of a movement that quickly made a great stir. I am speaking of the so-called 'joual' movement. Certain writers – Jacques Rénaud, André Major, and, later, Claude Jasmin – wished to make this diminished language a new vehicle of expression. Their attitude was fundamentally contradictory. 'Joual' was not for them a popular speech, the language of the masses, that must be raised to the level of literature. To them it was the proof of the enslavement of a people. Casting it into the face of the public constituted an appeal for liberation, since the language could only be 'reconquered' by social and political emancipation. But it is impossible to write in a language one despises and wishes to destroy. One cannot express oneself with words one scorns. So 'joual' literature was still-born, succumbing under the weight of its contradictions.

However, this did not mean the disappearance of the appeal for liberation. The young poets still wish to use poetry to liberate their people. Paul Chamberland, one of the most talented among them, is a nationalist poet. He is too lyric, however, to obey political cues or to be the prisoner of an ideology, even though he is himself one of its most fervent promoters.

The venture of the review *Parti Pris* also commenced in ambiguity. It was founded by writers. They perceived that the demands of literary expression could not easily be enclosed within the limits of ideology, the more so as this ideology was not completely formulated. *Parti Pris* would either become an avant-garde, political, and revolutionary literary review or change into the organ of an activist group concerned only with the elaboration of a platform and a programme. It has finally taken the latter direction, then ceased publication.

The young poets have gone much further than their predecessors. They not only affirm their accord with their people but wish to build a new society and plan a future. The much-desired harmony is no longer a lament but a programme of action.

Before the poets, the novelists provided a realistic description of the French-Canadian condition, a faithful mirror for a society in the process of urbanization. The realistic novels of Gabrielle Roy and Roger Lemelin did not form a school. Such off-shoots as they have had have been on television – for instance, the well-known and very successful *Les Plouffes*. It is André Langevin in *Poussière sur la ville*, *Évadé de la nuit*, and *Le Temps des hommes* that has best described the uncertainties and distress of the French Canadian in this era of transition. The spiritual anxiety that emerges from these novels, especially from *Le Temps des hommes*, is that of a great many Catholics. Religious structures have weakened, and the faith that was bound up with them grew fainter. Langevin does not reject Christianity but voices the need to revivify and renew it. His hopes and misgivings at that time were shared, it is true, by many Catholics, both laymen and clergy. Regrettably, Langevin has written no new novels for several years.

It would be useless to seek a common denominator among the dozens of novelists that have sprung up in these last years. It is possible, however, to discern in this diversity a single need – to take stock of reality. Women have played a full and generous part in this vastly increased production. With frankness, with a total lack of false modesty if not of modesty itself, these women novelists have described, candidly or insistently, their frustration and their thirst for fulfilment. From the sarcastic and bitter narratives of Claire Martin to the clinical details in the works of Yvette Naubert, French-Canadian women novelists have broken down all doors. Rarely have love and sexuality been discussed as openly as by Diane Giguère, Yvette Maheux-Forcier, and Hélène Ouvrard. In this openness there is often a vengeful discharge of a need too long contained.

Marie-Claire Blais has gone beyond the feminine condition. In her first novels, she released her private nightmares, but in *Une Saison dans la vie d'Emmanuel* she reveals herself as an accomplished novelist. She makes a humanity, still engulfed in a prenatal night, live before our eyes. We are far here from a demand for one's rights or an appeal for sexual liberation. The children Marie-Claire Blais describes to us refuse to face the light. They immerse themselves in sordid games to put off the moment when the world of the adults will swoop upon them, for this world is tainted and corrupt. But in this apprehension before life, this shrinking from its power, there is a song of hope. A real humanity will emerge, will spring from this opaque night, and the shadows will fade away before the rise of men and women eager to live.

The intention of the most significant novels of these last years has not been so much to describe reality, define, or limit it as it is to place the French Canadian and discover what his universe is. In other words, the novelists have been in quest of their identity – a quest that has manifested itself on various levels.

Gilles Marcotte placed it in his two novels, *Le Poids de Dieu* and *Retour à Coolbrook*, in relation to the religious conscience and a man's return to his native town. In the former, the central character is a priest at grips with social reality – here is the whole problem of the religious conscience in French Canada. In the latter, the problem is twofold. Can one live in a small town when one has known the freedom of the metropolis? And can love, embodied here by a woman, be dissociated from a return to the source and a rediscovery and acceptance of oneself?

In *Une Vie d'enfer*, André Laurendeau offers a man in conflict with himself, powerless to escape from the fascination of death and a destruction that takes the form of an inability to accept life and come to terms with a human community. Jean-Paul Fugère in *Les Terres noires* shows the fragility of an identity spontaneously acquired in a rural society. The French Canadians he portrays try vainly to reconstitute the village of their birth in an urban milieu. In *La Jument des Mongols* and *Le Grand Khan*, Jean Basile evokes a new marginal urban society in Montreal. In very dissimilar novels, *La Vie inhumaine* and *Prochain épisode*, Laurent Girouard and Hubert Aquin treat this search for identity directly. Girouard's central character is a French Canadian who sees his identity dwindle, destroyed gradually by social forces. The novel is a voyage to the end of the night, at the limit of which there is implicitly a call to revolution. The dark destiny imposed upon French Canadians cannot be checked and overcome except by overthrowing the social and political regime.

Like Girouard, Hubert Aquin is a Separatist. His protagonist splits in two. Entangled in a mad espionage adventure in Switzerland, in which he seems to be both pursuer and pursued, the French Canadian realizes that he can only find himself by eliminating his double. The novel ends before the characters are born and cancels itself out, in consequence, before it begins. Aquin attains the ultimate negation.

Other novelists have gone elsewhere in search of the fugitive identity. The number of Jewish characters in French-Canadian novels is worthy of note. In *Ethel et le terroriste*, Claude Jasmin makes a young Jewish girl serve as a mediator with reality. Unlike her lover, the French-Canadian terrorist, Ethel feels no uncertainty as to her identity. She does not need violence to discover her own face. In Claire Martin's novel, *Quand j'aurai payé ton visage*, the Jewish character represents a French Canadian free of the bourgeois conventions against which French Canadians are still struggling. Jacques Godbout (*Le Couteau sur la table*) has also sought in the portrait of an Anglo-Jewish girl a mirror that offers to her French-Canadian companion the reflection of his own face.

The French-Canadian novelist is seeking to enlarge his horizon by the affirmation of his identity. It is not surprising then that he presents Jewish characters. They do not threaten his minority status. Moreover, the Jew has been able to preserve his identity through the ages. The example is reassuring. To take a leap into the English-Canadian community would amount in a process of this sort to going over to the other camp and would be the equivalent of a betrayal. Thence the total absence of English-Canadian characters in the French-Canadian novel. It is true that these Jewish characters have no specific reality. They are Jews only externally. Their presence merely indicates a deeper and wider interest on the part of the French Canadian in his own community.

In comparison with poetry and the novel, French-Canadian theatre has developed only very slowly in recent years. Undeniably, television has paralysed it, if not atrophied it completely. Drawing upon the available resources of the creative élite, it has drained away a considerable number of talents. How many novelists and poets have abandoned the literary forms in which they had made brilliant debuts to launch themselves into this new medium? Television, it is true, might have created a climate favourable to theatre. It provided a living to a number of actors, scene designers, and directors. But it seems not to have been of much help to playwrights, and those that have set their pens to the service of television have more often than not forsaken the theatre. However, infrequent as new French-Canadian plays have been of recent years, it is possible to point out two tendencies. Dissimilar as they are, Gratien Gélinas and Marcel Dubé have both based their plays very strictly upon reality. Gélinas, by reflecting it, has exploited it to attract the public; and Dubé, by expressing it, has made himself the spokesman for those French Canadians who do not accept their condition and seek to modify it. The other tendency has not come to very much. It is exemplified by Jacques Languirand who has tried, by utilizing the discoveries and new techniques of the world avant-garde theatre, to renew that of French Canada.

The essay, a form too long neglected in French Canada, has recently had some distinguished practitioners, among them Jean Le Moyne, the success of whose *Convergences* is well known. This is an important book because it confirms the presence of an original French-Canadian thought. Le Moyne's rediscovery of his own roots is the result of the widening of his horizons upon the whole world and a familiarity with contemporary thought.

Like Le Moyne, Pierre Vadboncoeur in *La Ligne du risque* and Fernand Dumont in *Pour une nouvelle pensée chrétienne* and *Le Lieu de L'homme* proceed from an affirmation of their religious faith to renew and revitalize its framework. These essayists are contributing a philosophy to a society in ferment.

Translated by Joyce Marshall

Hector de Saint-Denys-Garneau

NOTES ON NATIONALISM

From *The Journal of Hector de Saint-Denys-Garneau*

At H—'s this evening, met C— who wants to define in a kind of manifesto *La Relève*'s position on nationalism.

What is nationalism?

A way of looking at problems with reference to the nation.

What problems can be properly considered from this standpoint, and to what extent?

The economic: it's impossible (so say R— and C—) to consider this from a nationalist standpoint. That would simply result in transferring the wealth of English capitalists to French-Canadian ones – leaving the people and the nation no better off. (Even if this gave French Canadians the money to develop their culture; for it's well known that when they have money they *close up* in the enjoyment of it and in the feeling of security it gives them.)

Nationalist politics, what does that offer? Political boycott of the English. And after that? No, what we want is not a nationalist government but simply an honest one. As for a programme by which the State takes over all initiative, that kind of centralization is good for nothing. (For my part, I can't see that it does much else.)

There remain the problems of culture. Can culture be considered from a nationalist point of view? I don't think so. Culture is something essentially human in its aims – it is essentially humanist. To 'form' French Canadians, that is to say to make them conscious of themselves as such, is perhaps a popular notion, but it lacks all sense. It's even against sense and against nature. The individual becomes conscious of himself in order to devote himself, to complete himself: yes, but not to complete himself as *self*, but as *man*. Besides, we find ourselves not so much by self-searching as by action. All movement towards the self is sterile. And especially, I believe, for a people. A people forms itself by acting, by creating – that is, by communicating. It finds itself through the act of communication.

For some time we have been awaiting the appearance of the creator, the poet who will give the F.-C. people their own true image. He will no doubt appear in his own good time, when the substance of the people is strong enough and real enough, and unique enough, sufficiently distinguished from all others to inspire this awaited genius with sufficient cogency. For the genius is not the product of a people. And yet he participates in their culture, their ambience; and being closer to them, he is the one who will see them most truly and will give them their truest form – the people, the nation, here playing the role of matter. (As for any generically French-Canadian way of looking at things, in which a French-Canadian artist could participate, I see nothing of the kind yet, and believe it will be a long time before such a thing appears in any distinct form.) It will then fall to this creator to present to the people their own countenance, recognizable and ideal. This will doubtless help the people to become conscious of themselves, to exist. But it will be the sign that their features are recognized, and not a sign by which one will recognize those features. Once again, all this retro-active *mystique* seems to me against nature, sterile and sterilizing.

(That way of looking at things, is it a way of facing problems, of facing life? Everyone has a different way. But could there be a residual principle according to which each, in order to obtain different results, might go through certain common processes? I can't say whether anything of this kind is going on here. In any case, I don't think any survey of this common and specifically French-Canadian field would be very fruitful. Moreover, I find it hard to see how anyone can base a culture on anything so diffi-cult to grasp. And to direct culture towards a heightening of these individualistic traits is out of the question.)

Culture, then, has a sense of human improvement. It is essentially humanist. It wishes to form men, not French Canadians. There is no contradiction here, only a distinction as to priority of values, as to direction. To make men out of French Canadians and not French Canadians out of men. A worthy intention – to make men more themselves by making them French Canadians. But any method not properly directed towards the essentially human is likely to be restrictive and short-sighted. And so is all education founded on historiography and nationalism.

It seems that the French-Canadian people must be considered, with reference to culture, as a datum, an accepted fact. A fact which humanist culture (in the sense of human, not that of a lettered élite) must develop and release in the way of humanity.

The whole task, I think, the whole problem consists in freeing the human spirit – not in freeing French Canadians. Nor would this lead to making human beings more uniform and to depriving the French-Canadian people of its characteristic traits; on the contrary, if this smooths out its disfiguring features, its defects and all its quality of restrictiveness, if it leads to fullness of life, to freedom of life, then communications more valid, healthy, simple and more vital within their own range (nature, work, etc.), will allow these essential and indigenous traits to glow with more character and firmness. It will then be a people truly itself, able to communicate unreservedly with other peoples.

But in any work designed to improve the culture of the French-Canadian nation, to free the human element in our people, this datum of nationality must be given its proper weight. And that is where the uncertainty lies. There are those who reduce everything to this datum, wish to make it the beginning and the end of our national character (whence the nationalist preaching which ignores the human element and advocates summary and short-sighted measures), when what is needed is to stress the human element of this datum, that is to say everything which opens and gives access, not that which closes by seeking to define.

In other words, we must take into account what is essentially human in this datum with a view to freeing it, and also the conditions under which it is found, so as to choose the methods of setting it free.

At present these conditions have several aspects. There is the fact that F.-C. nationality affects this human datum. And there are economic conditions, conditions of living, of work, of the state.

To be effective, action presumes a knowledge of the conditions affecting those towards whom it is directed. But here again, a consideration of the specifically French-Canadian aspect of these conditions does not seem a well-grounded guide to action. What we should like, for instance, is to improve the condition of the worker – not insofar as he is a French Canadian but insofar as he is a worker; and the same for the worker on the land. Unless the problems of both present a peculiarly French-Canadian aspect. In which case certain just claims would take on a properly nationalist character – as that of a brother demanding justice for a brother who is being exploited.

Thus there would be a certain truly French-Canadian aspect of the question which could justify a nationalist attitude. This attitude would consist above all in making common cause to press certain claims. The ground of agreement on the nature of these claims would be properly French-Canadian, and therefore nationalist. (Especially in the matter of the employment of French Canadians and in their gaining access to higher and better paid positions.)

But our ideas of action, which seek to embrace the whole life of our native land – *the* life and *our* life in the sphere in which Providence has placed us – have a deeper and more radical character. From our point of view the human problem extends on all sides far beyond the national problem. It is not as 'national' but as 'human' that it makes its most profound demand on us.

And it is by human measures that the ills of our compatriots can be remedied, not their human ills by nationalist measures. For man's ills go beyond the idea of the national, they are human, and only human measures can overcome them.

Are our ills national? Not at all. They may be more peculiarly ours, but they are human defects which affect French Canadians. They call for remedies which are entirely human.

So with the grand problem of 'national' education. And what is 'national' education? An education designed to create a nation in a French-Canadian mould? And then the holding up to the people of certain moulds, certain formulas, a national myth? Would that give our people the consciousness of nationhood? And then what? Can such an education even exist without a sense of restrictiveness?

As soon as we speak of education it seems that the word 'national' falls of itself, as something footless. The material offered us is completely human, and whenever our attention strays towards the national it seems the balance is destroyed in favour of immediate issues and action, and the material at once loses its depth – or rather, we lose contact with its depth. These educators steeped in the spirit of nationalism, are they not in danger of finding their minds soon closed, of failing to see our problems in all their breadth, their human breadth?

In any case, at the moment, the critical nature of the situation concerns us in all its breadth. The problem facing us is fundamentally human. By searching for what is human, human values and human justice, we shall contribute something to its solution. We must consider the human state of the nation.

The problem and the solution are human in their nature – with a rider of quite secondary importance in the nationalistic sense.

To distinguish: What is properly national, and what is human, in our problem. Which of these calls for remedies that are human and not national. Where national action is harmful. Where it is inadequate. Where it is permissible.

Translated by John Glassco

Alden Nowlan

FOR JEAN VINCENT D'ABBADIE,
BARON ST-CASTIN

Take heart, monsieur, four-fifths of this province
is still much as you left it : forest, swamp and barren.
Even now, after three hundred years, your enemies
    fear ambush, huddle by coasts and rivers,
the dark woods at their backs.

    Oh, you'd laugh to see
how old Increase Mather and his ghastly Calvinists
patrol the palisades, how they bury their money
under the floors of their hideous churches
lest you come again in the night
with the red ochre mark of the sun god
on your forehead, you exile from the Pyrenees,
    you baron of France and Navarre,
you squaw man, you Latin poet,
    you war chief of Penobscot
and of Kennebec and of Maliseet !

    At the winter solstice
your enemies cry out in their sleep
and the great trees throw back their heads and shout
    nabujcol!
Take heart, monsieur,
even the premier, even the archbishop,
even the poor gnome-like slaves
at the all-night diner and the service station
will hear you chant
    The Song of Roland
as you cross yourself
and reach for your scalping knife.

Claire Martin

FROM IN AN IRON GLOVE

From that very first day I suffered acutely in my new state as a
boarder. Apparently it had never occurred to the nuns that I might
be totally ignorant of the rules of the house. I have often observed
this feature of convent life since. What goes on within the walls
seems so important to those poor girls who have cut themselves off
from all contact with reality, that they simply cannot understand
how anyone could not know what occupies every minute of their
lives. I was expected to do what I was supposed to without ever
being told what it was. The other little girls who had known all the
rules since September seemed to think the same. Sometimes the
sisters would give instructions, but they meant nothing to me
because I was not familiar with the convent vocabulary. I was
immediately taken to be disobedient by nature and in the first two
days earned several reprimands. My fate for the next ten years was
sealed from that instant on.

Still I was very lucky to get no more than scoldings. Corporal
punishment was not as common as in my father's house, but it was
not altogether neglected either. A few days before my arrival there
had been a collective punishment that was still being whispered
about. Here is the story. At the end of each of the morning classes –
catechism, French and English – each pupil received a mark: very
good, good, or fair. The morning in question the mistress of this
division announced that girls who did not get their three 'very
goods' would be punished as an example to all. At eleven o'clock
came the separation of the wheat from the tares. The tares were
led off to the dormitory where they were ordered to take off their
dresses. Then, arming herself with a stiff brush, the sister scrubbed
their faces with laundry soap. It was a powerful detergent; even
without the brush it left the skin raw in no time flat. Dark girls
resisted a little better than the rest, but the poor little blondes – not

to mention the red-heads – came through the ordeal their faces peeling and oozing blood. I was quite shaken by this story, all the more so because my own sister, Françoise, was among the number of the skinned. I knew all about blows delivered in anger. But I had not yet heard of such meticulous and patient tortures. Decidedly, apart from Mother, Grandmother and Grandfather, grownups were not much good.

After the third or fourth day I found myself involved in my own first adventure. Even though a climate of strict puritanism reigned in our family, we were none the less used to calling certain functions by their proper names. At home we never used those ridiculous expressions which avoid the use of 'peepee' but which, since they mean the same thing, are scarcely more distinguished for all that. I once knew a family where they said, 'Do a wet', which is really the height of stupidity. But since there is no real ceiling to the ridiculous, these people went on to use the same word for the organ as for the function, all of which I find rather repulsive. The importance of a word lies in its meaning I should think, and if 'chair' meant 'whorehouse', the word 'chair' in that case would have to be replaced by another word, which would in turn rapidly fall into discredit, and so on until we had no place to sit down.

In short, one day I had to 'go upstairs', for that was the way the thing was said at the convent, even though we often might be on the same floor or the floor above. I happened to confide to my neighbour that I had a terrible urge to do a peepee. Hiding her mouth behind her hand, 'Ah dzou !' she exclaimed. 'Dzou', in that particular institution, was the strongest expression of horror imaginable. But, because I was so new, I didn't know the meaning of 'dzou'. The period ended just at that minute, and since we all went upstairs in a group, my problem was solved and I forgot the confidence I had shared with my neighbour.

At recess I was called over by the scrub-brush sister who made it her duty to get me to confess my sin. As it happened, I had completely forgotten it. One must really know nothing about children to think that they know what they said an hour earlier. Besides, since I had no idea of the organized tattle-taling that went on in convents, I couldn't understand what it was all about. I hadn't even spoken to that particular nun.

'You said a bad word.'

To whom? When? The soul of good will, I tried to remember. But I drew a complete blank.

'So you want to add a lie to your bad word?'

Oh-oh! I had heard that somewhere before, and I realized that I had just earned myself a double punishment on the heels of the single. The more I saw of life, the more it seemed the same. But this time, weary of the fray, the sister dismissed me. I thought that was the end of it. But I didn't know who I was dealing with. That evening at bedtime I was taken to a room adjoining the dormitory.

'You're not going to go to bed without owning up? Just think, you might die in your sleep.'

Good God! That didn't help matters much. Here I was now, to all intents and purposes threatened with death. I searched and searched. Nothing. The sister made me sit closeted alone with my crime, while the other little girls went to bed. From time to time she came to inquire into my disposition to confess. It wasn't good intentions that I lacked, it was a subject for confession.

I kept on searching and shivering in my nightgown. At last, after an hour perhaps, though it seemed as if half the night had gone by, she said : 'I realize it must be embarrassing for you to repeat the word. I'm going to help you. It begins with a "p"—'

It was good of her, but at my wits' end with all the unexpected, inextricable, petty, and insane confusion of the whole story, and overcome with sleep, 'p'— wasn't much to set me on the right track. I kept on searching.

'Well? p—p,e—'

'P,e'—? I can't have been very brilliant that night. 'P,e'—? I couldn't see what it was. Finally the sister, who wanted to go to bed, I suppose, but for all that didn't want to let me risk my eternal salvation, lost patience.

'You said "peepee".'

She hid her mouth behind her hand, just as my little schoolmate had done. She made me say an act of contrition and then let me go to bed.

Next Thursday during the visit, my sisters told that I had been scolded but said they didn't know why. Mother insisted on knowing. Well, I was so convinced that I had done a thing, not really dreadful but running counter to the spirit of the institution, that I didn't want to admit to something in front of my sisters which might have caused them endless embarrassment.

'I said the food was no good. I said it was no better than cat shit.'

In the end, that was not much better, but I felt there was an enormous difference between the two words: in the second there was no reference to human needs. The human had been duly rejected. Anyway, Mother laughed till the tears came, and my sisters too.

'Don't you worry about it any more, it's all forgotten.'

That remained to be seen.

I didn't like lying to Mother. It didn't happen often. With Grandmother, never. That was because though she might scold me for doing wrong, she never punished me. She thought that a scolding was enough. In Mother's case it was different. When we were quite patently at fault, when we had broken something for instance (I should point out that my father made no allowance for children's clumsiness and punished us just as severely for accidentally breaking a window as he would for deliberate badness), before inescapable evidence, Mother would have to tell what had happened. The first question my father would ask was, 'Has the child been punished?' Mother couldn't decently say yes unless we had been. It is impossible to bring children up in that sort of duplicity. She had to reply vigorously in the affirmative or else he would have taken charge of the punishment himself. Mother wanted to avoid that at all costs. This didn't prevent my father, I must add, from often administering a second punishment which was never the same variety as the first. Mother made us stand in a corner. I can't remember ever being sent there by my father.

It isn't really so bad to be sent to the corner. The reason I hated it was for fear my father might come in while I was there. I will never forget my terror one day when I had been really intolerable and was left in the corner until I could hear my father's footsteps shaking the staircase.

'Mother, please forgive me! Please! I promise to be good.'

Promptly pardoned and overcome with gratitude, for the next few days I behaved better than I ever had, and I was full of such tenderness for her – I remember this distinctly – that I even kissed her dress.

Lying to my father was quite another matter. It was a kind of vital necessity. Good sport, too. And vengeance, when you come to think of it. If all the lies invented by all of us over a period of, say, twenty years, had had to be totalled up, it would have kept a sharp accountant pretty busy. Children lie not only out of fear but also when they have to deal with people they don't respect. 'That kind doesn't deserve to be told the truth.' Truthfulness is not just a duty, it's a gift. To make matters worse, my father was not in the least observant. He always believed we were lying when we were telling the truth, and vice versa. The thoughts that such an attitude inspires in a child could hardly be called indulgent.

*

. . . One Sunday morning at sermon time, the chaplain announced that he had a long proclamation to read to us and with an imperial gesture unrolled a crackling scroll. It was the decree – people of my age will remember it well – that forbade dancing in the diocese of Quebec. It was as though the chapel had been hit by lightning! The big girls looked at each other aghast and even the tiny tots were horrified. It should be realized that we were, in general, the offspring of the very cream of what the sisters called 'society' in the city of Quebec, and stories about receptions, balls, evening gowns, et cetera, were the staple of our small talk.

Hereafter, under pain of mortal sin, the waltz, the tango, the foxtrot, the one-step, the two-step, the shimmy . . .

The list seemed interminable. The chaplain drew a few chuckles with all these tongue-twisters, most of them English, which he mouthed as best he could. You realized that a team of real experts – and it was dizzying to think where they had been unearthed – had taken stock of every solitary thing that bore a name in the whole realm of jiggling to music. Nor was a single obscure polka or bourrée forgotten that nasty-minded people would, of course, immediately discover and put into practice.

The emotion aroused by this decree filled the parlour that Sunday afternoon with a bustle of whispering. What a shame! No, but really, what a rotten shame!

'Pooh! Mother said we'd go dancing in Montreal,' said Bérangère with infinite scorn.

And that, in fact, is what people did for a while. Then, since the Château Frontenac kept its ballroom open, 'for the tourists' – belonging to the Canadian Pacific it had, by that token, acquired a sort of extraterritorial status – little by little Quebec parishioners began to steal in there until, less than five years after the ukase, practically no one paid any attention to it, which may at first sight seem surprising in a populace as docile as ours. However, on second thought, it seems to me that the dance is such a good way for people like us to let off steam that it would have been impossible to forbid it for long. It should be added that, unless I am mistaken, this order was never withdrawn. I draw this, in passing, to the attention of all good citizens of Quebec.

*

... My father was never able to understand that at a certain age a child ceased being a child. We could be fifteen, eighteen, twenty, he always kept on treating us as though we were four-year-olds. The age of reason wasn't for us.

Since I haven't any children and have never had occasion to pass over to the parents' camp, I have kept a very sharp memory of one thing in particular: when a child is right, it is useless trying to persuade him that he's wrong. It is also useless to try to make him believe that you are acting for the best according to your lights – he sees through that little farce very quickly. If, on top of that, you prevent him from answering back, from explaining why he thinks he's right, well, in that case, just let me say that the child's feelings are so unflattering that it's better not to comment on them. A child doesn't just hunger after tenderness, caresses and presents, but justice. And how hungry I've been!

At the root of my father's injustice lay a profound ignorance of a child's mental development. It wasn't because there was any shortage of them, but because he hadn't watched them grow up with interest and love. For instance, he could very well accuse us of having pencilled on the wall, even though we were ten or twelve and the scribbling was at the height of a child of three, mentally as well as physically. Furthermore, since we were no sooner accused than punished, the possibility of being found innocent absolutely never entered into it. A punished child remains guilty. What's done is done, and the father of the family – maybe not other ones, but mine at any rate – is infallible by divine right. If we were too patently innocent, his bad humour knew no bounds.

'And above all don't go thinking you're the victim of some injustice or other. God willed you to be punished for some other foolishness I didn't know about.'

He would march off with an angry stride, then turn back.

'I just mentioned some other foolishness I might not have found out about. But don't start thinking there's much that escapes me. You should know by now I always find out the truth in the end, and I don't think you could name a single fault you've committed without my learning about it.'

After I left the convent I was forbidden to write any letters to anyone without first asking his permission.

'You've disobeyed me again,' he said one morning, pulling me over into a corner. 'I had forbidden you to write letters without showing them to me.'

'I didn't write any letters.'

'Don't lie. I found your rough copy.'

And he waved a scrap of paper on which my sister Thérèse, who was still just a baby, had told some little convent friend how she played with her dolls, et cetera. The writing and the spelling were equally clumsy.

'It's Thérèse who wrote that.'

My father folded his arms in a Vercingetorixian gesture.

'Why don't you say straight out that I'm a fool? Thérèse? At her age? We'll soon see about that.'

Summoned to the stand, Thérèse was forced to admit that she had authored the document. With that, my father suddenly believed he had fathered a genius, and in his astonishment he completely forgot about me.

Later on, if he ever referred to an event that had taken place when we were twelve or thirteen, he would always say, 'You were much too young at the time, you couldn't remember that.' This was due, I think (and it was perfectly understandable), to the hope that we had forgotten a great deal.

Tyranny, of course, works much better on children than on adults. As the years sped by, he grew afraid of having to sacrifice a single scrap of his tyranny. That's why he refused to see that we had outgrown our childhood. He would have liked to control our least thoughts. Indeed, he thought he could. The certificate he had been awarded by Professor L. A. Harraden, Hypnotist, testified to that. It said that the recipient had faithfully studied and completed the course in Modern Hypnotism and was now a perfect hypnotist, thoroughly qualified to practise the art. You should have seen the way my father looked us in the eye when he wanted to make us own up to something ! This Professor Harraden – who described himself on the certificate as 'the greatest hypnotist in the world' was un-doubtedly a nut, and possibly the most obscure hypnotist in the world into the bargain; for to my knowledge not a single one of us, despite the blue paternal stare, ever yielded up anything but the first lie on the tip of his tongue. The push-button lie. We had to be past masters of that art, since we might be interrogated at any minute on any subject under the sun.

'What are you humming? Why are you humming that? Where did you learn that tune? Don't lie.'

'What are you thinking about? And don't tell me you don't know. Don't lie.'

'You smiled. Were you thinking about something dirty? Don't lie.'

We had the answers down pat. It was a tune we had heard played in church last Sunday. I was just thinking about mending some

socks for him. I was smiling to think of that awfully funny story
he had told us one day about the time he lived on Anticosti Island.
If he could be pushed on to the safe path of this period in his life,
you could be sure to be left in peace for a good long while. You
didn't even have to listen. We had heard those anecdotes a thousand
times, and we all knew the moral you were supposed to draw from
them : that it was he who was the wisest, strongest, bravest, purest,
smartest and most humble of all.

'I don't know,' he would say, squirming a little, 'whether it's
that I've got more common sense – or judgement, or memory, or
goodness or understanding – than others, but if the truth must be
known . . . et cetera, et cetera.'

Poor father ! He was really the only child among us, and – when
I had passed the age of adolescent intolerance – to hear him rave on
so made me feel something – it wasn't tenderness, you don't feel
tenderness for someone who is a stranger to you, but indulgence
perhaps – of the same kind one feels towards some young scamp in
the street who tries to show off to the passers-by.

The business about the socks was pretty good, too. He was never
happy unless the whole household was busy working for him. If I
was sewing a button on my blouse, he would begin to fidget, then
to grumble :

'I see you are sewing on a button. What about my buttons? I'll
bet it's donkey's years since you've looked them over.'

It would never do, however, to fix our buttons on a Sunday. That
wasn't allowed. On the other hand, we spent a good half of every
Sunday doing little jobs for him – shining his shoes, pressing his
suits, shortening this, lengthening that. He must have thought
that since we were working on a saint's things, heaven didn't just
turn a blind eye on it, oh no, but actually rejoiced. Hosanna !

If it was one of his days of high anger, he would feverishly hunt
through all his clothes to find something that wasn't in perfect
shape. That was hard to find, for we knew the price there was to
pay for the slightest neglect. Well, never mind ! He would cut holes
in his socks. Through the open door, we could sometimes see him,
reflected in a couple of mirrors, painstakingly occupied at this
modest task.

At table it was the same story. Everyone had to wait on him. As the girls grew up, it became impossible for them to get a hot serving. Although we made meals that were copious and elaborate – this had become easier because over the years he had started to forget about centenarian foods – no matter what trouble we took, he always found something missing.

'I'd rather have had peas with this.'

Dine would leave the table to quickly heat up a can of peas.

'What about some ketchup?'

Françoise would get up.

'Or, no, make that hot relish.'

I would get up.

'I'd like my bread toasted.'

Marguerite would get up.

'This meal wasn't enough for me. Fry me some eggs.'

Since Dine wasn't back yet, Françoise would get up again. Although the kitchen was huge we kept bumping into each other.

His appetite was limitless. Despite the four or five courses he tucked away, he always had room for a couple of fried eggs. Since he continuously told us that liars like us turned into thieves and assassins, that the person who steals an egg today will steal an ox tomorrow, we used to whisper to each other, splitting our sides laughing :

'The person who eats an egg today will eat an ox tomorrow.'

With this diet, he had a world of trouble keeping his weight down to two hundred and thirty pounds, which was enormous enough. Then Lent would come along. Naïve as always, he would use this occasion to try to cheat heaven. He would start on a diet to lose weight and call it penance. He thought that if he waited until Lent to start reducing they'd be taken in up there, and would tot it up in the column of mortifications. Incapable of moderation in anything, he would starve himself for forty days. The most immediate result of this fast was that it made him acutely jealous of us for all the things we allowed ourselves to eat in front of him. Even the plainest dishes seemed awfully tempting to him.

'Well! Carrots *à la poulette*. You never make them when I'm eating.'

'But we had them on Shrove Tuesday.'

'Anyway, you don't make them often. But it's the same thing every year. As soon as I start my Lent, you bring out all your best recipes . . . blah-blah-blah.'

Not only was his bad humour aggravated – in certain circumstances even the worst can be worsened – but his health also suffered. The year he decided to eat nothing but lettuce for forty days, he suffered from some kind of complication of malnutrition which left red splotches all over his skin. He finally went to show this to the doctor, but he was careful not to say anything about his diet. Somewhat perplexed, all the doctor could think of was to give him a Wasserman test, which turned out negative, as you can well imagine. Sure that we were completely ignorant of such matters (but my sister's boy friend was a medical student and told us all about it), he had left the results of the test lying out on his desk. Which was just one other occasion when we nearly died laughing.

So each year we saw the holy season of Lent approach in fear and trembling. In the end we had the inspiration to suggest to him that such privations, while they didn't exactly make him seem older – it wouldn't have been wise to say that – at least made him seem less young, and he decided to cut out the penance. All the same, for seven or eight years, besides the habitual rhythms that ruled our lives, we also had those seasons of mortification and of feasting.

Translated by Philip Stratford

Alice Munro

WALKER BROTHERS COWBOY

After supper my father says, 'Want to go down and see if the Lake's
still there?' We leave my mother sewing under the dining-room
light, making clothes for me against the opening of school. She has
ripped up for this purpose an old suit and an old plaid wool dress
of hers, and she has to cut and match very cleverly and also make
me stand and turn for endless fittings, sweaty, itching from the hot
wool, ungrateful. We leave my brother in bed in the little screened
porch at the end of the front verandah, and sometimes he kneels on
his bed and presses his face against the screen and calls mournfully,
'Bring me an ice cream cone!' but I call back, 'You will be asleep,'
and do not even turn my head.

Then my father and I walk gradually down a long, shabby sort
of street, with Silverwoods Ice Cream signs standing on the sidewalk, outside tiny, lighted stores. This is in Tuppertown, an old
town on Lake Huron, an old grain port. The street is shaded, in
some places, by maple trees whose roots have cracked and heaved
the sidewalk and spread out like crocodiles into the bare yards.
People are sitting out, men in shirt-sleeves and undershirts and
women in aprons – not people we know but if anybody looks ready
to nod and say, 'Warm night,' my father will nod too and say something the same. Children are still playing. I don't know them either
because my mother keeps my brother and me in our own yard,
saying he is too young to leave it and I have to mind him. I am not
so sad to watch their evening games because the games themselves
are ragged, dissolving. Children, of their own will, draw apart,
separate into islands of two or one under the heavy trees, occupying
themselves in such solitary ways as I do all day, planting pebbles in
the dirt or writing in it with a stick.

Presently we leave these yards and houses behind, we pass a
factory with boarded-up windows, a lumberyard whose high

wooden gates are locked for the night. Then the town falls away in a defeated jumble of sheds and small junkyards, the sidewalk gives up and we are walking on a sandy path with burdocks, plantains, humble nameless weeds all around. We enter a vacant lot, a kind of park really, for it is kept clear of junk and there is one bench with a slat missing on the back, a place to sit and look at the water. Which is generally grey in the evening, under a lightly overcast sky, no sunsets, the horizon dim. A very quiet, washing noise on the stones of the beach. Further along, towards the main part of town, there is a stretch of sand, a water slide, floats bobbing around the safe swimming area, a life guard's rickety throne. Also a long dark green building, like a roofed verandah, called the Pavilion, full of farmers and their wives, in stiff good clothes, on Sundays. That is the part of the town we used to know when we lived at Dungannon and came here three or four times a summer, to the Lake. That, and the docks where we would go and look at the grain boats, ancient, rusty, wallowing, making us wonder how they got past the breakwater let alone to Fort William.

Tramps hang around the docks and occasionally on these evenings wander up the dwindling beach and climb the shifting, precarious path boys have made, hanging on to dry bushes, and say something to my father which, being frightened of tramps, I am too alarmed to catch. My father says he is a bit hard up himself. 'I'll roll you a cigarette if it's any use to you,' he says, and he shakes tobacco out carefully on one of the thin butterfly papers, flicks it with his tongue, seals it and hands it to the tramp who takes it and walks away. My father also rolls and lights and smokes one cigarette of his own.

He tells me how the Great Lakes came to be. All where Lake Huron is now, he says, used to be flat land, a wide flat plain. Then came the ice, creeping down from the north, pushing deep into the low places. Like *that* – and he shows me his hand with his spread fingers pressing the rock-hard ground where we are sitting. His fingers make hardly any impression at all and he says, 'Well, the old ice cap had a lot more power behind it than this hand has.' And then the ice went back, shrank back towards the North Pole where it came from, and left its fingers of ice in the deep places it had gouged, and ice turned to lakes and there they were today. They were *new*, as time went. I try to see that plain before me, dinosaurs walking on it, but I am not able even to imagine the shore of the Lake when the Indians were there, before Tuppertown. The tiny share we have of time appals me, though my father seems to regard it with tranquillity. Even my father, who sometimes seems to me to have been at home in the world as long as it has lasted, has really lived on this earth only a little longer than I have, in terms of all the time there has been to live in. He has not known a time, any more than I, when automobiles and electric lights did not at least exist. He was not alive when this century started. I will be barely alive – old, old – when it ends. I do not like to think of it. I wish the Lake to be always just a lake, with the safe-swimming floats marking it, and the breakwater and the lights of Tuppertown.

My father has a job, selling for Walker Brothers. This is a firm that sells almost entirely in the country, the back country. Sunshine, Boylesbridge, Turnaround – that is all his territory. Not Dungannon where we used to live, Dungannon is too near town and my mother is grateful for that. He sells cough medicine, iron tonic, corn plasters, laxatives, pills for female disorders, mouth wash, shampoo, liniment, salves, lemon and orange and raspberry concentrate for making refreshing drinks, vanilla, food colouring, black and green tea, ginger, cloves and other spices, rat poison. He has a song about it, with these two lines.

> And have all liniments and oils,
> For everything from corns to boils . . .

Not a very funny song, in my mother's opinion. A pedlar's song, and that is what he is, a pedlar knocking at backwoods kitchens. Up until last winter we had our own business, a fox farm. My father raised silver foxes and sold their pelts to the people who make them into capes and coats and muffs. Prices fell, my father hung on hoping they would get better next year, and they fell again, and he hung on one more year and one more and finally it was not possible to hang on any more, we owed everything to the feed company. I have heard my mother explain this, several times, to Mrs Oliphant who is the only neighbour she talks to. (Mrs Oliphant also has come down in the world, being a school teacher who married the janitor.) We poured all we had into it, my mother says, and we came out with nothing. Many people could say the same thing, these days, but my mother has no time for the national calamity, only ours. Fate has flung us on to a street of poor people (it does not matter that we were poor before, that was a different sort of poverty), and the only way to take this, as she sees it, is with dignity, with bitterness, with no reconciliation. No bathroom with a claw-footed tub and a flush toilet is going to comfort her, nor water on tap and sidewalks past the house and milk in bottles, not even the two movie theatres and the Venus Restaurant and Woolworths so marvellous it has live birds singing in its fan-cooled corners and fish as tiny as fingernails, as bright as moons, swimming in its green tanks. My mother does not care.

In the afternoons she often walks to Simon's Grocery and takes me with her to help carry things. She wears a good dress, navy blue with little flowers, sheer, worn over a navy-blue slip. Also a summer hat of white straw, pushed down on the side of the head, and white shoes I have just whitened on a newspaper on the back steps. I have my hair freshly done in long damp curls which the dry air will fortunately soon loosen, a stiff large hair-ribbon on top of my head. This is entirely different from going out after supper with my father. We have not walked past two houses before I feel we have become objects of universal ridicule. Even the dirty words chalked on the sidewalk are laughing at us. My mother does not seem to notice. She walks serenely like a lady shopping, like a *lady* shopping, past the housewives in loose beltless dresses torn under the arms. With me her creation, wretched curls and flaunting hair bow, scrubbed knees and white socks – all I do not want to be. I loathe even my name when she says it in public, in a voice so high, proud and ringing, deliberately different from the voice of any other mother on the street.

My mother will sometimes carry home, for a treat, a brick of ice cream – pale Neapolitan; and because we have no refrigerator in our house we wake my brother and eat it at once in the dining-room, always darkened by the wall of the house next door. I spoon it up tenderly, leaving the chocolate till last, hoping to have some still to eat when my brother's dish is empty. My mother tries then to imitate the conversations we used to have at Dungannon, going back to our earliest, most leisurely days before my brother was born, when she would give me a little tea and a lot of milk in a cup like hers and we would sit out on the step facing the pump, the lilac tree, the fox pens beyond. She is not able to keep from mentioning those days. 'Do you remember when we put you in your sled and Major pulled you?' (Major our dog, that we had to leave with neighbours when we moved.) 'Do you remember your sandbox outside the kitchen window?' I pretend to remember far less than I do, wary of being trapped into sympathy or any unwanted emotion.

My mother has headaches. She often has to lie down. She lies on my brother's narrow bed in the little screened porch, shaded by heavy branches. 'I look up at that tree and I think I am at home,' she says.

'What you need,' my father tells her, 'is some fresh air and a drive in the country.' He means for her to go with him, on his Walker Brothers route.

That is not my mother's idea of a drive in the country.

'Can I come?'

'Your mother might want you for trying on clothes.'

'I'm beyond sewing this afternoon,' my mother says.

'I'll take her then. Take both of them, give you a rest.'

What is there about us that people need to be given a rest from? Never mind. I am glad enough to find my brother and make him go to the toilet and get us both into the car, our knees unscrubbed, my hair unringleted. My father brings from the house his two heavy brown suitcases, full of bottles, and sets them on the back seat. He wears a white shirt, brilliant in the sunlight, a tie, light trousers belonging to his summer suit (his other suit is black, for funerals, and belonged to my uncle before he died) and a creamy straw hat. His salesman's outfit, with pencils clipped in the shirt pocket. He goes back once again, probably to say good-bye to my mother, to ask her if she is sure she doesn't want to come, and hear her say, 'No. No thanks, I'm better just to lie here with my eyes closed.' Then we are backing out of the driveway with the rising hope of adventure, just the little hope that takes you over the bump into the street, the hot air starting to move, turning into a breeze, the houses growing less and less familiar as we follow the short cut my father knows, the quick way out of town. Yet what is there waiting for us all afternoon but hot hours in stricken farmyards, perhaps a stop at a country store and three ice cream cones or bottles of pop, and my father singing? The one he made up about himself has a title – 'The Walker Brothers Cowboy' – and it starts out like this:

> Old Ned Fields, he now is dead
> So I am ridin' the route instead...

Who is Ned Fields? The man he has replaced, surely, and if so he really is dead; yet my father's voice is mournful-jolly, making his death some kind of nonsense, a comic calamity. 'Wisht I was back on the Rio Grande, plungin' through the dusky sand.' My father sings most of the time while driving the car. Even now, heading out of town, crossing the bridge and taking the sharp turn on to the highway, he is humming something, mumbling a bit of a song to himself, just tuning up, really, getting ready to improvise, for out along the highway we pass the Baptist Camp, the Vacation Bible Camp, and he lets loose:

> Where are the Baptists, where are the Baptists,
>   where are all the Baptists today?
> They're down in the water, in Lake Huron water,
>   with their sins all a-gittin' washed away.

My brother takes this for straight truth and gets up on his knees trying to see down the Lake. 'I don't see any Baptists,' he says accusingly. 'Neither do I, son,' says my father. 'I told you, they're down in the Lake.'

No roads paved when we left the highway. We have to roll up the windows because of dust. The land is flat, scorched, empty. Bush lots at the back of the farms hold shade, black pine-shade like pools nobody can ever get to. We bump up a long lane and at the end of it what could look more unwelcoming, more deserted than the tall unpainted farmhouse with grass growing uncut right up to the front door, green blinds down and a door upstairs opening on nothing but air? Many houses have this door, and I have never yet been able to find out why. I ask my father and he says they are for walking in your sleep. What? Well if you happen to be walking in your sleep and you want to step outside. I am offended, seeing too late that he is joking, as usual, but my brother says sturdily, 'If they did that they would break their necks.'

The nineteen-thirties. How much of this kind of farmhouse, this kind of afternoon, seems to belong to that one decade in time, just as my father's hat does, his bright flared tie, our car with its wide running board (an Essex, and long past its prime). Cars somewhat like it, many older, none dustier, sit in the farmyards. Some are past running and have their doors pulled off, their seats removed for use on porches. No living things to be seen, chickens or cattle. Except dogs. There are dogs, lying in any kind of shade they can find, dreaming, their lean sides rising and sinking rapidly. They get up when my father opens the car door, he has to speak to them. 'Nice boy, there's a boy, nice old boy.' They quiet down, go back to their shade. He should know how to quiet animals, he has held desperate foxes with tongs around their necks. One gentling voice for the dogs and another, rousing, cheerful, for calling at doors. 'Hello there, Missus, it's the Walker Brothers man and what are you out of today?' A door opens, he disappears. Forbidden to follow, forbidden even to leave the car, we can just wait and wonder what he says. Sometimes trying to make my mother laugh he pretends to be himself in a farm kitchen, spreading out his sample case. 'Now then, Missus, are you troubled with parasitic life? Your children's scalps, I mean. All those crawly little things we're too polite to mention that show up on the heads of the best of families? Soap alone is useless, kerosene is not too nice a perfume, but I have here –' Or else, 'Believe me, sitting and driving all day the way I do I *know* the value of these fine pills. Natural relief. A problem common to old folks, too, once their days of activity are over – How about you, Grandma?' He would wave the imaginary box of pills under my mother's nose and she would laugh finally, unwillingly. 'He doesn't say that really, does he?' I said, and she said no of course not, he was too much of a gentleman.

One yard after another, then, the old cars, the pumps, dogs, views of grey barns and falling-down sheds and unturning windmills. The men, if they are working in the fields, are not in any fields that we can see. The children are far away, following dry creek beds or looking for blackberries, or else they are hidden in the house, spying at us through cracks in the blinds. The car seat has grown slick with our sweat. I dare my brother to sound the horn, wanting to do it myself but not wanting to get the blame. He knows better. We play I *spy*, but it is hard to find many colours. Grey for the barns and sheds and toilets and houses, brown for the yard and fields, black or brown for the dogs. The rusting cars show rainbow patches, in which I strain to pick out purple or green; likewise I peer at doors for shreds of old peeling paint, maroon or yellow. We can't play with letters, which would be better, because my brother is too young to spell. The game disintegrates anyway. He claims my colours are not fair, and wants extra turns.

In one house no door opens, though the car is in the yard. My father knocks and whistles, calls, 'Hullo there! Walker Brothers man!' but there is not a stir of reply anywhere. This house has no porch, just a bare, slanting slab of cement on which my father stands. He turns around, searching the barnyard, the barn whose mow must be empty because you can see the sky through it, and finally he bends to pick up his suitcases. Just then a window is opened upstairs, a white pot appears on the sill, is tilted over and its contents splash down the outside wall. The window is not directly above my father's head, so only a splash would catch him. He picks up his suitcases with no particular hurry and walks, no longer whistling, to the car. 'Do you know what that was?' I say to my brother. '*Pee*.' He laughs and laughs.

My father rolls and lights a cigarette before he starts the car. The window has been slammed down, the blind drawn, we never did see a hand or face. 'Pee, pee,' sings my brother ecstatically. 'Somebody dumped down pee!' 'Just don't tell your mother that,' my father says. 'She isn't liable to see the joke.' 'Is it in your song?' my brother wants to know. My father says no but he will see what he can do to work it in.

I notice in a little while that we are not turning in any more lanes, though it does not seem to me that we are headed home. 'Is this the way to Sunshine?' I ask my father, and he answers, 'No ma'am it's not.' 'Are we still in your territory?' He shakes his head. 'We're going *fast*,' my brother says approvingly, and in fact we are bouncing along through dry puddle-holes so that all the bottles in the suitcases clink together and gurgle promisingly.

Another lane, a house, also unpainted, dried to silver in the sun.

'I thought we were out of your territory.'

'We are.'

'Then what are we going in here for?'

'You'll see.'

In front of the house a short, sturdy woman is picking up washing, which had been spread on the grass to bleach and dry. When the car stops she stares at it hard for a moment, bends to pick up a couple more towels to add to the bundle under her arm, comes across to us and says in a flat voice, neither welcoming nor un-friendly, 'Have you lost your way?'

My father takes his time getting out of the car. 'I don't think so,' he says. 'I'm the Walker Brothers man.'

'George Golley is our Walker Brothers man,' the woman says, 'and he was out here no more than a week ago. Oh, my Lord God,' she says harshly, 'it's you.'

'It was, the last time I looked in the mirror,' my father says. The woman gathers all the towels in front of her and holds on to them tightly, pushing them against her stomach as if it hurt. 'Of all the people I never thought to see. And telling me you were the Walker Brothers man.'

'I'm sorry if you were looking forward to George Golley,' my father says humbly.

'And look at me, I was prepared to clean the hen-house. You'll think that's just an excuse but it's true. I don't go round looking like this every day.' She is wearing a farmer's straw hat, through which pricks of sunlight penetrate and float on her face, a loose, dirty print smock and running shoes. 'Who are those in the car, Ben? They're not yours?'

'Well I hope and believe they are,' my father says, and tells our names and ages. 'Come on, you can get out. This is Nora, Miss

Cronin. Nora, you better tell me, is it still Miss, or have you got a husband hiding in the woodshed?'

'If I had a husband that's not where I'd keep him, Ben,' she says, and they both laugh, her laugh abrupt and somewhat angry. 'You'll think I got no manners, as well as being dressed like a tramp,' she says. 'Come on in out of the sun. It's cool in the house.'

We go across the yard ('Excuse me taking you in this way but I don't think the front door has been opened since Papa's funeral, I'm afraid the hinges might drop off'), up the porch steps, into the kitchen, which really is cool, high-ceilinged, the blinds of course down, a simple, clean, threadbare room with waxed worn linoleum, potted geraniums, drinking-pail and dipper, a round table with scrubbed oilcloth. In spite of the cleanness, the wiped and swept surfaces, there is a faint sour smell – maybe of the dishrag or the tin dipper or the oilcloth, or the old lady, because there is one, sitting in an easy chair under the clock shelf. She turns her head slightly in our direction and says, 'Nora? Is that company?'

'Blind,' says Nora in a quick explaining voice to my father. Then, 'You won't guess who it is, Momma. Hear his voice.'

My father goes to the front of her chair and bends and says hopefully, 'Afternoon, Mrs Cronin.'

'Ben Jordan,' says the old lady with no surprise. 'You haven't been to see us in the longest time. Have you been out of the country?'

My father and Nora look at each other.

'He's married, Momma,' says Nora cheerfully and aggressively. 'Married and got two children and here they are.' She pulls us forward, makes each of us touch the old lady's dry, cool hand while she says our names in turn. Blind! This is the first blind person I have ever seen close up. Her eyes are closed, the eyelids sunk away down, showing no shape of the eyeball, just hollows. From one hollow comes a drop of silver liquid, a medicine, or a miraculous tear.

'Let me get into a decent dress,' Nora says. 'Talk to Momma. It's a treat for her. We hardly ever see company, do we Momma?'

'Not many makes it out this road,' says the old lady placidly.

'And the ones that used to be around here, our old neighbours, some of them have pulled out.'

'True everywhere,' my father says.

'Where's your wife then?'

'Home. She's not too fond of the hot weather, makes her feel poorly.'

'Well.' This is a habit of country people, old people, to say 'well', meaning, 'is that so?' with a little extra politeness and concern.

Nora's dress, when she appears again – stepping heavily on Cuban heels down the stairs in the hall – is flowered more lavishly than anything my mother owns, green and yellow on brown, some sort of floating sheer crepe, leaving her arms bare. Her arms are heavy, and every bit of her skin you can see is covered with little dark freckles like measles. Her hair is short, black, coarse and curly, her teeth very white and strong. 'It's the first time I knew there was such a thing as green poppies,' my father says, looking at her dress.

'You would be surprised all the things you never knew,' says Nora, sending a smell of cologne far and wide when she moves and displaying a change of voice to go with the dress, something more sociable and youthful. 'They're not poppies anyway, they're just flowers. You go and pump me some good cold water and I'll make these children a drink.' She gets down from the cupboard a bottle of Walker Brothers Orange syrup.

'You telling me you were the Walker Brothers man !'

'It's the truth, Nora. You go and look at my sample cases in the car if you don't believe me. I got the territory directly south of here.'

'Walker Brothers? Is that a fact? You selling for Walker Brothers?'

'Yes ma'am.'

'We always heard you were raising foxes over Dungannon way.'

'That's what I was doing, but I kind of run out of luck in that business.'

'So where're you living? How long've you been out selling?'

'We moved into Tuppertown. I been at it, oh, two, three months.

It keeps the wolf from the door. Keeps him as far away as the back fence.'

Nora laughs. 'Well I guess you count yourself lucky to have the work. Isabel's husband in Brantford, he was out of work the longest time. I thought if he didn't find something soon I was going to have them all land in here to feed, and I tell you I was hardly looking forward to it. It's all I can manage with me and Momma.'

'Isabel married,' my father says. 'Muriel married too?'

'No, she's teaching school out west. She hasn't been home for five years. I guess she finds something better to do with her holidays. I would if I was her.' She gets some snapshots out of the table drawer and starts showing him. 'That's Isabel's oldest boy, starting school. That's the baby sitting in her carriage. Isabel and her husband. Muriel. That's her room-mate with her. That's a fellow she used to go around with, and his car. He was working in a bank out there. That's her school, it has eight rooms. She teaches Grade Five.' My father shakes his head. 'I can't think of her any way but when she was going to school, so shy I used to pick her up on the road – I'd be on my way to see you – and she would not say one word, not even to agree it was a nice day.'

'She's got over that.'

'Who are you talking about?' says the old lady.

'Muriel. I said she's got over being shy.'

'She was here last summer.'

'No Momma that was Isabel. Isabel and her family were here last summer. Muriel's out west.'

'I meant Isabel.'

Shortly after this the old lady falls asleep, her head on her side, her mouth open. 'Excuse her manners,' Nora says. 'It's old age.' She fixes an afghan over her mother and says we can all go into the front room where our talking won't disturb her.

'You two,' my father says. 'Do you want to go outside and amuse yourselves?'

Amuse ourselves how? Anyway I want to stay. The front room is more interesting than the kitchen, though barer. There is a gramophone and a pump organ and a picture on the wall of Mary, Jesus' mother – I know that much – in shades of bright blue and pink with a spiked band of light around her head. I know that such pictures are found only in the homes of Roman Catholics and so Nora must be one. We have never known any Roman Catholics at all well, never well enough to visit in their houses. I think of what my grandmother and my Aunt Tena, over in Dungannon, used to always say to indicate that somebody was a Catholic. *So-and-so digs with the wrong foot*, they would say. *She digs with the wrong foot.* That was what they would say about Nora.

Nora takes a bottle, half full, out of the top of the organ and pours some of what is in it into the two glasses that she and my father have emptied of the orange drink.

'Keep it in case of sickness?' my father says.

'Not on your life,' says Nora. 'I'm never sick. I just keep it because I keep it. One bottle does me a fair time, though, because I don't care for drinking alone. Here's luck!' She and my father drink and I know what it is. Whisky. One of the things my mother has told me in our talks together is that my father never drinks whisky. But I see he does. He drinks whisky and he talks of people whose names I have never heard before. But after a while he turns to a familiar incident. He tells about the chamberpot that was emptied out the window. 'Picture me there,' he says, 'hollering my heartiest. *Oh, lady, it's your Walker Brothers man, anybody home?*' He does himself hollering, grinning absurdly, waiting, looking up in pleased expectation and then – oh, ducking, covering his head with his arms, looking as if he begged for mercy (when he never did anything like that, I was watching), and Nora laughs, almost as hard as my brother did at that time.

'That isn't true! That's not a word true!'

'Oh, indeed it is ma'am. We have our heroes in the ranks of Walker Brothers. I'm glad you think it's funny,' he says sombrely.

I ask him shyly, 'Sing the song.'

'What song? Have you turned into a singer on top of everything else?'

Embarrassed, my father says, 'Oh, just this song I made up while I was driving around, it gives me something to do, making up rhymes.'

But after some urging he does sing it, looking at Nora with a droll, apologetic expression, and she laughs so much that in places he has to stop and wait for her to get over laughing so he can go on, because she makes him laugh too. Then he does various parts of his salesman's spiel. Nora when she laughs squeezes her large bosom under her folded arms. 'You're crazy,' she says. 'That's all you are.' She sees my brother peering into the gramophone and she jumps up and goes over to him. 'Here's us sitting enjoying ourselves and not giving you a thought, isn't it terrible?' she says. 'You want me to put a record on, don't you? You want to hear a nice record? Can you dance? I bet your sister can, can't she?'

I say no. 'A big girl like you and so good-looking and can't dance!' says Nora. 'It's high time you learned. I bet you'd make a lovely dancer. Here, I'm going to put on a piece I used to dance to and even your daddy did, in his dancing days. You didn't know your daddy was a dancer, did you? Well, he is a talented man, your daddy!'

She puts down the lid and takes hold of me unexpectedly around the waist, picks up my other hand and starts making me go backwards. 'This is the way, now, this is how they dance. Follow me. This foot, see. One and one-two. One and one-two. That's fine, that's lovely, don't look at your feet! Follow me, that's right, see how easy? You're going to be a lovely dancer. One and one-two. One and one-two. Ben, see your daughter dancing!' *Whispering while you cuddle near me Whispering where no one can hear me* . . .

Round and round the linoleum, me proud, intent, Nora laughing and moving with great buoyancy, wrapping me in her strange gaiety, her smell of whisky, cologne, and sweat. Under the arms her dress is damp, and little drops form along her upper lips, hang in the soft black hairs at the corners of her mouth. She whirls me around in front of my father – causing me to stumble, for I am by no means so swift a pupil as she pretends – and lets me go, breathless.

'Dance with me, Ben.'

'I'm the world's worst dancer, Nora, and you know it.'

'I certainly never thought so.'

'You would now.'

She stands in front of him, arms hanging loose and hopeful, her breasts, which a moment ago embarrassed me with their warmth and bulk, rising and falling under her loose flowered dress, her face shining with the exercise, and delight.

'Ben.'

My father drops his head and says quietly, 'Not me, Nora.'

So she can only go and take the record off. 'I can drink alone but I can't dance alone,' she says. 'Unless I am a whole lot crazier than I think I am.'

'Nora,' says my father smiling. 'You're not crazy.'

'Stay for supper.'

'Oh, no. We couldn't put you to the trouble.'

'It's no trouble. I'd be glad of it.'

'And their mother would worry. She'd think I'd turned us over in a ditch.'

'Oh, well. Yes.'

'We've taken a lot of your time now.'

'Time,' says Nora bitterly. 'Will you come by ever again?'

'I will if I can,' says my father.

'Bring the children. Bring your wife.'

'Yes I will,' says my father. 'I will if I can.'

When she follows us to the car he says, 'You come to see us too, Nora. We're right on Grove Street, left-hand side going in, that's north, and two doors this side – east – of Baker Street.'

Nora does not repeat these directions. She stands close to the car in her soft, brilliant dress. She touches the fender, making an unintelligible mark in the dust there.

On the way home my father does not buy any ice cream or pop, but he does go into a country store and get a package of licorice. which he shares with us. *She digs with the wrong foot,* I think, and the words seem sad to me as never before, dark, perverse. My father does not say anything to me about not mentioning things at home, but I know, just from the thoughtfulness, the pause when he passes the licorice, that there are things not to be mentioned. The whisky, maybe the dancing. No worry about my brother, he does not notice enough. At most he might remember the blind lady, the picture of Mary.

'Sing,' my brother commands my father, but my father says gravely, 'I don't know, I seem to be fresh out of songs. You watch the road and let me know if you see any rabbits.'

So my father drives and my brother watches the road and rabbits and I feel my father's life flowing back from our car in the last of the afternoon, darkening and turning strange, like a landscape that has an enchantment on it, making it kindly, ordinary and familiar while you are looking at it, but changing it, once your back is turned, into something you will never know, with all kinds of weathers, and distances you cannot imagine.

When we get closer to Tuppertown the sky becomes gently overcast, as always, nearly always, on summer evenings by the Lake.

Earle Birney

WAY TO THE WEST

11 pm & sunset still going on
but that could be the latitude
whats wrongs the color
everywhere horseshit ochre   & roiling
like paper that twists&browns
before firing up on hot ashes
theres somebodys hell ahead
meantimes our lips prick
& the trees are dead
but its another 20 miles before the sign

YOU ARE ENTERING SUDBURY
HOME OF THE LARGEST
& christ there on the skull of a hill
3 manhattan-high stacks   a phallic calvary
ejaculating some essence of rotted semen
straight up   mass sabotage at cape kennedy

the damned are everywhere   the young
shrieking   (looking much like anyone)
drag race with radios up
from one smoldering stoplight to another –
under neon the older faces
assembled from half europe
screwcheeked & pitted all the same way
have something dignified about their devilship
that stares us down   till they come human
houcking brown on the cement

WELCOME TO SUDBURY 73% OF THE FREE
  WORLD'S NICKEL IS CREATED HERE
& the free world invented a special cough
not even 100 taverns can dampen
or all the jukes drown in the doorways
of pandemonium   milton thou shouldst
be living etc

DEAD END   wheres west?   sunset folded
our headlights finger dumped cans
wriggle through streets like crevasses
blasted in bedrock pink & folded
like glazed guts on a butchers marble

out of the starless dark falls the roar
of golgotha   how long before one stops
noticing?   & the sting in the eyes?

by a raped car an Indian sits
praying?   puking

YOU ARE LEAVING SUDBURY
  CENTRE OF...FREE ENTERPRISE
then 20 more miles of battlefield

at last a moon smolders out
& we are into the dumb firs again
       Turn Out   300 Yds
       Historic Site
       French River
what?   canoe route the Hurons found
& showed the whites –
the way to the west   silks   buffalo
vietnam   the moon
shines over the middle of nowhere –
dumb as the trees

we stop for a leak   silence
too late for other cars now
the trees listen back
nothing   the owls dead too?
suddenly some kind of low growl
coming up   we head back for the car –
only a night jet

but after it passes we realize
we'd been hearing the river all along

Jacques Godbout

FROM KNIFE ON THE TABLE

PAGES 15–17

It was a strange love almost one-way: I dreamed of her all week, but because we were of different languages and cultures, I had trouble imagining her days, her thoughts, her childhood. I wore myself out for her, I polished my brass, I waited. I was Waiting itself. I was indifferent to the others, and they returned the compliment. In camp men can only avoid total brutalization with their nerve-endings. When night came and the sun was endlessly setting, unable to dream on their beds because the rooms were as dreary as college dormitories, they would gather at seven o'clock around a fire, a few cases of beer, and rye whisky.

I remember whole evenings spent in semi-sleep contemplating the black wood of the piano – the only surface where graffiti could be gouged – scarred from chairs, pen-knives, use. The rest of the furniture, the chairs, the tables, was replaced almost monthly, after a donnybrook, just for the hell of it, or a mass battle between two sections carrying on the old French–English quarrel. Wearing the same uniforms, obeying the same orders, the soldiers in khaki green mixed it up. French Canadians used their boots to avenge the deportation of the Acadians, the loss of Louisiana, the sacrifice at Dieppe; the English defended their right over America and the little colony of Quebec.

The next morning the Camel, who could sense our quarrels but didn't understand them, would make us jump, run, and threatened us with barrack inspection: most slept that night beside their beds, on the carpet, so as to keep the covers smooth and the neat hospital corners.

The English caroused awkwardly and stupidly but, sunk in a leatherette chair, eyes half-shut, I soaked up a whole military folk-lore which used to make Patricia laugh. The songs were probably bawdier than I realized (they taught me English with a Prairie accent), and the puns often escaped me.

> Old King Cole
> was a merry old soul ...

'Are you cold?'
'Not at all.'
'You came back despite —'
Despite the cold, despite the creditors, despite the fear, despite hatred, despite a whole love to begin again, seize again, renew. Patricia, the first Patricia, the second as in the days of royalty, I came back for several days, for two hundred years perhaps.

PAGES 48–9

'I'm famished, starved, that's it.'
'Maybe you don't eat enough.'
'*Don't be ridiculous, Patty.*'
'You're all *exhausted*, you French, whether you come from France, Quebec, or Navarre ... you're sick over the fact that you didn't invent the civilization of the twentieth century, so you mumble in your corner like little old ladies in a Home...'
'There's so much to save.'
'Go to it, Christian! You want to save everything, go on, Jansenist!'
'Maybe you're right.'
'Just wait: Soon there'll be a new *earthly* adventure, you'll be at ease then, more than the Turks...'
'Why do you say that? Why the *Turks*?'
'Because I'm fed up with your shrunken skin, your sudden out-bursts of moralism, your continual lament, your groaning, and above all, your *ideas*.'
Our feet like ice, our toes curled up in fur boots, we go on tramp-ing about in the snow, going around in circles (I'll get a terrible cold

if this keeps up), bit by bit the Problem emerges: if only I had a black skin, a Jewish nose! Theirs are great cultures, known the world over! I speak French in America, that's *the* sin, the crime, if I were the bastard son of the Folies-Bergère and Paris by Night, the Salvation Army couldn't be any more scandalized...

But I'm not scandalized by myself any more; *the time-span of an adolescence.* ... Patricia begins to run down toward the Fairlaine Bookstore where we'll amuse ourselves pulling out the most bizarre of the American paperbacks.

Translated by Penny Williams

George Whalley

FROM THE LEGEND OF JOHN HORNBY

BEGINNINGS 1880-1907

One photograph of John Hornby preserves for anybody who has ever heard anything about the man an indelible and tantalizing image. Hornby himself approved of the picture and had copies made which for a time he would give to any friend who wanted one or to any stranger who seemed impressed. Nobody knows who took the photograph. All that can be seen of the setting is the inverse angle of a log building, the timbers squared with a broad-axe and dove-tailed at the corners in the best style. The place must be Fort Norman where the Great Bear River flows into the Mackenzie. The date must be the late spring or early summer of 1919. And there sits John Hornby on a log in a rare instant of repose: shock-headed, bearded, hawk-nosed, moccasined, the strong lean hands holding a thick illustrated catalogue. He is reading, it seems, with almost insolently withdrawn concentration. What the photograph does not show clearly – though it implies this in the way that some pen drawings can imply colour – is that John Hornby is a short wiry man, little more than five feet tall; that his eyes are an intense and memorable blue, and disconcerting because often vague in intention and always apparently looking at something a long way off.

At that time John Hornby was less than forty. It was ten years since he had first come into the North. Within the next five years he was to become a legend in his own lifetime; within less than ten years he would be dead. In the first quarter of this century there were plenty of colourful characters in the North-West Territories: old Klondikers, beachcombers, remittance men; frantic solitary men who got bushed and stayed behind; men of good family with neither past nor future; men empty of desire, impetus, or purpose; braggarts, ruffians, visionaries, unscrupulous men. These provided a variegated contrast to the respectable and hard-working people who were simply and quietly committed, through choice or birth, to living in an inhospitable country : the grave, self-reliant Scots and Orkneymen who served the interests of the great trading companies, and sometimes their own; and morose business-like trappers, often of Scandinavian or German stock, living often a tenuous and dangerous existence that depended upon skill, experience, dogs, and a judgement immune from hysteria. Restlessness, endurance, energy, cunning, a cold eye for probabilities and not too much of the gambler's instinct : these are the hall-marks of the best of them. Against such a background, the small little Chaplinesque figure that John Hornby cut – pathetic and endearing, with the laconic smile and piercing blue eyes, and an infuriating instinct of withdrawal – this would seem slender material for the making of a legend.

But John Hornby eluded all the categories. He had no commercial or scientific ambitions, no will-o'-the-wisp dream of gold or fur. His past was not notably disreputable even though his own account of it had some intriguing gaps in it. He was said to be wealthy – and that at times was about half-true. He was well-educated, a Harrovian, spoke in a soft scholarly voice, was not much given to profane language, and was even by some suspected of being a learned man because he knew a few colloquial phrases of French, German, and Italian. Professionally, during the ten years before the Fort Norman photograph, he was not an explorer, a trapper, a prospector; he was something of all these, but a caricature of them all. By instinct and habit he was most like a trapper, and could have been a good trapper but for his love of animals and his hatred of steel traps. Unlike many Indians, he never killed except for food; and like many Indians, he was often in the matter of food notoriously improvident. He was not a particularly good shot with a rifle, and was even rather careless in looking after his weapons; yet he managed to keep himself alive. And his name persists on the maps. The bay where he first wintered on Great Bear Lake; the elegant canoe-passage which had once been a York boat channel and which he rediscovered through the confusing islands and peninsulas at the eastern end of Great Slave Lake; a hill on the Coppermine River; the double turn in the Thelon River where he built a cabin and died –

all these still bear Hornby's name. And although his name is now overshadowed by the manner of his death, he lives still in the long Northern memory.

The legend is mostly to do with Hornby's feats of strength and endurance, and with behaviour which, even in the North-West Territories, was regarded as a little eccentric. Stories were told of him as a young man working with the railway gangs around the Yellowhead Pass, how he would go hatless in winter, and barefoot in the snow if need arose; and how, when he was at Onoway, he would frequently run the forty miles to or from Edmonton, had once trotted fifty miles beside a horse, and on another occasion ran 100 miles from Edmonton to Athabaska Landing in under twenty-four hours for a wager of a bottle of whisky (though he was not a drinking man). It was said that he could outrun an Indian, and pack more than his own weight at a portage; and his untiring crooked jog-trot, an Indian habit grafted on to his own more civilized endowments as a runner, was the despair of anybody who had the misfortune to travel with him. He had the reputation of fearing no man, of being crazily quixotic, always eager to help any person in distress, courtly and chivalrous to women.

On the whole he preferred the company of Indians to white men, and – to an increasing degree as time went on – he liked to travel light. His standard outfit even for a journey of indefinite duration (he was inclined to boast) was a rifle, a fishnet, and a bag of flour. Because he despised 'White man's grub', other men – from quite early years – were suspicious of travelling with him; yet it was said that he had several times kept indigent Indians alive by starving himself. (Others, however, said that there were several times when Hornby would have died if the Indians had not fed him.) Altogether his reputation for starving and for being impervious to hunger and hardships was impressive. He was said to have wintered once in a wolf-den south of Chipewyan when the freeze-up caught him there on the way to Slave Lake. And stories more agreeable and fanciful were also told : how he refused to travel with any brown-eyed man; how he had once turned up at Resolution with a group of Indians to collect Treaty Money, and would have got away with this harmless deception but for the colour of his eyes; how he knew of fabulous deposits of gold and silver but refused to form a company for fear of spoiling the country; and how he had been the first man to bring samples of pitchblende out of Bear Lake.

In the way of legends, the chronology of some of these stories is indistinct; but many of the legendary stories about Hornby have some root in fact. They have suffered accretion and transmutation in passing from one story-teller to another; for heroic elaboration of the truth is one of the chief forms of emotional release in the North, and a good story travels quickly and has a long life. Hornby did not deliberately manufacture or distort his own legend; but he was too human to destroy it, and intelligent enough to understand the rhetorical force of deftly managed silences. He delighted in providing his few friends with a fund of outrageous stories about himself. Because he was reticent and enigmatic – and not least reticent when most voluble – he was called a hermit and a mystic. Because he refused to plan, and did whatever he did with bland self-confidence, he was said by some to be a man of diabolical skill and dare-devil courage, a man capable of surmounting any difficulty by deft improvisation. The fact that he survived year after year did nothing to undermine the legend.

The legend constructed for itself an image of John Hornby that changed with time only in the exaggeration of the salient characteristics of solitariness, courage, and endurance. But behind the set mask of the legend John Hornby changed in many and sorrowful respects of which the exuberant fireside stories of the country gave no hint. In the early days around Edmonton and Bear Lake – young, buoyant, with a little anachronistic fringe of black beard – he was amiable, gregarious, amenable. Then suddenly he becomes solitary, resentful, withdrawn, inscrutable. Casual observers sometimes thought him mad; his few closest friends found him eccentric and almost entirely unpredictable. Privations at times brought him to the outer fringes of sanity. Northern travellers and trappers are remarkably tough : some remain agile and active enough to work well into their seventies. But by 1920 or so Hornby's physique – remarkable though it was – was breaking under the manner of his life, and it looked as though time might intercept him in his mortal folly. Made (it seems) of gristle and whipcord he would not rest for long;

yet he did not break, and remained, contrary to all reasonable prophecy, able enough in physique to undertake what he said would be his last journey. The trip had no distinguishable purpose. Late in April 1926 he landed at Quebec from England in the liner *Montrose*. One companion landed with him from the ship – a lad of seventeen, taller than Hornby, his clothes still showing the uneasy transition from school to manhood; his name was Edgar Christian and he was Hornby's nephew. At Edmonton Hornby collected another companion. Less than a year later Hornby had died of starvation and exhaustion in a very inaccessible part of the Arctic, and within a few weeks both of his companions were also dead. Hornby's death did not destroy his legend : it may even have given it a new energy and persistence. But the way he died has raised obstacles almost insurmountable to anybody who wishes to discover the true nature of that vivid and desolate man.

The Caribou Report of 1925

As part of his undertaking with the North-West Territories and Yukon Branch in 1924, Hornby agreed to prepare at the end of the Casba-Thelon journey, 1924–5, a report upon the caribou migrations and the distribution of musk ox in the country he had travelled. The MS. draft of his report was written in a large leather-covered exercise book ($7\frac{1}{2} \times 9\frac{3}{8}$ inches) which was in the end recovered from the Thelon cabin in 1929 after Hornby's death, the draft being written on pp. 37–72, 75, 79–85, 129–30. After the book was brought out from the cabin in 1929, the Public Administrator for the District of Mackenzie, H. Milton Martin, removed the leaves containing the draft report and sent them to Ottawa where they are now preserved in the files of the Department of Northern Affairs. Specimens of flowers and grasses collected on the first or on the final Thelon journey are still pressed between the leaves of the book. The other part of the book has now disappeared, is known to have contained on the first thirty-six pages the draft of part of Hornby's projected book *In the Land of Feast or Famine* (p. 1, title; pp. 3–28, Chapter 1, 'Brief Description of my First Trip into the Far North 1908'; pp. 29–36, 'The Animals').

The *Caribou Report* also exists in typescript with Hornby's signature and a few notes in his hand; in a copy of the typed version, drastically revised by the N.W.T. & Y. Branch for publication; and in the revised and expurgated version published posthumously in the *Canadian Field Naturalist* XLVIII (October 1934) 105–11. The MS. draft acknowledges, as the title of the typed version does not, that the report is based on observations made by both Hornby and Bullock. A few of the more interesting and characteristic passages – some of which are found only in the MS. draft or which were excluded from the printed version – are collected below.

(i) *The Natives*

'Both Indian and Eskimo have practically become dependent on white trappers for the majority of their supplies. It would be impossible for them to return to their own methods of living off the country. When once weaned from that, it is necessary to see that there is always an ample supply of white man's food in case there are times of hardship. In many instances Eskimo certainly could be encouraged to use nets especially those we met on the Thelon River who are now equipped with guns and rifles [and] slaughter any living wild creature which may be so rash as to come near. Like sheep they clean a country. Nothing will ever satiate the killing appetite of man which appears more conspicuously with the natives. The now ever increasing number of dogs kept by the natives ever tend to the great destruction of animals. Nothing except the fear of punishment will ever restrain them.

'It is a waste of time and energy to endeavour by talk to persuade natives from slaughtering caribou. Fear of punishment can alone prevent it. Indians, however, never attempt to make a clean up of fur bearing animals. When they make a reasonable catch they prefer either to go to a trading post or pay a visit to other Indians.'

(ii) *Caribou Migration and Feeding*

'The caribou in their migrations move northwards in the spring and southwards in the winter. Caribou do not migrate in one continuous stream but there are countless bands of caribou which migrate to the different sectors. In summer the caribou, to a great extent, feed on the grasses they can find. In the winter their food is chiefly the moss. It is difficult to say how long it takes to reproduce the moss eaten by the caribou. They do not totally clean up any special area consequently may be seen again in that area the following year or others even may be feeding there that very same year.'

(iii) Barren Land Caribou: Rangifer arcticus

'Though the caribou still winter in herds their area is now becoming more restricted. They are remorselessly slaughtered by the natives, killed in large numbers by the wolves which continually follow them and their remains are eaten up or devoured by the wolverines, white foxes and ravens. These caribou are very small and the largest bulls when they are in their fattest condition at the end of September will weigh only about 300 pounds. It is then that the back fat – the fat cut from the back – weighs twenty-five pounds. Besides this the Indian gets much grease from the meat and bones. It is said that the migrations of the caribou are very irregular but I found that they would be as regular as the seasons if their courses were not deflected by the Indians and Eskimo or on account of the sea or large lakes not being frozen over or the country having been burnt. Once I noticed it was on account of glare ice at Dease river – the caribou had come down to the edge of the lake in thousands and then turned back.

'There are, however, few places that caribou cannot go. They swim across lakes and go up and down very steep places and can even cross lakes or glare ice and are not afraid to cross any swift place in a river.

'The Indians are supplied with an unlimited amount of powder and ammunition and also can procure shells from the traders. They are all equipped with high power rifles. Nothing terrifies the caribou more than fire arms which combined with the awful and wanton slaughter cause the alteration of their movements. The lust for killing is human nature and the Indian certainly affords a good example. The Indians are still further encouraged to kill as the traders pay for both skins and tongue.

'Unlike most deer the male and female caribou may be seen together many times of the year but it is only because they happen to be moving in the same direction. It is about the first week in August that the Indians move up to the barren lands to meet the caribou as they make their first movement southwards. The caribou have now almost shed all their old hair and their skins are beginning to get good but not as a rule until about the third week in August are the caribou fat and the skins good. The young caribou are very small but can travel fast and swim perfectly. Black flies are now [early August] in myriads and keep the caribou constantly on the move. Of course they are very poor and it is not before the end of the month that they begin to get fat. During this time caribou could be seen moving for several days in small bands of ten to several hundreds. During the summer there were always bull caribou to be found along the barren points of the lake and on the high ridges and also on the islands close to Hunter's Bay where they could get some respite from the flies. . . . The hides of caribou are at their best towards the end of August and the beginning of September. The caribou are in the fattest condition from towards the end of September until the first week in October. About the beginning of October, during the first real cold spell, the mating season commences. The caribou now congregate in countless herds at the edge of the woods on the barrens, all the bull caribou having come out of the woods.

'At this time they generally move off in a north easterly direction in small bands with one bull caribou and two to twenty cows follow. Towards the end of October and the beginning of November the bull caribou come into the woods singly and in small herds of from two to twenty. At this time they are poor and are not at all good eating. In November – the old bulls cast their horns. Towards the end of November most caribou move southwards by many circles back into the barren lands, especially the females and the young and again in December large bands of caribou are moving southwards into the woods, females and young ones remaining outside the woods during the whole winter in large numbers but most of the bulls go into the woods. During the very stormy weather the caribou leave the woods and go on to large lakes, into open places, because when the winds are strong the caribou cannot detect any strange sounds and so are scared. In winter the caribou have long hair which affords good protection against the cold weather. They penetrate far into the woods but do not always frequent the same locality. This is mainly due to the fact that previous winters they have been well slaughtered and hunted by the Indians. Caribou generally, both summer and winter, are always on the Move. Indians require large numbers of caribou to feed both their families and dogs. One Indian family with their dogs can easily use up one caribou per day. In April the female caribou move out of the woods and by May there are no female caribou to be seen in the woods.

'In May the bull caribou have left the woods travelling northwards. They travel in bands from two to twenty and sometimes far more but later scatter out and in summer are to be seen wandering aimlessly about in ones and twos. Wounded and sick caribou endeavour to stay on the islands or close to the water during the summer so as to escape pursuit from the wolves. I do not think that the caribou move north and south in one large continuous mass but there are many distinct immense herds which, in their migrations, though, according to the seasons go north and south, scatter out in the different localities.'

(iv) Barren Land Wolf – Canis albus

'The barren land wolves vary greatly in colour – are pure white to dark which latter rarely belong to the timber. They are large and not ferocious. This is one of the finest animals we have but unfortunately it has a bad name and there is every desire to slaughter them all. Now it is a question if all the wolves were killed off would the caribou increase or would they die off through weakness? The wolves must undoubtedly kill off the weak and sick caribou and consequently only the hardy ones are left to reproduce. In summer wolves can be met with almost everywhere in the Barrens. After the mating season they go off in pairs. They have their young in any suitable spot generally facing south on the side of a ridge in a sandy place in a den about one yard from the entrance and sometimes only under a small spruce tree. When caribou are numerous in winter wolves are also fairly plentiful.

'I have never found the barren land wolves to travel in larger packs than seven. Once, however, where there had been a big slaughter of caribou I counted forty-one wolves but they had only collected in passing and were eating up the remains. In that country there is nothing that a wolf will not eat, especially in winter. These wolves are not dangerous and on several occasions I have had wolves come within a few inches during the night. Wolves can always be caught with large traps. When the men were sent to set poison I in vain protested. Last year these men, in the spring, even, went as far as Artillery lake to poison the wolves. They should never have been allowed into a district where there are other trappers or traders. No half measures are never of any use. If it is intended to set a little poison that meant only a beginning. (I think it would be better to give a free permit to all ['traders' deleted] trappers, for if one non resident is allowed to poison out a country, it must be at least justifiable for the residents to do the same.) Trappers are very jealous of their own rights and am certain would not hesitate to take any means. I was requested by them to make a complaint but these men are not in the country now so they should be satisfied. No one could ever convince me that it is possible to poison wolves in that country without poisoning foxes. However, since half measures are never any good and if it is required to poison off all the wolves in order to protect the caribou, it could be done regardless of white foxes. I do not think it could possibly hurt the caribou. White foxes could be easily raised in captivity and there might be a fox farming industry encouraged in that district. Of course I do not like to see the wolves totally destroyed until it was definitely approved that it was necessary. Wolves like all other predatory animals and birds must be put there for some purpose beneficial in destroying weaklings.'

Leonard Cohen

ALL THERE IS TO KNOW ABOUT ADOLPH EICHMANN

EYES:	Medium
HAIR:	Medium
WEIGHT:	Medium
HEIGHT:	Medium
DISTINGUISHING FEATURES:	None
NUMBER OF FINGERS:	Ten
NUMBER OF TOES:	Ten
INTELLIGENCE:	Medium

What did you expect?

Talons?

Oversize incisors?

Green saliva?

Madness?

STORY

She tells me a child built her house
one spring afternoon,
but that the child was killed
crossing the street.

She says she read it in the newspaper,
that at the corner of this and this avenue
a child was run down by an automobile.

Of course I do not believe her.
She has built the house herself,
hung the oranges and coloured beads in the doorways,
crayoned flowers on the walls.

She has made the paper things for the wind,
collected crooked stones for their shadows in the sun,
fastened yellow and dark balloons to the ceiling.

Each time I visit her
she repeats the story of the child to me,
I never question her. It is important
to understand one's part in a legend.

I take my place
among the paper fish and make-believe clocks,
naming the flowers she has drawn,
smiling while she paints my head on large clay coins,
and making a sort of courtly love to her
when she contemplates her own traffic death.

Brian Moore

PRELIMINARY PAGES FOR
A WORK OF REVENGE

The characters in this work are meant to be real.
References to persons living and dead are intended.

Are there fifteen people in the world who will be afraid when they read this paragraph? No. That, in itself, is a comment on my insignificance. Are there fifteen people who will become uneasy on reading it? I think so. Almost half my life is over and I have known many people. I know things about some of them which they would not like to see written down. Are you uneasy, S—? Or you, F—? Or you, my once dear T—? Why do I not spell out your names? Well, for one thing I have known more than one S— in my life. If I can make two of you uneasy, then so much the better. For another, were I to reveal your disparate identities you would possibly band together in order to silence me. In these preliminary pages I wish to engage you singly, yet collectively, to reveal my identity to each of you in turn, yet to preserve a final anonymity so that none of you will be sure you are thinking about the same person. That is my strategy.

My second preliminary page is reserved for a quotation. Authors usually offer a quotation as a propitiatory rite in hopes that the wise saying of some great man will induce in the reader a similar respect for the idiocies contained in the work which will follow it. My intention is not propitiatory. It is minatory. Here is my quotation.

'Life being what it is, one dreams of revenge.' *Paul Gauguin*

You know what I mean, don't you? Very well then, let us turn the page.

ACKNOWLEDGEMENTS

The author does not wish to express his gratitude to anyone. He has no reasons to be grateful. He does, however, wish to acknowledge that parts of this work have been provided him unwittingly by relatives and friends, enemies and acquaintances. The uses he intends to make of the facts, lies, rumours, scandals and secrets so provided shall be his own. He will attempt to make his own truth for, like Pilate, he knows only that truth is not the accurate rendition of facts. Was the man they crucified that Friday afternoon an obscure agitator who had made a small stir in Jerusalem? Or was he the son of God? We still have no facts. We have religions. Turn the page.

Some of you may have turned first to this page. Go back. I shall not reveal myself so easily. The name I have used on the first page of this work is mine, yet not mine. It is my *nom de plume*. If you do not believe that it is the name of a professional writer you have merely to look up certain volumes of bibliography published in the United States and Great Britain during the past five years. I say this to warn you that these pages are written in the expectation of seeing them published. I am not writing from an asylum. I know you and you know me. These pages reached you postmarked with the name of the city in which you were born. But I do not live there now. I merely had the letters sent from there as, shall we say, an *aide-mémoire* to some of you. The postmark ensured that you would open the letter, for no other postmark can compete in authority with the place of one's birth. It is what we fled: it may, at any time, reach up to reclaim us.

So there is no error. Your name and address have been carefully checked and unless you are at the moment reading someone else's mail, you are one of the persons with whom I am concerned. Or let me say that you may be one of the persons concerned: the decision is yours: However, I anticipate myself. So – about the author:

I am that person you insulted. I am that person you forgot. I am the one you do not speak of, the person you hope never to meet again. I am the one you said something mean and spiteful about and I have heard what you said. I am that friend who fell out of fashion, whose reminiscences about old times you found boring, whose dinner invitation you did not return, whose address you did not keep. I am that person you never phoned back. I am that person you flattered then ignored, the one who rang your doorbell many times while you sat like a statue inside, hoping I would go away. I am the one whose footsteps you heard going down the stairs, who knew you were there and hated you for it. For you did not deceive me. Did you honestly think that people like me are ever deceived by evasion and excuses? Unlike the successful friends you now court, we are not busy; we plan each visit and depend on it. Perhaps you *did* forget our appointment. Perhaps you *were* out. But then, if you really forgot, is that not a far greater wrong?

I am that person you betrayed. I am the one who confided my faults, my shames, my fears. I am the one to whom you swore secrecy, whose confidences you promised to respect. But one night at a party when someone wondered out loud, when someone told a garbled version of the facts I had confided to you and someone else contradicted them, you, who knew the truth, could not keep your mouth shut. You shook your head wisely at the talkers, took a deep breath and, for the moment's pleasure of having an audience, you told my secrets out. And then, having betrayed me once, you continued to do it. Two years later, all my shames and fears had been fitted into a repertoire of amusing stories to delight your new marriage partner. (Who does not know me; whom you did not even know when I told you those private things.) You know what I am talking about, don't you?

I am the person who loved you. You said you loved me but behind my back you told others that you were merely 'fond' of me. Yet I am the one in whose arms you wept, the one who sat up all night with you, the one who helped you when things went wrong. It was comforting to have me on display at that time for I so obviously loved you. I was the two ears, the tail and all four hoofs to hold aloft in the plaza while you waited for someone better. I am the one who walked away and did not look back, the one who hung up the receiver, the familiar voice which was never the same again. I can tell you now that I cried. I cried because you told me not to worry, that nothing was changed. I cried because I guessed then that you had already made your secret plans to leave me. I was right, wasn't I? Later, you remember, when it was all over and we knew it, you said you were trying to be honest. You said we were never suited to each other. You knew I would understand, you said. Did I understand? Do I? What would you think of you, if you were me? I know that you have been in and out of the place where I live many times. I know that you have never phoned me. I know that you never will phone me.

Some of you, reading this, may decide it is not addressed to you. You do not know me from these pages. That is true. To some of you, I was a child. To you, my classmates, I address the following.

As a child I did not believe that I was clever. I feared myself to be stupid and cowardly and believed that I would be a disappointment to all who knew me. I read a great deal and like many unsure children I had a taste for tragic endings. But in my reading I discovered that, to fall from the heights of tragedy, heroes must first scale the peaks of achievement. In books, I searched for a suitable daydream. When I was fourteen we were asked to write an essay about our ambitions in life. I wrote all night. I was, for the first time in my life, inspired. (The first and last time if you except this work.) I wrote that I would become a great poet, that I would devote my life to the composition of a masterpiece and that, at the age of thirty, coughing blood in a last consumptive frenzy, I hoped to die, my gift still clear and unmuddied. This essay I submitted to my English master who, the following day, came to my desk, took my ear between his nicotined thumb and forefinger and led me before the class to read my essay aloud. Oh, what a fine foil I must have seemed for the exercise of his lumpish pedagogic wit, what a perfect victim with which to win amusement from a class of captive boys!

But he is dead now, my master. I can no longer hate him for his use of me as hunchback for his sallies. Nor can I hate you my classmates for the larger diversion you staged after school. Why should I? At the time, the incident seemed the greatest triumph of my life.

You may remember how a much larger audience assembled as I was dragged to the school drinking fountain, ducked under it and held until water ran down my spine, dripped into my trousers, trickled down my skinny legs to fill my socks and shoes. You may remember that, after my ducking, I was forced to read my essay once more. Your motives were just, I suppose. You wanted to knock the pretensions from under me, to teach me the lesson I have been too long in learning. But I learned nothing. Soaking wet, my clothes torn, I read my essay, but with pride now, screaming out that I would do everything I had promised in it. And all of you, watching my pale face and trembling shoulders, hearing the true fanatic in my thin defiant scream, all of you turned away, uneasy of me. Because conviction – even a wrong conviction – makes the rest of us uneasy. For the first time in my life I had won. My own unsurety died and for the remainder of my years at school I grew in the wind of your disapproval. Your doubts that day made me victim – the victim I still remain – of my own uncertain boast.

For I did not become great. I had no vocation for greatness. At thirty, instead of coughing blood, I bled rectally from haemorrhoids. I who boasted to you that I would never settle for the ordinary avocations you proposed have settled instead for failure. Yet in writing this I show that I have not even the dignity of a man who has accepted a fate, no matter how despicable. I am still unable to agree to my failure because on that day, when by your fear of me you gave me a taste of what greatness might bring me, my course was set, suddenly, haphazardly, yet with no possible alternative routing, towards a destiny I was not fit to accomplish. Oh, how I wish you had succeeded in drenching all my foolish hopes under that fountain. For who is more unworthy than a fool who boasts of talents he does not possess? Who more contemptible than the false artist posturing through life as he spews out his tiny frauds? What spectacle more truly degrading than a would-be Rimbaud, covered in the vomit of sickly pastiche, crying out his genius and his purity from a mouth filled with rotten teeth? I am that man. Are you responsible for the monstrous impostor I have become? Not you alone. There are others.

I reveal myself to those others now. You are my peers. You are those who encouraged me, those who, sinning against uncomfortable truths, were always willing and eager to admit a new accomplice to the small smelly circles of your self-love and self-deceit. You are the members of cliques and coteries – do not deny it for, of course, everyone will deny that he is the member of a clique – but let me describe you to yourselves and ask if you can wear the shoe.

You are the small uncertain talents of our time, ever ready to arrange a panel, lunch a critic, flatter a would-be disciple, praise an enemy if he has the power to hurt you, betray a friend whose reputation you hear is on the fade. You are the readers of reviews, not of books, the hiders in your attics of pictures now said to have gone out of style. Must I go on? You know what I am talking about, don't you? I am one of you or was one of you until I lost my grip on the tiny fringe of the curtain we mutually clutched to hide our falsities from the light of truth.

Truth. I cry out that word with fetid breath. Truth was to have been my redemption from the things that you and you and I and I have made of me. I am my own Judas. In writing these pages I have once again demonstrated that I am not worthy to attempt the truth. I make you the confession now, that as I started to write I was at once deflected from the truth. Truth could wait, for, in the moment of writing, I knew it was money I sought. I excused myself by thinking that I cannot write my work of truth until I have enough money to complete it. And so I knew that if I could strike at the guilt in half your hearts, some of you might send me small sums of money which would help me continue in this work. I excused myself by swearing (falsely) that despite these sums of money I would not allow myself to be deflected from writing the truth about you : a blackmailer is under no obligation to keep his word. And so, by this muddled morality – despicable, of course, but an important part of the truth about me – I hoped to gain time to write a work so terrible in its truth that it would revenge me forever. But what is the truth I seek? On whom must I revenge myself?

On you who falsely flattered me? On you who did not love me enough? On you who scorned me? Can I hold you responsible for the man I was, the man I am, the man I will be? Which of us can tell who is at fault? I can only say that long ago your unwillingness to let me dream prevented for years my true awakening. I wonder what you would say if you could see me now. For that is the purpose of these preliminary pages. Before I begin to write this work I want to know that I am not, once again, mistaken in my purpose. I want to know if you have recognized me, if you remember me.

Can you see me? Can you see the man who sits at a desk, trying with a pen – that ludicrous weapon which conceit once forced into his hand – to reach you across the waste of twenty years? Look, look and you will see me. Here I am. I am here. Can you see me now? Do you laugh? Or do you weep?

Alfred Purdy

THE NORTH WEST PASSAGE

                              is found
needs no more searching
and for lack of anything better to do
waiting the plane's departure north from Frobisher
I lounge on the bed poring over place-names
on maps
                and baby it's cold outside
I amuse myself with the idea of
                                Martin Frobisher
'Admiral of the Ocean-Sea' who was
'hurte . . . in the Buttocke with an Arrowe'
running down the beach near here
to escape the blood-mad Skraelings hoping
to reach Mrs Frobisher in time for tea
But Frobisher didn't make it either
in 1576
                and it's two hours until dinner
tho I'm not really very hungry just now
Locate Fury and Hecla
                on the orange-coloured paper
north west of where I am on Baffin
and go rocking thru history
in search of dead sailors
suspended from Ariadne's quivering cord
and find them at the precise point
where the meter registers 'alive'
when a living man remembers them
and the Minotaur's bull-roar
trembles in the northern lights
and a red needle flickers

on the playback device
Locate the Terror and Erebus that way
Franklin's ships preserved in ice
with no place-names for them
it'd be much too close to hell
and the big jets might take a wrong turn
skimming over the top of the world
or the ICBM computers make a quarter inch error
and destroy the illusion of paradise by mistake
and Capt. James' letter to the Emperor of Japan
suddenly gets delivered three centuries later
Or take the Ringnes boys
                              Ellef and Amund
heroic Norwegian brewers whose names
cling alcoholically to islands up there
or Boothia after an English gin distiller
Names like Ungava and Thule
                              The Beaufort Sea and Ellesmereland
places to drop cigarette butts in
while the big jets go popping over the horizon
to Moscow and you can snooze 5 minutes
before the stewardess brings dinner
or read the New Yorker with a double whiskey
and make it last a thousand miles
for it's a long time since Luke Foxe's cook
served 'beer in small cans' to the sailors
and it didn't last one nautical mile

The North West Passage is found
and poor old Lady Franklin well
she doesn't answer the phone
tho once she traded her tears for ships
to scour the Arctic seas for her husband
but the Terror and Erebus sank long ago
and it's still half an hour before dinner
and there isn't much to do but write letters
and I can't think of anything more to say

about the North West Passage
but I'll think of something
maybe
a break-thru
to strawberries and ice cream for dinner

FROBISHER BAY

TREES AT THE ARCTIC CIRCLE

(*Salix Cordifolia* – Ground Willow)

They are 18 inches long
or even less
crawling under rocks
grovelling among the lichens
bending and curling to escape
making themselves small
finding new ways to hide
Coward trees
I am angry to see them
like this
not proud of what they are
bowing to weather instead
careful of themselves
worried about the sky
afraid of exposing their limbs
like a Victorian married couple

I call to mind great Douglas firs
I see tall maples waving green
and oaks like gods in autumn gold
the whole horizon jungle dark
and I crouched under that continual night
But these
even the dwarf shrubs of Ontario

mock them
Coward trees

And yet – and yet –
their seed pods glow
like delicate grey earrings
their leaves are veined and intricate
like tiny parkas
They have about three months
to ensure the species does not die
and that's how they spend their time
unbothered by any human opinion
just digging in here and now
sending their roots down down down
And you know it occurs to me
         about 2 feet under
those roots must touch permafrost
ice that remains ice forever
and they use it for their nourishment
use death to remain alive

I see that I've been carried away
in my scorn of the dwarf trees
most foolish in my judgements
To take away the dignity
         of any living thing
even tho it cannot understand
         the scornful words
is to make life itself trivial
and yourself the Pontifex Maximus
         of nullity
I have been stupid in a poem
I will not alter the poem
but let the stupidity remain permanent
as the trees are
in a poem
the dwarf trees of Baffin Island

PANGNIRTUNG

ESKIMO HUNTER
(New Style)

In terylene shirt and suspenders
sun glasses and binoculars
Peterborough boat and Evinrude motor
Remington rifle with telescope sight
making hot tea on a Coleman stove
scanning the sea and shore for anything
that moves and lives and breathes
and so betrays itself
one way or another
All we need in the line of further equipment
is a sexy blonde in a bikini
trailing her hand thru the sunlit water
maybe a gaggle of Hollywood photographers
snapping pictures and smoking
nationally advertised brands
Like bwana in Africa
pukka sahib in Bengal
staked out on a tree platform
a tethered goat underneath wailing
Papa Hemingway's bearded ghost on safari
or fishing for giant turtles in Pango Pango
            Maybe it is phony
(and all we're after is seal)
but over the skyline
where the bergs heave and glimmer
under the glacier's foot
or down the fiord's blue water
            even under the boat itself
anywhere the unhappened instant is
real blood
            death for someone or some thing
            and it's reassuringly old fashioned

KIKASTAN ISLANDS

Roland Giguère

POLAR SEASONS

No flame. No warmth.
It was a cold life, the heart gripped in a ring of ice.

The sun had withdrawn its rays and finally left the humans who had insulted it for so long. They had spat in its face, in broad daylight; they had desecrated love like a whore, right on the street; they had dragged liberty through the mud and barbed wire. The noblest reasons for living torn to shreds under our windows and thrown to the four winds.

In autumn, we watched the dead leaves fall and, mentally, counted them among the green ones that we should not forget the colour of our hope. In our deepest selves, secretly and timidly, there still wavered the idea of the dignity of man.

But the centre of the earth was growing colder and colder. . . .

No flame. No warmth.
It was a cold life, the heart gripped in a ring of ice.

The eyes drained away, pierced by needles of cold. We that were brands became icicles, and everything froze in a terrible transparency.

White dominated, a cold white. A white that hid more than one festering wound of black, thick blood. But on the surface, to the eye, it was white. . . .

And the eye-sockets grew still, the flutter of eyelashes grew still, the beat of the wing grew still in a sky crystallized red and low while the other beating, of the heart, still kept on but now reached us deadened, muffled as though from far away, as though it moved farther and farther from the breast.

Those who continued to believe in something, no matter what, remained haggard. They were as lost as children in a railway station. They raved, adrift.

No flame. No warmth.
It was a cold life, the heart gripped in a ring of ice.

After death we would not rot but it would have been better to rot – to leave well-washed skeletons, clean remains, without a speck of flesh or blood, bones bleached and like new as the carcasses of horses that one finds on desert sands with skulls as beautiful as sculptures.

No, we would not rot but it would have been better to rot, for what was waiting for us was even worse : we were to be mummified at the foulest and most revolting moment of our lives and the image of our suffering preserved unchanged for ages and ages, reflected and magnified on the sky in humiliating auroras.

At any cost some other traces of ourselves had to be left, or none at all. None.

And we were there, caught in the ice, longing for a scorching summer.

No flame. No warmth.
It was a cold life, the heart gripped in a ring of ice.

And yet, a single night of universal love could save everything. A single white night of love and the earth is lighter; the sea withdraws into its bed taking with it the rags with which we are covered. Everything is washed clean. Man can sleep in white sheets without fear that his slumbers may be murdered.

But at this time from which I speak to you, one saw even in the eyes of man a longing for man and it is in the eyes of animals that one found again the gentleness that causes you to be torn from the ground and to soar in the pure air, caught up in the ecstasy of the dream lived in flesh and bone. The flower, too, in spite of everything, clung to its petals, and after their migration the swallows came back to us as though there had always been a spring.

Silently, we sought a new horizon on which to find a foothold for a new life, to start all over again, to re-invent everything beginning with ourselves.

Translated by F. R. Scott

George Woodcock

LOST EURYDICE

THE NOVELS OF CALLAGHAN

Morley Callaghan's best book for a quarter of a century is that
which he probably wrote with the least effort and the least intent of
producing a masterpiece. It is not one of the three ambitious but
imperfect novels he has published since the last war; it is the volume
of autobiography, *That Summer in Paris*.

That Summer in Paris is more than a satisfying book for the
great stock-market crash, when Montparnasse was enjoying its
last fling as an international literary centre and when Morley Callaghan, a young man from Toronto, mingled closely with several
of the great figures of the Lost Generation. It is self-revealing to an
extraordinary degree, honest and, despite some curious vanities,
more modest than a first reading immediately suggests, for it is a
naïve wonder that really comes through when he tells how Sinclair
Lewis said 'Flaubert would have loved your work' and Hemingway
remarked that 'Tolstoy couldn't have done my "Wedding Dress"
story better.' In a rare feat of reminiscent concentration, Callaghan
really does bring back the spirit of Paris a generation ago and he
offers some extraordinarily interesting insights into the personalities
of Hemingway, Fitzgerald and even Joyce; he also recreates very
convincingly his own personality of those far-off days. He not
merely recollects his past self, he seems to rebecome it; and the
achievement affects even his writing. The tone is that of *They Shall
Inherit the Earth* rather than that of *A Passion in Rome*. The flabbiness of prose and thought that have characterized his most recent
novels is absent; everything is crisp, clear, unpretentious. Callaghan
writes with the air of a man knowing the limitations of his powers
and then using them to the full, as he did in the three novels of his

middle period which are still unexcelled among his longer works of fiction – *Such is My Beloved, They Shall Inherit the Earth* and *More Joy in Heaven.*

That Summer in Paris is more than a satisfying book for the reader interested in literary personages. It is in its own way a fascinating handbook to Callaghan's own other writing. For example, we come across incidents and characters which we recognize from his fiction, and so we begin to get some insight into his methods of building up a book. Callaghan's realistic theories – even if they have never really dominated his essentially moralistic novels – have justified him in appropriating anything that life happened to offer which was suitable to his purposes of the moment. Like many better novelists, Callaghan is less inventive than imaginative. He is always ready to use a good character or a good situation time and again under various guises, so that the priest whom he portrays in real life in *That Summer in Paris* (the priest who loved drink too well and has walked with sixteen men to the death chamber) appears, variously transformed, in both his early novel, *It's Never Over,* and his middle-period novel, *More Joy in Heaven.*

But even more interesting than the buds of character and situation which Callaghan has more or less successfully transplanted into his novels from the life portrayed in *That Summer in Paris* are the statements of his literary principles which are scattered through the pages of his Paris memoirs. Like Samuel Butler, George Orwell and Ernest Hemingway, Callaghan came in his own way (which he does not very clearly reveal to us) to the conclusion that – in our age at least – writing must be uncomplicated and direct. It should present the object – not seek to transform it into something it is not or use something else to suggest or describe it.

I remember deciding that the root of the trouble with writing was that poets and storywriters used language to evade, to skip away from the object, because they could never bear to face the thing freshly and see it freshly for what it was in itself.

Hence metaphor must be avoided. At this point in the argument it is ironical to find Callaghan picking for the special target of his attack the man who wrote in the Preface to *Lyrical Ballads* that the language of poetry should be 'a selection of the language really spoken by men'.

Those lines, 'A primrose by the river's brim, a yellow primrose was to him, and it was nothing more,' often troubled me, aroused my anger. What the hell else did Wordsworth want it to be? An orange? A sunset? I would ask myself, Why does one thing have to remind you of something else?

It goes against the grain to defend Wordsworth at his most inane, but there is a certain obtuseness about Callaghan's argument which suggests that he did not even attempt to consider the uses of metaphor; at least, however, he makes quite clear the practice he intends to follow in his own work.

He follows this first statement with hostile references to 'arty writers' and uses 'too literary' as a regular term of condemnation. He remarks that 'it was part of my writing creed to distrust calculated charm in prose,' and he shows a hostility towards critics and 'writers about writers' which – even if his later actions have shown it to be rather suspect can be interpreted as part of his general reaction against literary self-consciousness. Elsewhere he talks of aiming at a writing 'as transparent as glass', and in what is probably his most significant statement he tells us this:

But I knew what I was seeking in my Paris street walks, and in the typing hours – with Loretto waiting to retype a chapter. It was this: strip the language, and make the style, the method, all the psychological ramifications, the ambience of the relationships, all the one thing, so the reader couldn't make separations. Cézanne's apples. The appleness of apples. Yet just apples.

Wandering around Paris I would find myself thinking of the way Matisse looked at the world around him and find myself growing enchanted. A pumpkin, a fence, a girl, a pineapple on a tablecloth – the thing seen freshly in a pattern that was a gay celebration of things as they were. Why couldn't all people have the eyes and the heart that would give them this happy acceptance of reality? The word made flesh. The terrible vanity of the artist who wanted the word without the flesh. I can see now that I was busy rejecting even then the arrogance of the spirit, that fantasy running through modern letters and thought that man was alien in this universe. From Pascal to Henry Miller they are the children of St Paul.

The philosophy is clear and, as Callaghan expresses it, consistent. Writing is concerned with, in the old Godwinian phrase, things as they are. Its purpose is statement. It should be simple – so 'transparent' as to be self-effacing. The style and the content should become one, indivisible. Writing should not detach itself from the visible world which, for Callaghan as for Gautier, exists. Callaghan shared his attitude, as I have remarked, with many writers of his time; it was part of the great reaction against the reign of Symbolism. At the same time, he did not reject entirely those who followed other directions. We find him admiring Joyce, that most deliberately 'literary' of all writers, and Fitzgerald, though he also says of him:

And what could be left for Scott when the glamorous wandering was over? When 'a primrose by a river's brim, a yellow primrose was to him, and it was nothing more.' My old theme. Nothing more; the wonder of the thing in itself. Right for me. But not for Scott.

The theory of writing Callaghan puts forward in *That Summer in Paris* is rational enough, but literature is not produced by logical consistency. Carried to extremes, such a theory would result in a total atrophy of feeling, but no real writer works by theory, and Callaghan as often deserts his ideal of stark, direct statement as Zola does his vaunted scientific realism. Every Callaghan novel deals with man as a moral being, and hence it is led into realms where the statement cannot be direct; here, even when metaphor is not used obviously, it enters in the larger symbolic sense. A whole essay could be written on the significance of the cathedrals which appear at crucial points in every novel that Callaghan wrote, from the Canadian cathedral in his first novel, *Strange Fugitive*, of which he says, 'You can't get away from it. It's right in the centre of things,' to the universal cathedral, St Peter's, in *A Passion in Rome*, where the ceremonies connected with the death of the Pope proclaim the endurance of universal verities which reflect on the morally tortured life of the novel's characters.

Strange Fugitive is probably nearer than any other Callaghan novel to being a textbook example of his writing theory carried into practice. The narrative style is simple and for the most part decorated only by a frequent use of vernacular. At times the tone is that of a rather naïve person laconically telling a tale.

> The practice was over, he went into the dressing-room and talked with some of the players. He watched a fellow stretched out on his belly getting a rub down. He smelled the liniment, and thought maybe the fellow had a charlie horse. Most players undressed slowly, singing and telling stories. They talked loudly and happily. Harry picked up a fellow's ball-shoes and whacked them on the floor, knocking the mud out of the spikes.

There is no need to seek far among the companions of Callaghan's youth to find something very similar. In the passage I have quoted, Callaghan was speaking as author; here Hemingway speaks through the mouth of one of his characters.

> Walcott had been just hitting him for a long time. It was like a base-ball player pulls a ball and takes some of the shock off. From now on Walcott commenced to land solid. He certainly was a socking-machine. Jack was trying to block everything now. It didn't show what an awful beating he was taking. In between the rounds I worked on his legs. The muscles would flutter under my hands all the time I was working them. He was as sick as hell.

Of the two passages Callaghan's is perhaps the better, but the similarity shows that, in their duller moments, both Callaghan and Hemingway slipped into an almost anonymous period style. Because it contains so much writing of this kind, *Strange Fugitive* is the most dated and the least individual of Callaghan's early works.

In content, *Strange Fugitive* is already typical Callaghan, a novel of consequences. The very first sentence strikes the note.

> Harry Trotter, who had a good job as foreman in Pape's lumberyard, was determined everybody should understand he loved his wife.

What follows is Harry's fall from this respectable niche because of his failure to control his passions. His predilection for violence loses him the good job in the timber yard. The attractions of an easy-going divorcée lead him away from his wife; here, incidentally, we find a situation that recurs constantly in Callaghan's work – the conflict between sacred and profane love, between the slender, somewhat frigid wife figure and the abundantly fleshed amoral mistress, the Jocasta figure of men who, like Harry Trotter, loved their mothers too well. Infidelity and careless violence lead to lawlessness and deliberate violence. Harry becomes a bootlegger, kills the boss of a rival gang, and dies under the sawn-off shotguns of his enemies. It is a fate that rolls on with massive inevitability, like a Buddhist Karma; in fact the very symbol of Karma fills Harry's eyes as he lies dying.

He saw the wheels of the car going round and round, and the car got bigger. The wheels went round slowly and he was dead.

Strange Fugitive is a Canadian Rake's Progress. At first sight its inexorable and highly formalized pattern of retribution seems at variance with Callaghan's expressed aim of direct and natural writing. Is this really, one wonders, Cézanne's apples? But the inconsistency is only apparent. For the aim of stripping the language, of seeing things as they are and using writing to make statements about them is as much a moral as an aesthetic aim; it is part of the puritanical or Jansenist revolt against luxury in art and thought as well as in life. The great moralist writers have always sought for a renewed directness of language, from Bunyan and Swift to Orwell and Gide. But in none of them is this simplification of style an expression of fictional realism; in fact it tends to remove such writers from the true business of the realist novel, that objective exploration of character which, as Flaubert and Tolstoy knew, requires all the subtlety, all the mutability and all the richness of suggestion of which language is capable. *Pilgrim's Progress* and *Gulliver's Travels* are neither novels nor realistic, and even the typical works of the later moralists, like *Strait is the Gate* and *1984*, deliberately abandon plausibility to achieve the highly formal and artificial pattern of the moral parable. Callaghan belongs in this company; his view of style is essentially moralistic, and every one of his works fails or succeeds according to the ability with which he manipulates the element of parable within it.

This is the underlying motivation of Callaghan's desire to 'strip down' which, as his art grows, he carries forward into such larger elements as action and character. It is the essence of the parable-novel to keep attention focused closely on the moral question which the author is posing to the reader. Hence the multiplication of sub-plots is to be avoided, the leading characters must be few and well-defined, the minor characters must be used at crucial points to perform actions or make statements that help to illuminate the theme. Gide and Camus found in the peculiarly French *récit* the ideal form and volume for the moral parable, and Orwell's best work in this vein was his slightest and least complicated, *Animal Farm*.

Similarly, in Callaghan, we see a progression in his earlier novels toward the simplification of structure. At the same time there is a compensating enrichment of the language which reveals an in-evitable relaxation of the rules Callaghan had set himself as an apprentice writer. It is true that his characters continue to speak in that peculiar rough patois which is his personal version – a kind of Basic Vernacular – of the impoverished language of contemporary North American man; in fact the dialogue becomes more laconic from novel to novel, but when it is well done the very sparseness provides an effective contrast to the fuller narrative style.

Callaghan, even at this point, rarely resorts to obvious metaphor. But there are ways of being metaphorical without seeming so. The Imagists discovered one of them, for the objects they presented with such clear delineation were so evocative as to acquire metaphorical status. When an orthodox Imagist like H. D. says:

> In my garden
> even the wind-flowers lie flat
> broken by the wind at last . . .

those wind-flowers are a great deal more than botanical specimens. The very absence of specific links, like those which are made in a simile, makes images of this kind productive of a rich overgrowth of association. That objects have their own ambiguity and mean more in the mind than facts has been well understood by a later genera-tion of writers, like Robbe-Grillet and Butor.

It is to this quasi-metaphorical use of imagery that Callaghan turns abundantly in his second novel, *It's Never Over*. This is a novel of the everlasting return; it begins and ends with a street-car journey; it concerns three people who are close to a man hanged for murder and who find themselves drawn into an inescapable circle of emotions which arouse unadmitted hatreds and loves and which lead the hero – the dead man's friend – to the edge of a second murder. At one point the hero and the sister of the hanged man sit on the back porch of the house where he had lived.

'Practically all the flowers are gone now,' Isabelle said.

Stems of flowers were still standing in the garden earth; withered flowers with broken stems; a few asters and zinnias still in bloom but fading in the daytime sun; tall stalks of flowers lying dry and dead against the fence. The leaves were still thick on the grapevine.

'I hate to see the last of them go,' she said. 'I worked with them all summer.'

The fading of the flowers is clearly linked with Isabelle's appearance on that day.

Since she had become so much thinner her nose now was almost too large for her face, and her forehead and chin were too prominent. . . . She had on a black crepe dress, a collar high on her neck. The dress was a little too large, there was no movement under it, the cloth folds were unnaturally still.

Everything in this passage, even if Callaghan does not present it as metaphor, in fact means something more than itself. The withering of the flowers suggests the withering of Isabelle's hopes of life, the ending of summer is linked with the winter of death that hangs over the minds of the characters throughout the novel, and Isabelle's black dress, with no movement beneath it and its 'unnaturally still' cloth folds, brings to one's mind the idea of a mortcloth and recalls the funeral of the hanged man that had taken place earlier in the day. In fact, as we see, Callaghan's primrose is no longer 'nothing more'. He is using, like other writers, the traditional devices of literature.

This becomes increasingly evident in his third novel, A *Broken Journey*, written at the beginning of the thirties. This is a very undisciplined novel in which the characters are far less clearly realized than the central trio in *It's Never Over*. It is also a longer book than either of its predecessors, and it anticipates such later long novels as *The Many Colored Coat* and *A Passion in Rome* in its failure to focus clearly on significant action, in its limping pace and in the author's inability to provide a structure that will discipline the volume of material.

A Broken Journey deals with such themes as love and infidelity, the aspects of innocence and the contrast between the indifferent natural world and the ideals by which we try to approach it. In their own ways, all the characters suffer tragedy because of the distortions of love which their own natures conspire with external circumstances to force upon them. Peter Gould, temporarily paralysed after being pushed downstairs by a rejected mistress, and thus rendered incapable of becoming the lover of Marion Gibbons on the trip they take into the wilderness, represents on a physical level the deprivation of the other characters. Marion loses her prized virginity to the boatman, Steve, a man of the wilderness, and feels only disappointment and 'a strange impersonal tenderness'. She departs, defeated, and leaves Peter to the closeness of his clearly symbolic 'small white room'. Indeed, *A Broken Journey* is packed with symbolic objects – the roses that stand for doomed innocence, the threatening waterweeds that clog the river in the wilderness, the white unattainable mountain peak 'that looked like an immense, crude, rugged cathedral of rock. . . .' Furthermore, in this novel Callaghan introduces long stretches of landscape description which is intended partly to evoke the impersonal power of the natural world and partly to deepen the shadows of mood in the depiction of a series of doomed relationships.

In the two years – 1932 to 1934 – that separate *A Broken Journey* from *Such is My Beloved*, the leap forward is extraordinary. *A Broken Journey* might have been the product of a young promise disintegrating; *Such is My Beloved* is the work of a writer who has – at least for a period – found his true direction. Since this and Callaghan's other novels of the 1930s form a closely related group, it may be well to start by indicating some of their common characteristics. All of them are novels of their time, in which the writer shows a deep consciousness of existing social ills; it is depression conditions that originally drive Ronnie to prostitution in *Such is My Beloved* and scar Michael Aikenhead's young manhood with unemployment in *They Shall Inherit the Earth*. At the same time there is no suggestion – at least in Callaghan's own attitude – of the political messianism that spoilt so many novels in the thirties; he is well enough aware of the arguments of those who call themselves the socially conscious, as the harangues of Bill Johnson show in *They Shall Inherit the Earth*, but he passes no Marxist judgement, and the effects of a depression environment on his characters are observed objectively. But, while at times Callaghan appears to present a realistic picture of the social landscape of his decade, and skilfully reinforces the illusion by an effectively controlled description of the physical setting in which his characters move, these are no more novels of social analysis than they are of political propaganda.

They are essentially, as their biblical titles suggest, novels of moral predicament. Each asks its questions. What are the bounds of Christian love? How far can a man be free when all his acts affect the lives of others? Can the prodigal ever return to the world against which he has risen in rebellion? Can the individual assert and maintain his human dignity in an acquisitive society? Each novel asks its questions; none provides the glib and easy answer.

It is these moral questions that dominate and shape the novels of Callaghan's middle period to the virtual exclusion of other considerations. While the apparent plausibility of background and of minor action may at first deceive the reader, neither the characters nor the structures of action in these novels are in any sense realistic. Considered as probable human beings, Father Dowling and Kip Caley are absurd; considered as the God's Fools of moral allegory they at once assume authenticity. Similarly the two Aikenheads, Michael and his father Andrew in *They Shall Inherit the Earth*, are radically simplified individuals who live fully only in terms of their essential moral predicament; everything else about them – their relationships with people outside the circle affected by the death of Dave Choat, their naïve loves and ambitions – is roughly sketched. As in a picture by Tintoretto, the almost slurred vagueness of detail has the effect of concentrating our attention on the central pattern, the moral heart of the work.

The patterns of action are equally simplified, and, as in Callaghan's first novel and in all the novels of the classic moralist tradition, the chain of consequences works out inexorably. Kip is not allowed to become merely disillusioned with the society to which he returns; he has to be physically as well as morally destroyed. Andrew Aikenhead is only reprieved after he has endured all the bitter stages of a moral crucifixion. The actions of the characters themselves are as unrealistic as the destinies that rule them. Father Dowling's haunting of the prostitutes he decides to befriend is plausible only as a manifestation of neurotic obsession; but, despite the priest's eventual mental breakdown – another blow of relentless fate – it is obvious that Callaghan is not wasting his time on a clinical picture of mental aberration. Father Dowling's actions, like his character, assume meaning – even in merely aesthetic terms – only if we regard them as contributing to the symbolic structure of a moral statement. Kip Caley's gross naïveté, his optimism, his extraordinary blindness to the implications of anything outside the almost messianic mission that inspires him – all of these characteristics and all of the actions that stem from them would seem improbably childish if we did not apply in reading *More Joy in Heaven* similar standards to those we apply in reading *Don Quixote*. Kip Caley is not a likely human being, nor does he seem intended to be one, in spite of the fact that the record of a real-life criminal provided the hints on which Callaghan worked in writing the novel.

It is in fact within a clearly established moral spectrum that all the characters and their actions in Callaghan's three central novels are to be observed. They range from the innocent full circle to innocence's parody, the amoral. The innocence of Julie in *More Joy in Heaven*, an innocence which experience cannot soil, is doubled by the frightening cynicism of the fur-thief Foley who leads Kip to his doom. In *They Shall Inherit the Earth* the joyful natural innocence of Anna saves Michael morally and brings him to the final reconciliation with his father and his own conscience, but Anna herself is for one perilous evening endangered by the ophidian lust of the amoral Huck Farr, every man's comrade and every woman's enemy. The amoral characters in these novels always appear as tempters; it is another of them, Lou, who holds the prostitute Ronnie in *Such is My Beloved* to her path of degradation and profits by it. Hence the ultimates of the spectrum must be regarded as the innocent and the diabolical, and in the gulf between them the central characters wage their struggle not merely within their own hearts, but also externally, with the great amorphous being of a conscienceless society represented by the chorus of minor characters, the indifferent, the cowardly, the proud and the corrupt.

Callaghan's rebels, as he presents them, are not anarchistic rebels; it is essential to the drama of Kip Caley that he should return to society repenting just such a rebellion. The actual martyr figures in all three novels suffer acutely because normal society misunderstands and rejects them. It is the knowledge that his fellow citizens are wrongly accusing him of the murder of his stepson that breaks Andrew Aikenhead's spirit; Father Dowling's calvary begins when he discovers that a devout Catholic family, famous for its charitable works, will not accept as human beings the prostitutes he befriends; Kip Caley's catastrophe comes when he realizes that the people who appeared full of enthusiastic admiration for his desire to live by good works have been merely enjoying the thrill of associating with a notorious and reformed ex-criminal and have never understood the moral urge that burnt within him. Not merely do such characters seek reconciliation with the society that rejects them; they also try to bring about the reconciliation of other rejected ones who have sought refuge in the sub-societies of prostitution and crime. The sinister unresponsiveness of society, and the moral insensitiveness of its symbolic figures – judges, bishops, politicians – suggests that Callaghan is posing the classic opposition between moral man and immoral society, between the actions urged by conscience and the actions dictated by custom and institution. The ambiguous symbolism of the cathedral, particularly in *Such is My Beloved*, extends this dichotomy into the world of religion, into the difference between acts spurred by Christian compassion and acts necessary for the institutional stability of the church on earth.

In writing these novels Callaghan used effectively the limited resources of a talent which his own statements on his early aims in writing have defined. Like the French writers of the *récits*, he chose a simple moral theme and gave it flesh and substance through the lives of his characters. Economy of structure and action, simplicity of language and imagery, a bold use of a few key symbolic settings in each novel, such as the hotel room in *More Joy in Heaven*, the lake and the rooming house in *They Shall Inherit the Earth* – these elements provide an appropriate form for the kind of parable Callaghan set out to write at this period. The novels are not flawless. At times the feeling softens into sentimentality; at times the clear writing muddies into dullness; at times the characters are not plausible even within their own allegorical framework. But as a group these three novels, all published between 1934 and 1937, represent Callaghan's best work outside some of his short stories, and one of the real achievements in Canadian writing.

Fourteen years passed before Callaghan's next novel, *The Loved and the Lost*, appeared in 1951, and another nine years before *The Many Colored Coat* was published in 1960, to be followed by *A Passion in Rome* in 1961. I do not know the reason for the long interval between the novels of the 1930s and *The Loved and the Lost* (with its curious Fitzgeraldish title) in the 1950s. But for the purposes of this essay the biographical details are unimportant. What is important is that since the last war Callaghan has been trying a somewhat different kind of novel, which has brought him on a long and not entirely successful journey away from his early aims in writing. Abandoning the *récit*-like form of his best period, he has sought the complexity of the classic realistic novel. *A Passion in Rome* is described twice on the dust jacket as 'A Major Novel', and, while the publisher may have been responsible for this so patently inaccurate description, there is no doubt that ever since the war Callaghan had been seeking to produce a successful work of greater dimensions than anything he had written before.

Unfortunately his three most recent novels have been large in size but not in texture. Even the monolithic grandeur of moral tragedy that lingers in the mind after reading *Such is My Beloved* or *More Joy in Heaven* is totally absent from one's recollection of *The Loved and the Lost* or either of its successors.

On reading *The Loved and the Lost* one immediately perceives an absence of the unity of conception that marked its predecessors. There is a moral theme of a kind, rather indistinctly embodied in former Professor McAlpine's inner conflict over his infatuation for the ambiguous Peggy Sanderson and his neglect of the cold, career-ensuring Junior Leaguer, Catherine Carver. But in the main Callaghan is seeking other goals, and *The Loved and the Lost* becomes a curious grafting together of the social novel and the romance. The overworld of the Carvers and their quasi-patrician 'society' set is opposed by the underworld of the Negro cabarets where Peggy Sanderson, even if she rejects conventional society, vainly seeks acceptance by its unconventional substitute. Peggy herself becomes in Jim's sentimental vision a kind of *princesse lointaine*, accompanied by symbolical devices – the carved leopard and the church which the hero can never again discover – that belong in the tradition of courtly romance. Jim's desire for Peggy never seems much more real than its object, and their relationship enters a further stage of romantic mistiness as the novel assumes the form of an Orpheus myth, with Jim going into the underworld to rescue his Eurydice and losing her to death when gaining her seems most assured. The world of the Carvers is hardly more convincing or consistent than that of Peggy Sanderson; one cannot take seriously either Catherine Carver's combination of gentility and vulgarity or McAlpine's odd values when in her company, values which make a scholar of history imagine that he has really found his vocation when he is allowed to become a columnist for the Carver newspaper with its dubious aims.

In some respects *The Many Colored Coat* is nearer the earlier novels. The moral question of the nature of innocence is elaborately posed. A respectable bank manager, Scotty Bowman, is fascinated by the personality and the company of a free-spending, good-natured publicity man, Harry Lane. The glamour of Harry's world and the easy charms of one of the tarts who move within it arouse in Scotty a longing for the kind of extravagant living he has never allowed himself. He offers Harry a bank loan to buy speculative stocks; he makes a false statement to his head office, and then the stocks crash. Scotty is arrested for embezzlement, and at the trial Harry is shown in a dubious light by a doggedly loyal but rather thick-witted friend of Scotty, the boxer-turned-tailor Mike Cohn. Scotty commits suicide in prison. The hatred between Harry and Mike grows, and it excites the mocking laughter of the Montreal bar-flies when Harry starts to wear, in and out of season, a shoddy jacket Mike has made for him. In the end, provoked beyond endurance by Harry's clowning, Mike knocks him down a flight of stairs, and Harry is paralysed temporarily (an echo of Peter Gould's misfortune in *A Broken Journey*). At the trial which follows, Harry, who has suddenly seen the relationship between himself and Scotty in another focus, does not appear; Mike seems triumphant, only to abdicate at that moment the right of judgement he has previously exercised. The moral of the novel – and there seems no description quite so adequate as that old-fashioned term – is summed up in a reflection of Harry's:

. . . he wondered if innocence was like a two-edged sword without a handle, and if you gripped it and used it, it cut you so painfully you had to lash out blindly, seeking vengeance on someone for the bleeding.

This is a theme of the same order as those which inspired Callaghan's novels of the thirties, but it is not served by the same simplicity and economy of writing. Rather like Hemingway in *The Old Man and the Sea*, Callaghan drags out to tedium an idea that could have been admirably treated in half the 318 pages to which *The Many Colored Coat* actually runs. The looseness of construction is paralleled in the characterization, which hovers uneasily between the sharpness of caricature and the flabbiness of sentimental pseudorealism. The women characters are the most ill-drawn. Like most Canadian male authors, Callaghan has always had difficulty in portraying women except as types – the cold, proud pseudo-saint and the easy-hearted, loose-legged floozie; the leading women in *The Many Colored Coat* represent these types at their worst, Mollie an insufferable prig and Annie a kind of soft-centred candy doll.

A *Passion in Rome* is Callaghan's most recent, ambitious and least successful novel. Unlike his earlier novels, in all of which the characters were seeking justification and acceptance in their own worlds, A *Passion in Rome* concerns two lonelinesses meeting in an alien setting. From the very moment when Sam Raymond reaches Rome, feeling scared and alone, the emphasis is on the need, not to find one's world so much as to find oneself. Sam, an unsuccessful painter turned news-photographer, is another latter-day Orpheus who discovers his particular Eurydice in Anna, a television singer ruined by drink. Each of the two seeks some new accepting world; Sam wonders 'if there couldn't still be some one place in the world where a man's life might take on meaning', and Anna, with Italian blood in her veins, lives in a displaced American's fantasy of being 'a Roman woman'. Both learn that one cannot fly through space away from oneself. The only Rome they can find is the false Rome of tourists, pilgrims, newsmen; the real Rome of the little dark Romans is always closed and hostile, and they are forced to face each other in the closeness of a symbolic single room, where Sam searches into the darkness, draws Anna into the light and then loses this Eurydice whom he is too anxious to keep. In the moment of loss he finds himself, and so the two part heroically to face their individual futures; the novel ends, if not happily, at least triumphantly, as Callaghan tells us in an excruciating last sentence, 'He felt all at once fiercely exultant.'

A *Passion in Rome* is clumsily constructed and so verbose that one wonders what has happened to the old vows to achieve a writing 'as transparent as glass'. The set pieces of the Pope's funeral and the election of his successor project a background of stuccoish unreality against which the human drama never emerges into authenticity. Sam is the kind of improbable romantic fool who in Callaghan's earlier phase might have been raised to something approaching allegorical grandeur. But A *Passion in Rome* has all the signs of being intended as a realistic novel, and in a setting described with such crowded detail a hero of this kind is out of place. Anna comes into the novel fighting, interesting in her sulky perversity, and one expects much of her; but Sam's devotion irons out her individuality to a self-abnegating silliness which the author himself seems to have found unendurable, since at this point he quickly draws the novel to an end.

As characters Sam and Anna are too mechanically exemplary to have any place in a novel in the realist tradition, but at the same time insufficiently distilled to form the core of an effective moral parable. Ultimately the test of characters lies in what they say and how they speak. Callaghan's earlier characters are often laconic in their peculiar Callaghanese way of speaking; but they are usually idiosyncratic enough to be acceptable. The language in which Sam and Anna converse is undifferentiated substandard North American. One opens the book at random and is faced, usually, by something like this:

'Do you really have to go singing there, Carla?' he asked, surprised.

'He'll pay me, Sam. I'll be getting some money. Singing and getting some money.'

'You just said he wouldn't pay you much.'

'Look, Sam. You're the boss. Don't you want me to sing there?'

'I don't care,' he said, laughing awkwardly. 'I mean the thing was to have you see you could sing anywhere. There's nothing to stop you doing anything you want. It's settled now, and you're free in your mind about it.'

'It means some money for just being myself, Sam. It's easy.'

'How much?'

'A couple of hours a night. See that you get ten thousand lire a night out of him, Sam.'

'About a hundred a week, eh?'

Such passages proliferate, filling up pages but achieving very little else. Thus the search for transparency in writing has ended in a kind of dialogue so dull that its effect is one of complete opacity.

Has another Eurydice vanished into the darkness? Certainly *A Passion in Rome* demonstrates more convincingly than ever that Callaghan is never likely to be a good novelist in the grand manner; the moralist allegories of the thirties remain his best works of longer fiction. Yet perhaps it is not too late to expect a turn in that devious path which Callaghan's inspiration has followed. The freshness and honesty and directness of *That Summer in Paris*, springing up unexpectedly between two such laborious works as *The Many Colored Coat* and *A Passion in Rome*, showed that Callaghan has not yet lost the qualities which – however he may have recently neglected them – have made him a Canadian writer who cannot be overlooked.

William Weintraub

FLUXATION AND SLURRAGE

Until recently, the New Cinema knew Ron Chaffinch only for his 'proems' (*Basilisk One, Basilisk Two, Basilisk Three*, etc.). These films run from seventy to ninety seconds each and, in terms of their avowed intention – 'to fragment the instant' – I have found them moderately successful. But I have never been able to share the unreserved enthusiasm of most critics, as each succeeding proem (there have been twenty-three so far) has left me with a nagging feeling of promise unfulfilled.

In the *Basilisks*, Chaffinch never fully exploits the opportunities for ambiguity inherent in his subject-matter, although I admit that the effects of this are mitigated by the very brevity of the films. Also, there is a troubling lack of fluidity-within-the-frame, and without Chaffinch's highly-personal use of the hand-held projector we would probably never feel the full impact of his granitic images.

There was, therefore, considerable surprise at the recent premiere of his latest film when Chaffinch entered the hall and conspicuously took a seat among the audience. Obviously he would not be handling the projection himself. This added to the air of anticipation, for there had been much rumour of a radical change in Chaffinch's style, and Chaffinch had been uncharacteristically secretive about his new project. Thus none of us had the slightest idea of what to expect when the lights were dimmed for this first showing of *Dig My Holocaust*.

Four hours later, when the lights went up again, one thing was stunningly apparent: Ron Chaffinch had abandoned the short form.

But beyond this stark fact lay a richly ambiguous texture of filmic intent and effect. This was reflected in the hubbub from the audience as voices rose to exclaim about this or that aspect of the *oeuvre*. Had anyone since Antonioni so completely captured the bone-crushing boredom of life? Had anyone since Godard so adumbrated the random nature of perception? Had anyone *ever* superimposed the Hiroshima mushroom on the female breast so courageously often?

Despite varying interpretations of the nature of Chaffinch's accomplishment, there was complete agreement that he had now thrown off any vestige of *retardataire* shackles. Here was a truly subversive film. In its evisceration of the middle-class ethos, no entrail had been left unturned.

But what interested me most were *Holocaust*'s frequent ventures into the narrative form. This, of course, was not 'plot' in the Pauline Kaelic sense, nor even in the Robbe-Grilletian sense; there was no sacrifice here of the aleatory for 'story line'. It was, rather, narrative of the sort that fully expresses the film maker's contempt for the chloroform that Hollywood distils from literature.

In this vein, Chaffinch's nonprofessional actors (so free of sophistic gloss!) gave us moments that will not easily be forgotten. One that keeps returning to my mind is that climactic scene in the fourteenth reel of *Holocaust*. Surely it must be one of the most electrifying Pregnancy Announcement Sequences screened in recent months. Suffice to say that when Chaffinch's high-school heroine, Immolata, said, 'Gregory, I've got something to tell you,' a choking sound ran through the audience.

Some viewers thought that Chaffinch's impact derived from the fact that he had symbolically buried Immolata up to her neck in sand for this scene, but credit must also go to Gregory's unconventional rejoinder to the dread phrase, 'I am with child.' (All dialogue, of course, was improvised by the actors.)

Unlike Mario, in Bognor's *Negation 17*, Gregory does not say, 'Are you sure?' And unlike Hubert, in Trent's *Bitter Elixir*, he does not say, 'Ya sure?' No, Gregory's reply, which promises to become a byword on the nation's campuses, gets its effect by being far more mosaic than linear.

It seems to me that the Pregnancy Announcement, by its climactic nature, frequently throws into sharp focus the film maker's efforts to break new ground in the narrative form, often through a painterly approach. One therefore immediately compares Chaffinch's master stroke in *Holocaust* with the Announcements in earlier films, like Kretschmer's pioneer work *Lydia* (1965). One recalls that Lydia, wishing to impart the news of her parturient state, tugs at Ludwig's beard and says, 'Ludwig, I've got something to tell you.' But Ludwig, absorbed with his yo-yo, affects not to hear. In order to attract his attention, Lydia dances on the beach and turns from positive to negative every eight frames. Though this may appear primitive today, it was epochal for its time (since then, of course, Kretschmer has grown enormously, thanks to his unique technical innovations like focus-mangling, fluxation and slurrage).

In later works by 'Kretsch' (as the film makers call him), what is probably the best Pregnancy Announcement comes in *Medusa* (1967). One recalls how Medusa, tugging at Harold's Iron Cross, cries, 'Harold, I've got something to tell you.' This, naturally, causes Harold to crash the motorcycle, and Medusa's next remark ('I'm five weeks late'), uttered as she staggers from the wreckage, is surely a landmark in the Expanded Cinema. The fact that Medusa addresses this observation to a tree stump has been attributed by some critics to a parallax problem that dogged Kretschmer's view-finder throughout the shooting, but the *cinéaste* himself assures me that Harold was *meant* to be out-of-frame, and that the tree stump embodies a symbolism that will not be lost on Suburbia.

Bligh, on the other hand, has chosen a more documentary approach in *Black Forceps* (1966). In this film, one recalls that when Jocko says, 'Are you sure?' Althea goes to her chiffonier and produces a calendar, a table of logarithms and a sundial. As the young couple sit down to do their arithmetic, one is spared any *longueurs* in the ensuing twenty-minute obstetrical discussion thanks to the haunting overlay of song and guitar by Dow Jones and the Industrials.

Though Bligh's somewhat archaic, sequential logic has a curious power, the full use of irrelevance is still probably the film maker's most cunning sledgehammer. And in this *genre*, of course, Porchester has no peer.

In *A Chick Too Groovy* (1966), where we see one of the few non-dream sequences Porchester has ever attempted, he shows us his heroine, Rosamund, on the telephone. She is about to make her

Announcement when her parents saunter into the room. Rosamund's abrupt switch to four hours of small-talk, on the phone, is surely Porchester at his most savage. As she speaks her monologue, the parents' continuous performance of Swedish calisthenics, in the foreground, heightens the effect of Porchester's bold refusal to compress time. And the father's callous remark ('If you ask me, that girl's got one in the oven') must surely be one of the underground's most searing comments on middle-class values.

But probably the most impactful of all will be *Orpheus Nacreant*, which Ruttenberg is making in multi-screen and Fujichrome color for the World Youth Pavilion at the Osaka World's Fair in 1970. 'Rut' has just vouchsafed me a peek at the draft script, and I can only say that as an experience the film will probably compare with Chaffinch at his uttermost.

In *Orpheus*, Ruttenberg puts the Announcement Sequence at the very end of the *oeuvre*. The sequence begins with Screens 2 and 3 dark. On Screen 1, Lisa is dialling a number. She is a swinging young item from Prince Edward Island, a hostess at the Pulp and Paper Pavilion at Expo '67.

The gigantic Screen 3 lights up as Kevin answers. Kevin is assistant manager of the maple syrup boutique in the State of Vermont Pavilion.

'Kevin, I've got something to tell you,' says Lisa.

'What makes you think it was me, my little doxy,' says Kevin. 'I haven't seen you since the Youthfest at the Katanga Pavilion. If you're preggers, it could have been any one of those wops, coons, kikes, krauts, pepsis, gyppos, greasers, squareheads, micks, hunkies, limeys, frogs, spicks, japs, chinks or reds from the other pavilions. So it's strictly *your* problem, baby.'

As Kevin hangs up on Screen 3, Lisa dissolves in tears on Screen 1 and, for the first time, Screen 2 lights up, in the middle. On it, from its cushion of flame, a Saturn rocket lifts hissingly off its pad at Cape Kennedy. As we follow it up into space, the Narrator says: 'The Family of Man ... Earth ... One planet in the heavens ... Childbirth, death ... Beauty, terror, as World Youth wanders through the Yin in search of its Yang.' (The words 'United States' stencilled on the rocket will not be lost on audiences at Osaka.)

Ruttenberg, of course, is able to paint a massive canvas, thanks to sponsorship by the Kyoto Specie Bank, but today equally pungent statements are being made by the shoestring film maker. One immediately thinks of Rakor's mini-film *Hudibras Spangled* (1968).

Hudibras opens with the telephone ringing in a young man's pad. The young man picks up the phone, listens for a moment, puts down the receiver and shoots himself. End titles, credits. The audience has not heard a single word; there has been no whisper, even, of an Announcement. Yet everyone understands. For such is the grammar of the New Cinema.

Robert Fulford

GALBRAITH IN DUTTON

John Kenneth Galbraith's recent book, *The Scotch*, has once again put him on the best-seller lists and once again demonstrated his style, wit, and insight. But in his old home, the Dutton-Wallacetown area in southwestern Ontario, Galbraith is the villain of the year.

The rest of the world may know Galbraith as the author of *The Affluent Society* and, indeed, the inventor of that famous phrase. It may know him as a distinguished Harvard economist, a journalist of high ability, an essayist of grace and charm, a confidante of Stevenson, Kennedy, and Nehru. But in Dutton this week he is regarded as a local boy who went away and told the world some unpleasant facts about his own people.

Galbraith's book, which he wrote in odd moments when he was American ambassador to India, is touching and funny, and most outsiders will see it as an honest and mainly sympathetic memoir. But it describes the Scotch he knew in his childhood as sometimes dirty, sometimes drunken, sometimes miserly, and rarely very smart. To the descendants and friends of those so described, the book seems a monumental insult.

Mrs Herb Green, the librarian at the Dutton Public Library, is one of the most outspoken members of the anti-Galbraith faction. She has only two copies of the book in the library, and there is a waiting list of fifty people for them. But Mrs Green doesn't like the book and would have preferred not to stock it at all. She did so only because of the demand.

'Most of the people here are fairly disgusted with it,' Mrs Green told me when I telephoned her yesterday. 'It's very crudely written. I don't know how to explain it to you. Rough – a rough way of writing, if you get my meaning. I'm surprised that a person of his supposed stature would lower himself to write such a book. He wrote another book, you know, called *The Affluent Society*, and we have one copy. He was a neighbourhood boy and we thought we should patronize him. I don't think it's ever been taken out. I figure that the other was a kind of washout and he turned to this, figuring that if he made it controversial enough it would sell. I haven't heard anyone here say they liked it. One woman said, "There's an insult in every paragraph." '

Mrs Green objected especially to the rough handling Galbraith gave the high-school principal who made his adolescence a kind of hell. Mrs Green's brother-in-law went to his school and spoke well of the man. Mrs Green herself knew him slightly and thought him very nice.

Like it or not, however, the people of the area are buying it. They may not have read *The Affluent Society*, but they can't ignore *The Scotch*. The drugstore in Dutton, which normally doesn't sell books, has sold fifty copies and has an order in for fifty more. In St Thomas, thirty-five miles away, Richard Cochrill's bookstore has sold about 165 copies (at $3·95 each). In London, Roberts Bookstore has sold close to six hundred and Holmes told me yesterday it's the biggest seller since Orlo Miller's 1962 book, *The Donnellys Must Die*, another local scandal.

On Saturday Galbraith himself visited Dutton for a few hours, to make a film for the C.B.C. television show, *The Observer*. With cameras following him he walked into the McIntyre House, which he celebrates in his book as a scene of wild Saturday-night drinking; it's a beer parlour now. Galbraith had a beer and a ham sandwich with the locals. They all knew about the book.

'Did you have to be so personal?' one of them said. 'Did you think it was fair?' Many Dutton people think he should have used false names.

Galbraith replied by quoting Oliver Cromwell's remark that he wanted his portrait painted, 'warts and all'. He felt this was the only honest way to do it.

A week before, a C.B.C. man had gone to Dutton to arrange for Galbraith's visit. When he told one merchant Galbraith was coming to town, the man said, joking, 'Do you think that's safe?' But of course it turned out to be safe. The local people were politely cool.
30 September 1964

J. K. Galbraith

FROM *THE NON-POTABLE SCOTCH*

II

In many cultures obloquy attaches to unlicensed intercourse, especially if it becomes, in one way or another, a matter of record. This is rarely sufficient to prevent it. Thus the continence and fidelity of the Scotch call for additional analysis.

More must be attributed to the absence of opportunity than would be first imagined. There was no place, literally none, where a questing husband could take an interested wife and go to bed. He couldn't visit her house when her husband was away for the reason that husbands were rarely if ever away for as much as over-night. In any case, a man's horse and buggy were as firmly identified with his personality as his nose, hair or gait and they would be seen passing down or up the road or tied in the yard. In the centre of Khatmandu, the capital of Nepal, is a temple and around all four sides of it couples engage imaginatively in copulation for all eternity. (One talented woman rewards two well-endowed and highly aroused lovers simultaneously.) A visit by the couple to the McIntyre House in Dutton would have been almost equally unreticent.

Unmarried affection encountered similar barriers. The girl's dwelling was filled with parents and siblings and thus unavailable to anyone less adept at second-storey operations than the aforementioned McCallum. Resort to the barn, the classical arena of bucolic love, was an outright admission of intent. Also it would have been regarded by the better or even the average class of girl as rather vulgar. The couple could go riding together; chaperones were unknown and boys and girls, engaged or otherwise, went anywhere together. This, however, was allowed not out of liberalism but from a knowledge of the Canadian climate. In winter a cutter lent itself to love-making only at the cost of extreme contortion and an occasional chilling exposure. The alternative was a snowbank. Things were not appreciably more agreeable in the autumn on the frozen ground, in the spring in the mud or in summer under the onslaught of the mosquitoes. Chastity was everywhere protected by a vigilant Nature. With closed and heated automobiles, things have doubtless changed but that is only conjecture based on a general view of human nature.

III

Something had also to be attributed to the uncompromising Calvinism of our upbringing. We were taught that sexual intercourse was, under all circumstances, a sin. Marriage was not a mitigation so much as a kind of licence for misbehaviour and we were free from the countervailing influence of movies, television, and John O'Hara. Among the rougher element of the community, after the weather, the wisdom of selling cattle, and the personality of the school teacher had been touched upon, conversation would often be taken over by one or another of the acknowledged masters of salacious detail. However, in contrast with other cultures, no one ever boasted of his own exploits, presumably because there was no chance he would be believed. More often a shy or especially puritanical participant would be accused of fornication with some highly improbable lass. Interest would centre on the way he denied it. The charge would then be repeated, and coupled with more graphic, though even more imaginary, detail, and a pleasant hour or two would thus be whiled away. Members of the more prestigious clans never participated in such pastime. In our family we would have been visited by a Jovian wrath had it been known that we even listened. The mere appearance of my father at a neighbourhood gathering would turn the conversation back to crops.

An important feature of an austere education in such matters is that it need influence only one of the two people involved to be fully effective. And uncertainty as to the state of conviction of the other person, plus the moral consequences of miscalculation, can be a powerful deterrent. One such experience had a durable effect on me.

At some time during adolescence, I encountered a novel by Anatole France which made unlicensed sexual transactions, especially if blessed by deep affection and profound mutual understanding, seem much more defensible than I had previously been allowed to suppose. It was summer and I was deeply in love. One day the object of my love, a compact, golden-haired girl who lived on Willey's Sideroad, a half-mile away, came over to visit my sisters. They were away and we walked together through the orchard and climbed on to a rail fence which overlooked a small field between our place and Bert McCallum's. Our cows were pasturing on the second-growth clover in front of us. The hot summer afternoon lay quiet all around.

With the cows was a white bull named O. A. C. *Pride* for the Ontario Agricultural College where my father had bid him in at an auction. As we perched there the bull served his purpose by serving a heifer which was in season.

Noticing that my companion was watching with evident interest, and with some sense of my own courage, I said: 'I think it would be fun to do that.'

She replied: 'Well, it's your cow.'

Gilles Hénault

THE PRODIGAL SON

The child who used to play see him now thin and bowed
The child who used to weep see now his burned-out eyes
The child who danced a round see him running after a streetcar
The child who longed for the moon see him satisfied with a mouth-
    ful of bread
The wild and rebellious child, the child at the end of the town
In the remote streets
The child of adventures
On the ice of the river
The child perched on the fences
See him now in the narrow road of his daily routine
The child free and lightly clothed, see him now
Disguised as a bill-board, a sandwich-man
Dressed up in cardboard laws, a prisoner of petty taboos
Subdued and trussed, see him hunted in the name of justice
The child of lovely red blood and of good blood
See him now the ghost of a tragic opera

The prodigal son
The child prodigy, look at him now as a man
The man of 'time is money' and the man of bel canto
The man riveted to his work which is to rivet all day
The man of the Sunday afternoons in slippers
And the interminable bridge parties
The numberless man of the sports of the few men
And the man of the small bank account
To pay for the burial of a childhood that died
Toward its fifteenth year

                                        Translated by F. R. Scott

Marie-Claire Blais

FROM *A SEASON IN THE LIFE OF EMMANUEL*

II

Then, tottering with fever but still laughing, Jean-Le Maigre offered his head up to the torture. Like a conqueror, Grand-mère Antoinette drew the lamp toward her, then the bowl, and counted the lice as they fell under her cruel comb. His sisters (The Little A's, Helena, Maria), with wild, shy eyes and sulky lips, approached on tiptoe. They huddled against one another or hung back against the wall as they waited for their turn. They fiddled with the ends of their braids. It's too crowded, Grand-mère Antoinette said, I don't want to see all these children around me like this! No, oh heavens no!

And the moment she began to push Jean-Le Maigre away from her, his proud head was already raised, he had already escaped from his grandmother's hands with the agility of a fox, just as Number Seven, whom they no longer expected to see, whom they had thought buried beneath the snow or devoured by wolves, turning head over heels as he was hurled into the room by his gang of brothers, burst in with his orange hair, Grand-mère abandoned her task, broke through the line of little girls: *What has he been doing this time?* ah! I know all! The little monster, he reeks of alcohol!

His mother sometimes began to make a gesture, an imperceptible sign of weakness or agonized pity, when, escaping from the blows of his elder brothers, Number Seven threw himself on his knees in front of his father. 'No forgiveness this evening,' Grand-mère Antoinette said.

(Jean-Le Maigre and the little girls were giggling in the shadows away from the lamp.) 'No, it's all over, I won't let you forgive him again ...'

Number Seven pretended he found it funny too. (What he most feared was when his father unbuckled his belt and his grandmother cried out as each blow fell: 'There, there, on your behind, my boy!')

Afterwards he felt better. It was warmer now, and there was a delicious flame flickering up his throat. 'This time I was beaten till I bled,' Number Seven thought as he stood up again, but he also seemed to be saying to them all: 'Thank you very much, I had a marvellous time.' He put his hat and his worn-through mittens back on again. 'Get undressed,' Grand-mère Antoinette said. 'Next time I shall throw you back out again. Not today, there's a storm coming up. Tomorrow!'

The snow was melting on Number Seven's boots. It was running off his stiffened clothes and hair. Jean-Le Maigre, already long accustomed to his brother's caprices, wiped up the trickles of water behind him and brushed off the snow still clinging to his coat.

'I don't like seeing them together,' Grand-mère Antoinette said. 'No, I don't like seeing devils plotting together at all!'

'Ah,' Number Seven said, staggering with drunkenness against Jean-Le Maigre's shoulder, 'ah, you just don't know how warm it makes you! How good it makes you feel . . .'

'Take off your hat,' Jean-Le Maigre answered. 'You heard, take off your hat. Tell me, is it burning a bit?'

'It's all right for you. You're lucky, being so thin. Who's going to beat you like that, eh?'

'No one,' Jean-Le Maigre replied, lying as usual and thinking with pride of the burning weals across his body, of all the blows borne in silence, head high and heart light.

'At your age I always got to school first, you know! I really am ashamed for you,' said Jean-Le Maigre with a shrug of his shoulders.

'Liars, hoodlums,' Grand-mère Antoinette called out as she saw the pair of them staggering and laughing past her, their arms around each other's necks.

'Your father is right, Jean-Le Maigre, you're rotten to the core!'

And the old woman, picking a blonde braid at random, tugged one of the little girls over her knees, where the child bent, sobbing, not knowing why this rasping and violent hand, only too skilled at hunting lice, had fallen upon her timid head . . .

At that late evening hour, Jean-Le Maigre and Number Seven, careless of their grandmother's scolding cries, were in the cellar, singing and drinking as they smoked the butts that Number Seven collected after school, during his idle wanderings along the road.

'Drinking with me is one thing, but drinking without me is not allowed. Do you understand?'

Number Seven signalled his assent with a wink. His face was so white in the flickering candlelight that Jean-Le Maigre thought he must be sick.

'Give me that candle,' Jean-Le Maigre said severely.

Sitting on an enormous crate of potatoes, Number Seven was playing at making the holes in his socks bigger.

'I feel good, hic .... It's hot, but I feel good, hic! I could even write a poem now, just like that, without stopping .... Hic! Hic!'

'You've got the hiccups! For God's sake, do you want them to hear us in the loft?'

'Hic ... hic ... they'll go away soon, hic ... hic ...'

'At least I know how to drink, it doesn't make me sick.'

(But his hand shook slightly as it held the candle. 'How strange the moon is this evening in the sky!' Jean-Le Maigre sighed, gazing at the slender beams of light striking the brick floor. 'Heavens, I've never seen it look like this!')

'But there isn't a moon tonight,' Number Seven replied, turning incredulously toward Jean-Le Maigre, his little face ravaged with fatigue. 'Where can you see a moon, eh?'

'You drink too much,' Jean-Le Maigre said (pouring himself another glass, ignoring his brother's). 'At your age I was doing something useful, learning Latin, having brilliant conversations with Monsieur le Curé. But you ...'

Number Seven was dozing against his shoulder ... 'Hic ... hic...' he murmured, like a baby complaining in its sleep, nestling his face beneath Jean-Le Maigre's pointed chin. 'Hic ... I feel really good!'

Abandoning his brother to his drunken sleep, Jean-Le Maigre opened his book, its pages yellowed by the damp. The book was full of fabulous meals, and as the scent of new bread suddenly wafted out from its pages, Jean-Le Maigre felt a slight pang in his empty stomach. 'The girl,' Jean-Le Maigre read silently, 'the girl brought in the fresh bread and the steaming soup, the girl . . .'

Jean-Le Maigre was hungry, there was no further doubt.

'I'm going to look for something to eat in the kitchen,' he said, shaking his sleeping brother by the arm. 'I'm not afraid of my father, not me. I never ask his pardon. I slip under the table, between their legs, and zip . . . I steal a piece of meat, a slice of bread. And that's it. Then we can eat it together in peace.'

'If I were you,' Number Seven said, 'I'd ask his pardon. Yes, before I stole the meat.'

But Jean-Le Maigre was no longer there.

There was not much to eat, but the father and the elder sons had brutish appetites that filled Grand-mère Antoinette with indignation as she sat there at the end of the table, looking down from a chair that was too high for her. Perched there like a crow, she gave a little curt 'Ah' of disapproval every time some froth-coated sliver of food fell from her son-in-law's greedy lips. The men and the boys sat as if in a trance around the table, protecting their plates like so many hoards of treasure, and they ate without raising their eyes. Taking advantage of their miserly silence, Jean-Le Maigre slid under the table on all fours, and sitting there surrounded by the heavy, apparently lifeless legs sloping toward him, he imagined himself lost in the middle of a field of bitter feet, watching the strange movements of those naked extremities beneath the table. Between his father's legs, as though through the dark balusters of a staircase, he could see his mother coming and going in the kitchen with plates of food. She always looked exhausted and dead-eyed. Her face was the colour of the earth. He watched her preparing the thick, greasy food that the men devoured, with customary greed, as fast as she could bring it in. He felt sorry for her. He felt sorry too for those heavy children she carried absent-mindedly around with her every year, dark burdens against her heart. But sometimes he forgot his mother's presence completely and thought only of the companion imprisoned in the cellar, with whom he would later share his evening meal. Grand-mère Antoinette was an accomplice in these thoughts. Salt, cheese, small pieces of food snatched up here and there with a fearless hand, all vanished beneath the table. But meat, no ! 'If you think,' she said to herself, 'if you think I'm going to give you meat for Number Seven – no, I'll never consent to that !'

Jean-Le Maigre tickled his grandmother's ankle under the table. 'Oh, if he could only live till spring,' Grand-mère Antoinette thought. 'December, January, February, if he could only live till March, oh Lord, if he could only live till summer comes. . . . Funerals are such a nuisance for everyone !' But this computation of the months that were still separating her from Jean-Le Maigre's tragic death did not prevent her grandson from behaving as usual like a little devil ! Though he was making painful efforts not to betray his presence : fighting down the sharp cough rising in his throat. He was afraid of awakening his father's slumbering wrath. His grand-mother was meanwhile imagining the good meal that would follow his funeral. (A consoling image of death, for Monsieur le Curé was so generous toward families in mourning; she could see him already, eating and drinking on her right; and on her left, as though in heaven already, Jean-Le Maigre, clean, his hair neatly combed, and dressed in clothes as white as snow.) There had been so many funerals during the years that Grand-mère Antoinette had reigned in her house, so many little black corpses, in the wintertime, chil-dren always disappearing, babies who had lived only a few months, adolescents who had vanished mysteriously in the fall, or in the spring. Grand-mère Antoinette allowed herself to be rocked gently in the swell of all those deaths, suddenly submerged in a great and singular feeling of content.

'Grandma,' Jean-Le Maigre begged under the table, 'just one piece, just a crumb . . .'

Grand-mère raised the corner of the tablecloth and saw a great, black eye shining in the darkness. So you're there, are you, she thought, disappointed at finding him still alive as usual, with one hand stretched out toward her, like a dog's paw. But when all was said and done, she'd rather have him like this; yes, it was better than the splendour of a scrubbed and sparkling angel sitting up to that macabre banquet – it was better, this vision of an ordinary Jean-Le Maigre in his rags beneath the table, raising a wild and timid forehead as he begged from her.

How well I've eaten, said Jean-Le Maigre, astonished to be lying once again, and above all to be lying with such joy! Suddenly he saw only one remedy for all these lies that flowed from his lips in such an inexhaustible flood: confession, a real confession on his knees in front of the stinking confessional (but Jean-Le Maigre was not aware of unpleasant smells, thanks to his blocked-up nose, and only sensed the rare perfumes that sometimes came within his ken), and so he saw himself, murmuring his sins into the indiscreet ear of a priest, taking pleasure in his self-betrayal, stirring up his basest secrets in a fantasy of delight!

'Well,' Number Seven asked, lying in pale collapse among the brown potatoes, 'can you still see the moon?'

'I was just thinking that you've drunk too much,' Jean-Le Maigre answered. 'You ought to make your confession, yes, right away, without thinking about it.... A real confession, a general confession! In other words, you must tell me about all the wicked things you've ever done, and there are lots of them, as I know only too well! You must tell me everything, and then I'll give you absolution. Afterwards you can start all over again, if you want.'

After this speech, Jean-Le Maigre, bending his head and imitating the Curé's voice, said solemnly: 'Speak my child, I am listening.'

'Evening prayers!' Grand-mère Antoinette cried. 'Everyone into the living-room!'

But as soon as they left the meal table the elder brothers had vanished behind the smoke from their pipes, followed by their father, who was yawning with fatigue, the fly of his trousers flapping in front of him. (Grand-mère Antoinette would pull them, one by one, from behind the shelter of their beards and their newspapers; and they would kneel down with her on the cold floor.)

If they weren't in the cellar, Jean Le-Maigre and Number Seven would escape through the kitchen and out into the snowy night as soon as it was time for prayers. All tangled up in their bootlaces, coats hurriedly thrown over their shoulders, the little girls too ran eagerly out to the latrines. Jean-Le Maigre and Number Seven stood and made fun of them as they came back, coughing into their hair. The two boys smoked while they waited standing under the trees, or sometimes, when they couldn't push their way past the file of little girls tripping and shoving their way into the backhouse, they urinated into the snow, without interrupting their peaceful conversation. Once shut in the latrines, they sat and read the whole of the Curé's library, or wrote verses of slender inspiration, such as Jean-Le Maigre's poem that began and ended with the lines:

How funereal the snow
Beneath the black flight of the birds ...

Whereas Number Seven, alas, could often find nothing in his head but lines like 'My heart is full of garbage' and 'I'm cold, I'm losing my teeth and my hair ...'

At eight o'clock, Grand-mère Antoinette came out to retrieve with imperious hand any deserter, girl or boy, still dreaming on the wooden seat, outside in the night-filled cabin.

Jean-Le Maigre stood up. 'That's enough,' he said. 'I don't want to hear any more. As heaven is my witness: I don't wish to hear any more!'

'I only did it once,' Number Seven said, by way of excuse.

'And now he is lying too! He has dared to lie!'

Then he leaned toward Number Seven and in a low voice asked: 'But what was it like, exactly?'

Number Seven lowered his eyes. 'The candle's almost out,' he said gloomily.

'I see,' Jean-Le Maigre said. 'In other words, you feel no remorse.'

'I do feel remorse,' Number Seven answered in a timid voice, 'but it was very nice at the time.'

'Ah! That's it, that's what vice is like,' Jean-Le Maigre exclaimed, 'I understand. But tell me everything. I have to know. First of all, there you were, outside, in the snow. Is that it?'

'Heavens, no. You've got the wrong story,' Number Seven replied. 'It was in May, and it was hot, in the schoolyard. There were flowers, and raspberries too.'

'There aren't any raspberries in May,' Jean-Le Maigre said sententiously.

'It must have been later on then,' said Number Seven, who, despite his few years, had already wandered idly through more than one summer and winter (seasons that Jean-Le Maigre liked to keep separate in his recollections – remembering how it had been a burning summer along the road, still retaining a deep memory of his hunger and his fatigue – or a harsh winter, spent running through the woods. Jean-Le Maigre loved to recall all these vanished moments endlessly . . .).

'For heaven's sake, tell ! Tell what it was like !'

Number Seven told about the little hunchback girl they had undressed together, in the schoolyard, one day in spring.

'It's your sin, not mine !' Jean-Le Maigre protested. (All the same, there were raspberries, Number Seven insisted, and the bees were buzzing . . .)

'What a nice little hunchback she was !' Jean-Le Maigre sighed. 'Next day she gave me some pancakes. Another day she brought me some paper and pencils. I wrote some poems.' (He did not add that his grandmother threw them into the fire that same night, exclaiming that they were scandalous, that Jean-Le Maigre would go to hell, so shocked by the title, 'To the Warm Beloved', that she had been afraid to read any further.)

'She was nice,' Jean-Le Maigre said, 'she always went to Mass. She had a beautiful missal with gilt edges.'

'And now ?' Number Seven asked.

'Ah, now ! Now she's a young miss, a lady, she lives in town, she still makes pancakes. But she's aged a great deal,' Jean-Le Maigre said in a tone of respect. 'I suppose all the little hunchback girls age quickly. And they're the ones I like best.'

He stopped speaking to spit on the floor before Number Seven's admiring gaze.

Translated by Derek Coltman

Margaret Atwood

THE LANDLADY

This is the lair of the landlady.

She is
a raw voice
loose in the rooms beneath me,

the continuous henyard
squabble going on below
thought in this house like
the bicker of blood through the head.

She is everywhere, intrusive as the smells
that bulge in under my doorsill;
she presides over my
meagre eating, generates
the light for eyestrain.

From her I rent my time:
she slams
my days like doors.
Nothing is mine

and when I dream images
of daring escapes through the snow
I find myself walking
always over a vast face
which is the land-
lady's, and wake up shouting.

She is a bulk, a knot
swollen in space. Though I have tried
to find some way around
her, my senses

are cluttered by perception
and can't see through her.

She stands there, a raucous fact
blocking my way :
immutable, a slab
of what is real,

solid as bacon.

JOURNEY TO THE INTERIOR

There are similarities
I notice : that the hills
which the eyes make flat as a wall, welded
together, open as I move
to let me through; become
endless as prairies; that the trees
grow spindly, have their roots
often in swamps; that this is a poor country;
that a cliff is not known
as rough except by hand, and is
therefore inaccessible. Mostly
that travel is not the easy going
from point to point, a dotted
line on a map, location
plotted on a square surface
but that I move surrounded by a tangle
of branches, a net of air and alternate
light and dark, at all times;
that there are no destinations
apart from this.

There are differences
of course : the lack of reliable charts;
more important, the distraction of small details :

your shoe among the brambles under the chair
where it shouldn't be; lucent
white mushrooms and a paring knife
on the kitchen table; a sentence
crossing my path, sodden as a fallen log
I'm sure I passed yesterday

>   (have I been
walking in circles again?)

but mostly the danger :
many have been here, but only
some have returned safely.

A compass is useless; also
trying to take directions
from the movements of the sun,
which are erratic;
and words here are as pointless
as calling in a vacant
wilderness.

>   Whatever I do I must
keep my head. I know
it is easier for me to lose my way
forever here, than in other landscapes.

Franklin Russell

THE DEVIL'S DRIVEWAY

From *The Secret Islands*

The summer light of Newfoundland is gentle but piercing. It implies the arctic and indicates how the island is caught midway between two extremes: pole and equator. This was the centrepiece of my travelling. From Newfoundland I would jump outward to smaller islands. On it, I would meet my first islanders, men whose lives had been directed by their separation from the mainland.

I landed on Newfoundland in July, and snow clung to distant lines of low hills. The road stretched before me through bulges of bare, grey-green doughnut hills. The rocks and black heathlands on either side of me seemed only recently freed of ice. I did not know it, but I was on the Devil's Driveway, the island's main road, a Frankenstein creation that interposed itself between me and my goal.

The road turns in a half-moon across the heart of Newfoundland, beginning at Port aux Basques, where I had landed from a car ferry, and ending on the south-east coast at the island's capital, St John's. It is a pity, in my mind, that in the mid nineteen-sixties the road was tamed, paved, straightened and fitted with picnic tables. When I first drove it, nothing encouraged the traveller to press on to his destination. The driveway discouraged tourists, but it also gave Newfoundland a flavour of its own. The highway said damnation to foreigners: come to this island at your own risk; you are not welcome. I saw a car with front *and* back windows punctured by a single stone. I met a woman driver whose foot was bleeding because a stone had penetrated the steel floor of her car, the carpet, *and* her thick leather sole.

The Devil's Driveway was merciless to all automobiles. Foreign cars, vaunted for durability, fell apart even more quickly than domestic U.S. cars. The most vulnerable machines turned out to be ostensibly rugged cross-country vehicles with hard suspensions. If the automobile survived the potholes, corrugations, washouts, and areas under construction, it still faced the pungent possibilities of collision with wandering moose, caribou, sheep, goats, cows, and horses.

But on this bright July morning, as I swung through sleek hills and headed inland, the highway was black and smooth as glass. It was built to what is known locally as 'trans-Canada specification', those of the extremely fast, two-lane road that now crosses the continent from coast to coast. I rushed past still ponds which transmitted flying pictures of snow, and my speed climbed to seventy. The end of the idyll was sudden.

I rounded a curve, and the blacktop ended abruptly. White gravel began. At first, the new surface was a dull throb of sound from jittering wheels, but gradually the road became Dantesque. A curtain of dust particles moved sluggishly between me and the windshield. A car ahead of me threw up an explosion of dust into which I drove grimly, seeing its tail-lights, six red eyes, gleaming from time to time. Quadrilights glared suddenly as trucks roared past, ten feet high with gravel; metal clanged as stones struck the car.

Each second, I expected the dust to end. But an hour passed; I had a near escape when a stalled dump truck squatted in the middle of the road and I skidded away from it. I seemed to have lost all contact with the normal world. The dust would have to end immediately. I insisted on it. Another hour passed, and my nerve ends became pinpoints of agony as I glared into the stuff boiling away behind a car ahead.

Later, I was to hear stories about the effect of the Driveway. It induced a stupor which sapped the driver's will. In the end, many motorists pulled to the side of the road, where they sat stunned and disbelieving. Hardier fellows got out of their smoking cars and walked through forest and marsh to regain their composure. If he was tough enough to keep driving, the driver felt the need to scream himself weak, give up, let the wheel go, and slump back in the seat.

The hammering road prepared me for any new horror, although scarcely for anything so prosaic as a hitchhiker. He stood beside the road, so well buried in dust that I almost ran him down. He looked just like any other hitchhiker, which was surprising. Somehow, I expected a special kind of hitchhiker, space-suited, perhaps, oxygen tanks on his back.

I would not have stopped, true to the tradition of my suspicious city world where any man without an automobile is a thief and a vagrant, but Newfoundland was, after all, an island, and its people were islanders. I stopped.

The man was tall and thin; his body stooped slightly in the effort to hold himself erect. His pale face looked tubercular and ill (a common sight in Newfoundland), and he slid into the seat with a smile. 'Thank you, sir.'

Was he going far?

'Just a little way up the drive, thank you.'

We pushed on through the dust which covered the instrument panel, seats, floor, and even the inside of the windshield. I started the ventilating fan and cyclones of dust billowed in the car. Covertly, I watched the man. His tapered fingers, cut and ripped by manual work, were flexing slowly in his lap. We ploughed through five miles of deep sand that would have stalled us had I stopped. Mercifully, the gravel road ended. The man was silent as we hummed over three miles of blacktop. The radio, released from competition with road noises, asserted itself and played hillbilly music, interspersed with personal messages from Newfoundlanders who lived beyond the reach of telephone.

Bill will be back Monday. Please feed the pigeons. Aunt Mabel sends her love.

The blacktop ended and the road plunged into a stretch of craters, some of them so big that the bottom of the car struck rock as we pitched into them. It was a hard road, the hitchhiker observed unexpectedly. Yes, it was. I noticed that his left forearm was bent and the fingers of the hand misshapen. Had he been wounded in the war? Puzzled, he looked at me and then understood. Oh no, nothing like that. He had broken his arm when he was a youngster.

For the next five minutes, conversation was impossible as I drove over teeth-shaking corrugations. The hitchhiker ignored the uproar until the car slewed into sand again. So I didn't know very much about Newfoundland, eh? Well, not much. Hmm. Things were different from where I came from. Yes, clearly. But he wanted to explain the scope of the difference, not have me assume it.

He had broken his arm when he was a kid living in an outport, one of a number of isolated fishing villages which dot the island's coast. There was no doctor within two hundred miles, and the arm set itself, crooked, of course. When he had reached a doctor, the arm was broken again and reset. But the doctor was incompetent and set it crooked, worse than the original set of the fracture.

Martha taken to hospital. Due for exploratory tests Monday. Keep your fingers crossed. How are Albert and Joe? Much love.

The hillbilly music resumed. Yes, it had happened in an outport. His father had been a fisherman, a dory fisherman. He used to row out of the village every morning at three o'clock and stayed offshore fishing until nearly dusk. He had been drowned in the big wind of 1926.

Dad died Friday. Mum taken to hospital with heart attack. Please come soon.

We drove through a construction site, pale with yellow dust and noisy with trucks, cranes, and shovels. Through a rift in the dust I caught a glimpse of a barren landscape, rolling, tundra-like country, a river, blue hills set against black clouds. It was blotted out as the car tipped into a river bed and bounded over water-washed rocks.

The hitchhiker's uncle had left the outport and had become the skipper of a banker, a fishing schooner that worked on the Grand Banks, the great fishing territories south-east of Newfoundland. He had returned to the outport when the hitchhiker's mother died and had taken the seventeen-year-old boy away with him. He felt the boy should have some schooling; it was ridiculous for such a bright youngster to be unable to read. But no school would take him. The banker captain had taught the boy to pick out words and to add. Since that time, he had read hundreds of books, but 'I don't write so well.'

We climbed a curved and dusty incline which led into mountains, the caps of which were obscured in mist. Suddenly, it was dark, although it was still morning. The lights of other cars moved in the misted hills. The hitchhiker saw nothing, intent on examining his memory.

His uncle had died in 1937, leaving the eighteen-year-old boy to take care of himself. It was depression time. The youngster walked, sometimes on roads, sometimes across the barrens. He caught a rabbit and slept where some caribou had camped. He came to a coastal village and a storekeeper gave him fifty cents worth of food on credit. If the youngster could catch a couple of barrels of Christmas fish, he wouldn't owe the storekeeper a thing. Christmas fish? What were they?

He learned they were small fish that could be caught through the ice. He stole a net, borrowed an axe, and went fishing. He got the two barrels, all right, and lived on fish and slept in an old shed. In fact, he caught a dozen barrels of fish, and with the credit, bought shotgun shells. The storekeeper lent him an old gun and he hunted ducks all winter. He sold them to the storekeeper for ten cents each. He enjoyed that winter, he did, and was sorry when the ducks disappeared to breed in the north.

John due at Joe Batt's Arm Tuesday. Please arrange to meet the boat.

He got through the summer. But in the fall he took sick. It was the T.B. Everybody had it then. Something to do with a lack of green vegetables, people said. He spent the next two years in and out of hospitals, and then got into the war. The army doctors never found out about his T.B. But the English officers were a problem. Perhaps he was biased against them. It was difficult, though, to talk about the British. The British had always run Newfoundland. It was their first colony and they regarded it as their own. They took the codfish out of the sea and carried them home. But they put nothing back into Newfoundland, and this left the island in poverty, at the fringe of the greatest fish bounty on earth. Yet, somehow, they made Newfoundland glad to be British.

The darkness lightened suddenly and it began to rain, torrential, tropical-style rain. In seconds it filled the craters in the road. Cascades of water rose from under the wheels of passing cars. The car crawled with mud. Water hit like a wet towel whacking a concrete floor. The wipers could barely deal with the muck and the grille under the windshield clogged with what looked like the spoilings of a sluice dredge.

The hitchhiker's father had run his life on credit, perforce, because he rarely saw money in cash form. He ran up a bill at the village store for his fishing provisions, and it was a funny thing, you know, that it did not matter how many fish he caught, he could never pay off the bill. He never really knew how much he got paid for his fish. He trusted the storekeeper, who was a man of education, a man who could *read* and *write*!

Bill and Mary arriving from Boston on the car ferry Thursday. Expect to see you all at the reunion.

When the store bill got out of hand, the storekeeper asked his father to build him a dory, or maybe two dories, if it was a big bill. Dory-building was hard work in a land where the forests had been exploited for lumber and firewood for hundreds of years. Forests grew slowly on the islands. His father spent his winters building dories, and counting the time he spent travelling to the nearest woodland and bringing out his lumber, he worked for a little more than five cents an hour. The store was owned by a merchant in St John's, and *he* sold the dories, presumably for a nice profit.

The hitchhiker's uncle had lived according to the same rules, though by island standards he was a successful man. He worked for merchants who owned the schooner he skippered. In those days, the fishing business was always in hard times, at least, so his uncle claimed. Markets were bad. He was lucky to be a skipper for those people. They would always take care of him, they would. And they did. After fifty years at sea, he was pensioned at seventy-five dollars a month. In his best year at sea, he made twelve hundred dollars and his men made two hundred and fifteen each. That was for more than four months at sea. It had to last them for the year, though, because there was no other work. The owners travelled a lot, in Europe mostly, and the uncle sometimes got letters from them with pretty stamps on the envelopes. Their children went to school in England. Of course, you had to understand that everything in England was much better than here. Newfoundlanders were a poor people and they had to be thankful that England had always tried to take care of them.

Ahead, the road turned black, smooth, straight. With relief, I drove the car on to blacktop again. But to my astonishment, I found the surface had emulsified to a depth of half an inch. I was driving over molasses spread between the shoulders of the Driveway. It was so thick that it lifted from the wheels reluctantly, like a wet wool blanket pushed by wind. I slowed, thinking I would wait until the rain stopped; but a truck passed me and buried the car under a solid wave of the muck. The windows were blacked out. The wipers crawled across the windshield, half cleared it, but another car passed and I was blacked out again.

I passed two cars whose drivers had decided to stop. The cars were rounded, shiny-black cocoons. Higher speed helped, I found. The harder the black stuff was struck, the more it tended to disintegrate. But at higher speed, even a second's loss of visibility was dangerous. I changed my driving technique. I approached a black wave fast, smashed into it, wound down the window, and drove with my head out the window until the wipers cleared the windshield. I risked meeting another car, of course, in the window-down phase, with consequences too horrible to think about.

At last, the melted blacktop ended and the car slewed into deep sand. The sand and the liquid asphalt created a magnetic union. Within a mile, the car was caked in sandpaper.

Dave leaves for Toronto in a few days. Can we all get together?
How had the hitchhiker managed since the war?

Well, it had been a bit of this, and a bit of that. A man could sometimes get work in a fish plant or in the lumber camps. For the last three months, he had been helping build the Driveway, working for a mainland contractor.

What doing?

He was driving a bulldozer, and there was a bit of a story to *that*. The road builders were desperate for skilled men because few mainlanders wanted to work on the island. So he had hidden in the bushes and watched the men at work. After a few days, he had memorized the things the bulldozer drivers did, the levers they pulled, and so forth. He had applied for a job, and the foreman had said, 'All right, let's see you drive this one,' and, no doubt about it, he had been some scared then. But he had got up and yanked those levers and away he went with a rush. He had been getting good money ever since. Now, if I would slow down a bit here, he would get out.

We were on a lonely stretch of road, with only a rough, tar-paper shack visible against a hill.

Here?

'Yes,' he said. 'I'm going fishing for a few days, and that's my shack. Much obliged for the lift, and good-bye, sir.' He nodded.

In that last word was almost all I ever needed to know about these island people. He walked through some alders and disappeared.

The schooner is bringing Dad down from the Labrador this week. We are making all the arrangements at this end. He will be laid to rest on Friday.

Today, the Devil's Driveway has gone. The dust, the potholes, the insane stretches of mud and sand, the washouts and the liquid asphalt have disappeared. You drive through a blur of beech and spruce on a road almost indecently civilized in such primeval territory. You may stop, get out, and listen. The silence is perfect at first; then you hear the faint music of songbirds. A flock of redpolls twinkles overhead and a hidden stream mutters among a glistening line of aspens. Hills sweep down to earth. A solitary raven circles.

I remember the old Driveway. To me it was a symbol of the island's four hundred years of history, a history that Newfoundlanders had accepted as being the way of the world.

At the height of its dishevelled life, it personified an island people entering the twentieth century. They were late, exploited, poor, but they very definitely were arriving. Determined to escape from the old days of their isolation, they wanted to be like the rest of us. In the same way as the running eiders, they had to abandon the island, or at least, the traditional idea of it. They had to find out what the world was all about.

Margaret Laurence*

FROM A JEST OF GOD

I've been teaching in Manawaka for fourteen years.

A faint giggle. I've been walking with my eyes fixed downwards. Who is it?

'Hello, Miss Cameron.'

'Oh – hello, Clare. Hello, Carol.'

I taught them in Grade Two. Now they're about sixteen, I guess. Their hair is incredible. Piled high, finespun, like the high light conical mass of woven sugar threads, the candy floss we used to get at fairs. Theirs is nearly white and is called Silver Blonde. I know that much. It's not mysterious. It's held up by back-combing, and the colour sprayed on, and the whole thing secured with lacquer like a coating of ice over a snowdrift. They look like twins from outer space. No, not twins necessarily. Another race. Venusians. But that's wrong, too. This is their planet. They are the ones who live here now.

I've known them nearly all their lives. But it doesn't seem so. Does thirty-four seem antediluvian to them? Why did they laugh? There isn't anything to be frightened of, in that laughter. Why should they have meant anything snide by it?

I have my hair done every week at Riché Beauty Salon. It used to be Lou's Beauty Parlour when I got my hair done first, at six-teen. They'd find that amusing, probably. I say to the girl, 'As little curl as possible, if you can.' So it turns out looking exactly as it's always done, nondescript waves, mole brown. What if I said some week, 'Do it like candy floss, a high cone of it, and gold'? Then they would really laugh. With my height. How silly I am to think of it. But what beats me is how the Venusians learn to do all these things for themselves. They don't have their hair done. Who

*Wrongly printed as 'Margaret Lawrence' on the back cover of this volume – Ed.

teaches them? I suppose they're young enough to ask around. At that age it's no shame not to know.

Japonica Street. Around our place the spruce trees still stand, as I remember them for ever. No other trees are so darkly sheltering, shutting out prying eyes or the sun in summer, the spearheads of them taller than houses, the low branches heavy, reaching down to the ground like the greenblack feathered strong-boned wings of giant and extinct birds. The house is not large – it often surprises me to realize this. The same way it will surprise my children to return when they're grown and look around the classroom and see how small the desks are. The house used to seem enormous, and I think of it that way yet. Rust brick, nothing to set it off or mark it as different from the other brick houses near by. Nothing except the sign, and the fact that the ground floor doesn't belong to us.

When I was a child the sign was painted on board, pale-grey background, black lettering, and it said CAMERON'S FUNERAL PARLOUR. Later, my father, laughing in some way incomprehensible to me then and being chided for it by Mother, announced other times other manners. The new sign was ebony background and gilt lettering, CAMERON FUNERAL HOME. After he died, and we sold the establishment, the phraseology moved on. The blue neon, kept lighted day and night, now flashes JAPONICA FUNERAL CHAPEL. All that remains is for someone to delete the word FUNERAL. A nasty word, smacking of mortality. No one in Manawaka ever dies, at least not on this side of the tracks. We are a gathering of immortals. We pass on, through Calla's divine gates of topaz and azure, perhaps, but we do not die. Death is rude, unmannerly, not to be spoken to in the street.

It was in those rooms on the ground floor there, where I was told never to go, that my father lived away his life. All I could think of, then, was the embarrassment of being the daughter of someone with his stock-in-trade. It never occurred to me to wonder about him, and whether he possibly felt at ease with them, the unspeaking ones, and out of place above in our house, things being what they were. I never had a chance to ask him. By the time I knew the question it was too late, and asking it would have cut into him too much.

We were fortunate to be able to stay on here, Mother and I. We sold the place outright, but for much less than it was worth, for the right to stay. Hector Jonas got a bargain. He already had a house. He didn't want the top floor of this one. At least we live rent free in perpetuity, or near enough to suit our purposes. I sometimes wonder what I'll do when Mother dies. Will I stay, or what?

'Hello, dear. Aren't you rather late tonight?'

'Hello, Mother. Not especially. I had some clearing up to do.'

'Well, I've got a nice lamb chop, so I hope you'll eat it. You're not eating enough these days, Rachel.'

'I'm fine.'

'You *say* you're fine, but don't forget I know you pretty well, dear.'

'Yes, I know.'

'You're too conscientious, Rachel, that's your trouble. Other people don't allow their work to get on their nerves.'

'It's not. I'm fine. A little tired tonight, perhaps, but that's normal.'

'You fret about them too much, whether they're doing well or not. But mercy, you didn't bestow their brains on them, did you? It's not up to you. Small thanks you'll get for it, if you ask me anything.'

She stands beside the stove. Her heart is very tricky and could vanquish her at any moment. Yet her ankles are still slender and she takes pride in wearing only fine-denier nylons and never sensible shoes. Her hair is done every week, saucily stiff grey sausage curls, and the frames of her glasses are delphinium blue and elfin. Where does this cuteness come from, when she's the one who must plump up the chesterfield cushions each night before retiring and empty every ashtray and make the house look as though no frail and mortal creature ever set foot in it?

'What are you having tonight?'

'Asparagus rolls, I thought,' she says earnestly, 'and that celery and ham mixture. I've got it made. All you have to do is spread them. Can you do the asparagus rolls or shall I do those first?'

'I can do them. It's all right.'

'Well, we could do them and put them in the fridge. It might be easier.'

'If you like. We'll do them after dinner, then.'

'I don't mind, dear – whatever you like,' she says, believing she means it.

How strange it is that I do not even know how old she is. She's never told me, and I'm not supposed to ask. In the world she inhabits, age is still as unmentionable as death. Am I as far away as that, from the children who aren't mine? She's in her seventies, I can guess with reasonable accuracy, as she bore me late, but the exact positioning is her wealth, a kept secret. And it matters. It means something. Does she think someone cares whether she's sixty or ninety?

I could have gone to Willard's for dinner. I could have gone with Calla. I wish I had. Now that it comes to it, I do not know why I didn't, one or the other.

It's her only outlet, her only entertainment. I can't begrudge her. Anyone decent would be only too glad.

As I am, really, at heart. I'll feel better, more fortified, when I've had dinner. I don't begrudge it to her, this one evening of bridge with the only three long long friends. How could I? No one decent would.

Thank God, thank God. They are finally gone. The last cup is washed and put away. The living-room is tidied enough to suit her. It might be the midsummer gathering of a coven, the amount of fuss we go to, lace tablecloth, the Spode china, the silver tray for sandwiches, the little dishes of salted nuts to nibble at. Well, it's only at our place once a month. I can't complain, really. And it *is* nice for her. She enjoys it. Her face grows animated and her voice almost gay – 'Verla, you're not going into no-trump – you wouldn't dare! Oh girls isn't she the meanest thing you ever saw?' She doesn't have much to interest her these days. She never reads a book and can't bear music. Her life is very restricted now. It always was though. It's never been any different. Just this house and her dwindling circle of friends. She and Dad had given up conversing long ago, by the time I was born. She used to tell him not to lean back in the upholstered chairs, in case his hair oil rubbed off. Then she put those crocheted doilies on all the chair backs. And finally on the chair arms as well, as though she felt his hands could never be clean, considering what he handled in his work. Maybe she didn't feel that way at all. Maybe it only seemed so to me.

This bedroom is the same I've always had. I should change the furniture. How girlish it is, how old-fashioned. The white spindly-legged dressing-table, the round mirror with white rose-carved frame, the white-painted metal bed with its white-painted metal bow decorating the head like a starched forgotten hair-ribbon. Surely I could afford new furniture. It's my salary, after all, my salary we live on. She'd say it was a waste, to throw out perfectly good furniture. I suppose it would be, too, if you think of it like that.

I always brush my hair a hundred strokes. I can't succeed in avoiding my eyes in the mirror. The narrow angular face stares at me, the grey eyes too wide for it.

I don't look old. I don't look more than thirty. Or do I see my face falsely? How do I know how it looks to anyone else? About six months ago, one of the salesmen who was calling on Hector Jonas, downstairs, asked me out and like an idiot I went. We went to the Regal Café for dinner, and I thought every minute someone I knew would see me and know he sold embalming fluid. Of course someone has to sell it. But when he told me I had good bones, it was too much. As though he were one of the ancient Egyptians who interred the pharaohs and knew too intimately the secrets of the core and marrow. Do I have good bones? I can't tell. I'm no judge.

Go to bed, Rachel. And hope to sleep.

The voices of the girls, the old ladies, still echo, the prattling, the tiny stabs of laughter making them clutch their bosoms for fear of their hearts. They feel duty bound to address a few remarks to me, remarks which have fallen into a comfortable stability. 'How's school, Rachel?' Fine, thank you. 'I guess they must keep you pretty busy, all those youngsters.' Yes, they certainly do. 'Well, I think it's marvellous, the way you manage – I always think that anyone who's a teacher is marvellous to take on a job like that.' Oh, I enjoy it. 'Well, that's marvellous – don't you think so, May?' And Mother nods and says yes it certainly is marvellous and Rachel is a born teacher.

My God. How can I stand –

Stop. Stop it, Rachel. Steady. Get a grip on yourself, now. Relax. Sleep. Try.

Doctor Raven would give a few sleeping pills to me. Why on earth don't I? They frighten me. What if one became addicted? Does it run in the family? Nonsense, not drugs. It wasn't drugs with him. 'Your father's not feeling well today.' Her martyred voice. That sort of thing is not physical, for heaven's sake, not passed on. Yet I can see myself at school, years from now, never fully awake, in a constant dozing and drowsing, sitting at my desk, my head bobbing slowly up and down, my mouth gradually falling open without my knowing it, and people seeing and whispering until finally –

Oh no. Am I doing it again, this waking nightmare? How weird am I already? Trying to stave off something that has already grown inside me and spread its roots through my blood?

Now, then. Enough of this. The main thing is to be sensible, to stop thinking and to go to sleep. Right away. Concentrate. I need the sleep badly. It's essential.

I can't. Tonight is hell on wheels again. Trite. *Hell on wheels.* But almost accurate. The night feels like a gigantic ferris wheel turning in blackness, very slowly, turning once for each hour, interminably slow. And I am glued to it, or wired, like paper, like a photograph, insubstantial, unable to anchor myself, unable to stop this slow nocturnal circling.

This pain inside my skull – what is it? It isn't like an ordinary headache which goes through like a metal skewer from temple to temple. Not like sinus, either, the assault beginning above my eyes and moving down into the bones of my face. This pain is not so much pain as a pulsing, regular and rhythmical, like the low thudding of a drum.

It's nothing. How could it be a tumour? It's nothing. Perhaps I have a soft spot in my head. This joke doesn't work. I can't hold on to the slang sense of it, and its other meaning seems sinister. Fontanelle.

Something meaningless, something neutral – I must focus on that. But what? Now I can't think. I can't stop thinking. If the pain is anything, then I'll see Doctor Raven, of course. Naturally. It wouldn't hurt to go in for a check-up soon anyway. It might be a very good idea. I can't afford to let myself get run down.

I can't sleep.

– A forest. Tonight it is a forest. Sometimes it is a beach. It has to be right away from everywhere. Otherwise she may be seen. The trees are green walls, high and shielding, boughs of pine and tamarack, branches sweeping to earth, forming a thousand rooms among the fallen leaves. She is in the green-walled room, the boughs opening just enough to let the sun in, the moss hairy and soft on the earth. She cannot see his face clearly. His features are blurred as though his were a face seen through water. She sees only his body distinctly, his shoulders and arms deeply tanned, his belly flat and hard. He is wearing only tight-fitting jeans, and his swelling sex shows. She touches him there, and he trembles, absorbing her fingers' pressure. Then they are lying along one another, their skins slippery. His hands, his mouth are on the wet warm skin of her inner thighs. Now –

I didn't. I didn't. It was only to be able to sleep. The shadow prince. Am I unbalanced? Or only laughable? That's worse, much worse.

I feel myself sinking at last into the smooth silence where no lights or voices are. When the voices and lights begin again, in there where I am lying, they are not bright or loud.

– Stairs rising from nowhere, and the wallpaper the loose-petalled unknown flowers. The stairs descending to the place where I am not allowed. The giant bottles and jars stand there, bubbled green glass. The silent people are there, lipsticked and rouged, powdered whitely like clowns. How funny they look, each lying dressed in best, and their open eyes are glass eyes, cat's eye marbles, round glass beads, blue and milky, unwinking. He is behind the door I cannot open. And his voice – his voice – so I know he is lying there among them, lying in state, king over them. He can't fool me.

He says run away Rachel run away run away. I am running across thick grass and small purple violets – weeds – dandelions. The spruce trees bend, bend down, hemming in and protecting. My mother is singing in a falsetto voice, the stylish tremolo, the ladies' choir voice.

Bless this house dear Lord we pray, keep it safe by night and day.

Jean-Guy Pilon

THE STRANGER HEREABOUTS

He came from a country of devout pirates
Where indifference was taken for dogma
The idiot for master
The sick man for the seer

It was a country of useless struggles
And magnificent ruins
A country eaten out by vermin

When he wished to shout out his rage
They would not allow it

They hardly allowed him to die

Translated by F. R. Scott

John Herbert

Nathan Cohen, drama critic of the *Toronto Star*, writes: '*Fortune and Men's Eyes*, by John Herbert (the pen name of John Brundage), is set in a Canadian reformatory and deals with the rape of a young man and his conversion into an aggressive homosexual. Just as Mr Brundage makes no secret of the fact that he is John Herbert, he also makes it clear that the play is autobiographical. Although he is not Smitty, the adventures of Smitty are based to a large extent on his experiences more than twenty years ago following his arrest and imprisonment on a morals charge. He claims that it was a frame-up. What no one disputes is that the conditions he describes are as applicable in Canadian prisons today as they were in 1948.

'Brundage is no Genet, and *Fortune and Men's Eyes* no first ripple in a tidal wave of stories by him depicting the fantasy world of the defiant outcast. In the decade that he has been writing plays Brundage has written on a variety of subjects. Indeed the two plays he now has scheduled for presentation clearly illustrate the diversity of his material. *Closer to Cleveland* shows the effect of bigotry at an exclusive country club. *Queen City Blues* deals with derelicts at an all-night café.

'What these plays have in common is that they are autobiographical. Until the success of *Fortune and Men's Eyes*, Brundage worked as a waiter and bartender in several private clubs. When he was an adolescent he used to buy his cup of coffee in one of those all-night restaurants and linger for hours. He draws directly on what he has seen and heard, and thinks he knows, for inspiration.

'Now true confession, old hat as it may be everywhere else, remains a daring novelty on the Canadian theatre scene. What really startled Canadian audiences was not the candour of the situation and the speech in *Fortune and Men's Eyes*. With all its bluntness, there is a naïveté about the language which makes transparent the honesty of Brundage's artistic intentions. Nor was it the controlled vigour of the staging and acting. What was really shocking was that the author obviously was writing from his own experience.

'When you look over the original plays staged by the half-dozen professional native theatres in Canada, from the Stratford Festival, which in fifteen years has made itself the most invulnerable sacred cow in North American cultural history, to the most recently organized Theatre Toronto, one thing which hits you is how seldom the author bases himself on his own involvements and observations, or how rarely he takes for his point of artistic departure the social tensions of life in his own backyard.'

FORTUNE AND MEN'S EYES

From ACT ONE, SCENE ONE

Mid-October, evening.
Overture: three songs – 'Alouette' (sung by Group of Boys' Voices);
'Down in the Valley' (One Male Voice); 'Jesus Loves Me' (sung by
Group of Boys' Voices).
A Canadian reformatory, prep school for the penitentiary. The inmates are usually young, but there are often older prisoners, as indicated by the dialogue in places. We are primarily concerned here with four who are young, though they tell us others exist. The overwhelming majority of prisoners in a reformatory are in the late teens and early twenties. Those who are older have been convicted of offences that do not carry a sentence large enough to warrant sending them to a penitentiary. The setting is a dormitory with four beds and two doorways. One door leads to the corridor, but we do not see it. There is a stone alcove, angled so that we get the impression of a short hall. We hear the guard's key open this unseen door whenever he or the four inmates enter or exit. The whole upstage wall is barred so that we look into the corridor where the guard and inmates pass in entrance and exit. Another doorway leads to the toilet and shower room.

ROCKY *is stretched on his bed like a prince at rest;* QUEENIE *sits on his own bed upstage;* MONA *leans against the wall of bars, upstage of* QUEENIE. *In the distance we hear the clang of metal doors, and a gruff voice issuing orders.* MONA *turns at the sounds, and looks along the hall.*

Just before lights come up, after curtain has opened, a BOY'S VOICE *is heard singing, at a distance – as farther along a corridor.*

BOY'S VOICE [*singing*] :
>Oh, if I had the wings of an angel
>Over these prison walls would I fly –

[*Sound of metal doors clanging open and shut. And sound of heavy boots marching along corridor.*]

VOICE [*English accent*] : Halt ! Attention ! Straighten that line ! Guard ! Take this one down and put him in Observation !

GUARD : Yes sir ! Smith ! Step out – and smartly !

[*Lights come up.*]

BOY'S VOICE [*singing*] :
>Oh, if I had the wings of –

QUEENIE [*on stage*] :
>Oh, if I had the wings of an angel,
>And the ass of a big buffalo,
>I would fly to the heavens above me,
>And crap on the people below.

VOICE [*English accent; raised now, the voice is not only gruff as before, but high and shrill in overtone, like Hitler's recorded speech*] : And you, Canary-Bird – shut that bloody row, or I shall cut off your seed supply.

[*Repeated sound of metal doors, and of boots marching away.*]

QUEENIE : Oh, oh ! That's Bad Bess. The Royal Sergeant don't come this close to the common folk, except when they're bringin' in a batch o' fish.

ROCKY : What's the action out there, Queenie?

MONA [*who stands nearest the bars*] : It's the new arrivals.

ROCKY : Anybody ask you to open your mouth, fruity?

QUEENIE : Oh, lay off the Mona Lisa, for Christ sake, Rocky.

ROCKY : Always getting her jollies looking out that hole.

QUEENIE : Does Macy's bother Gimbel's?

ROCKY : They got their own corners.

QUEENIE : Well she ain't in yours, so dummy up !

ROCKY : Don't mess with the bull, Queenie !

QUEENIE: Your horn ain't long enough to reach me, Ferdinand.

ROCKY: You might feel it yet.

QUEENIE: Worst offer I've had today, but it's early.

ROCKY: Screw off! [*Turning toward* MONA] Look at the queer watchin' the fish! See anything you can catch, Rosie?

QUEENIE: How's the new stock, Mona? Anything worth shakin' it for?

MONA: They're all so young.

QUEENIE: That'll suit Rocky. If he could coop a new chicken in his yard, he might not be so salty.

ROCKY: Where'd you get all that mouth . . . from your Mother?

QUEENIE: The better to gobble you up with, Little Red Riding Wolf!

ROCKY: Tell it to your old man.

QUEENIE: Which one? Remember me? I'm my own P. I.

ROCKY: You got a choice?

QUEENIE: I don't mean pimp, like you, I mean political influence, like me!

ROCKY: So you got a coupla wheels in the office! Big deal!

QUEENIE: I like it that way . . . makes it so I don't have to take no crap from a would-be hippy like you.

MONA: They're coming this way.

QUEENIE: Hell! And I didn't set my hair in toilet-paper curls last night. Oh well! I'll try to look seductive.

ROCKY: You better turn around then.

QUEENIE: Well, my backside looks better than your face, if that's what you wanta say.

ROCKY [*with disdain*]: Queers!

[*Enter* GUARD *with a youth who is about seventeen.*]

ROCKY: Hi, screw! What's that . . . your new baby?

GUARD: You planning a return trip to the tower, smart boy?

ROCKY: Just bein' friendly, Captain! I like to make the kids feel at home.

GUARD: So I've noticed. [*To the new boy*] Okay Smith, this is your dormitory for now. Try to get along with the others and keep your nose clean. Do as you're told, keep your bunk tidy, and no talking after lights out. You'll be assigned your work tomorrow. Meanwhile, follow the others to washup and meals. Pick up the routine and don't spend too much time in the craphouse, or you'll end up in an isolation cell.

ROCKY: He means Gunsel's Alley. Too bad all the queers don't make it there.

QUEENIE [*to the* GUARD]: Now he wants a private room. Take him away, Nurse!

GUARD: Okay you two! Turn off the vaudeville. You'll get your chance to do your number at the Christmas concert. [*He exits.*]

QUEENIE: The Dolly Sisters! After you got your royal uniform, in the delousing room, did Bad Bess challenge you to a duel?

SMITTY: Who?

QUEENIE: Little Sergeant Gritt – that chalk-faced, pea-eyed squirt in the rimless goggles! He's always goin' on about the 'Days of Empire' and 'God and Country' and all suchlike Bronco Bullcrap.

SMITTY: Oh, yes! He did most of the talking.

QUEENIE: That's our Cockney cunt – never closes her hole. Didn't he want you to square off for fisticuffs, old chap? Sporting chance an' all that stale roast beef an' Yorkshire pudding?

SMITTY: Well, he did say he'd been boxing champion at some school in England, and that, if any of us thought we were tough, this was our chance to prove it – man to man, with no interference.

QUEENIE: Yeah – that's his usual pitch. Corny, ain't it? It makes him feel harder than those stout lions out front o' Buckingham Palace. Yellow-bellied little rat! When he's outa that uniform, he's scared to death o' any eleven-year-old kid he meets on the street. Did his Lordship get any challengers?

SMITTY: Well, no! I wasn't surprised at that. I felt sure it was just a way of letting the prisoners know who's boss.

QUEENIE: I must say – you ain't exactly a idiot.

ROCKY: One o' these farty Fridays, he's gonna get it good, from some guy faster'n that goddam Indian.

QUEENIE: How stupid kin a Iroquois be? Imagine this jerky Indian from Timmins, takin' that fish-faced little potato chip at his word. The only one ever took the chance – far as I know.

SMITTY: He'd have to have a lot of guts.

QUEENIE: Oh yeah – and they showed them to him fast. He was a brave brave all right – an' stupid as a dead buffalo. The second he an' Bad Bess squared off at each other, two guards jumped Big Chief Running Blood, an' the three British bully boys beat the roaring piss outa him. Heroes all!

ROCKY: What a mess they made o' that squaw-banger!

QUEENIE: You couldn't exactly put that profile on a coin no more – not even a cheap little copper. Oh, well – let's look on the bright side o' the penny; he's in pretty good shape for the shape he's in. After all, he got a free nose-bob an' can pass for a pale nigger now. A darkie can get a better job 'n a redskin any day.

ROCKY: Whoever heard of a Indian what worked? They git government relief.

QUEENIE: Howda think he got here, Moronia? He was one o' them featherheads from Matachewan Reservation, tryin' t' get a job in the mines. There was this great big ol' riot, an' the cowboys won again. Pocahontas' husband is up here because he tried t' scalp some Timmins cop. An', believe you me, that's the wrong way to get yourself a wig in that tin town.

ROCKY: An' you believe that crap, like he tells you his stories about how some stinkin' bird got its name? Jeez! Maybe you should git yerself a blanket an' become a squaw – you dig those tepee tales so much.

QUEENIE: I dig all kinds o' tail, pale-ass – except yours.

ROCKY: All Indians is screwin' finks an' stoolies, an' I woulden trust 'em with a bottle o' cheap shavin' lotion; and that Blackfeet bum probably slugged some ol' fairy in a public crapper, t' git a bottle o' wine.

QUEENIE: Always judgin' everybody by yourself! Tch! Tch! That's the sign of a slow con man, Sweetie.

MONA [*to new boy*]: What's your name? I'm Jan.

SMITTY: Smith.

QUEENIE: But you can call her Mona, and I'm Queenie.

ROCKY: Look at the girls givin' the new boy a fast cruise. Give him time to take his pants off, Queenie.

QUEENIE: So you can get into them, Daddy-O? Don't let him bug you, Smitty. He thinks he's the big rooster here.

ROCKY: You know it too. Welcome home, punk.

SMITTY: This is my first time.

ROCKY: Braggin' or complainin'?

SMITTY: Neither. It's just a fact.

ROCKY: Well, that's nice. You shouldn't be here at all I guess. Got a bum beef?

SMITTY: A . . . a what?

ROCKY: Crap! A beef! A rap! Whose cookies did you boost . . . your mother's?

QUEENIE: What the judge wants to know, honey, is what special talent brought you this vacation . . . are you a store-counter booster or like myself do you make all your house calls when nobody's home?

SMITTY: Neither!

QUEENIE: Rolled a drunk . . . autographed somebody's checks . . . raped the girl next door . . .?

SMITTY: No, and I . . . I don't want to talk about it.

QUEENIE: You might as well spill it, kid. I can't stand suspense. Ask Mona . . . she screwed all around the mulberry bush until I finally had to go find out in the office.

ROCKY: I coulda saved you the trouble and told you she reached for the wrong joy stick. Did you ever get one you didn't like, Mona?

MONA [to SMITTY]: I've learned it doesn't matter what you've done. If you don't say, everyone assumes it's something far worse, so you might as well get it over with.

SMITTY: I just can't.

QUEENIE: OKAY Smitty . . . skip it! I'll find out on the Q.T., but I won't spill it.

ROCKY: Ottawa's First Lady! How did you do it, Ladybird?

QUEENIE: Well . . . I lifted my left leg and then my right, and between the two of them, I rose right to the top.

ROCKY: Of a pile of bull!

MONA: How long is your sentence?

SMITTY: Six months.

MONA: Same as mine. I have a few to go.

SMITTY: Does . . . does it seem as long as . . . as . . .

MONA: Not after a while. You get used to the routine, and there are diversions.

ROCKY: That's an invitation to the crapper.

MONA: Do you like to read?

SMITTY: I never did ... much.

MONA: Well, this is a good place to acquire the habit.

ROCKY: Yeah! Let Mona the fruit teach you her habits, then you can go and make yourself an extra pack of weed a week.

QUEENIE: She don't go as cheap as you, Rocky. We're tailor-made cigarette girls or nothin'.

ROCKY: I get what I want without bending over.

QUEENIE: Sure! You can always con some stupid chicken into doing it for you. How many left in your harem now, Valentino?

ROCKY: My kids wouldn't spit on the best part of you.

QUEENIE: Who's interested in a lot of little worn-out punks? I've seen them all hustling their skinny asses in the Corner Cafeteria, and if it wasn't for the old aunties who feel them up in the show and take them for a meal, they'd starve to death. Did you tell them before they left that you'd provide them with a whole bus terminal to sleep in when you get out?

ROCKY: After I smarten them up, they don't have to flop in your hunting grounds. They go where the action is and cruise around in Cadillacs.

QUEENIE: Yours, of course?

ROCKY: What I *take*, you can call *mine*.

QUEENIE: What a pity you couldn't get a judge to see it the same way.

ROCKY: You're cruisin' for a bruisin', bitch!

QUEENIE: Thanks awfully, but I'm no maso-sissy, sad-ass. I always kick for the balls when attacked.

    [*Sings to the tune of 'Habanera' from* Carmen]

> My name is Carmen,
> I am a whore,
> And I go knocking
> From door to door.

ROCKY: I'll meet you in front of the city hall next Christmas.

QUEENIE: Lovely, but don't ask me for a quarter, like last time.

ROCKY: Since when did you walk on the street with more than a dime?

QUEENIE: After I stopped letting bums like you roost at my place overnight.

ROCKY: Cripes! You'll never forget you played Sally Ann to me once. When you sobered up and felt like a little fun, did you miss me?

QUEENIE: ... Yeah – also my marble clock, my garnet ring, and eleven dollars.

ROCKY [*laughing*]: Oh jeez, I wish I coulda seen your face. Was your mascara running?

QUEENIE: He's having such a good time, I hate to tell him I like Bob Hope better. So where did you come from Smitty ... the big corner?

MONA: That means the city ... it's a slang term. You'll get used to them.

SMITTY: I feel like I'm in another country.

ROCKY: What's your ambition kid? You wanna be a Square John ... a brown nose?

QUEENIE: Ignore the ignoramus. He loves to play the wise guy.

SMITTY: I'm willing to catch on.

QUEENIE: You will, but you gotta watch yourself ... play it cool and listen to the politicians.

SMITTY: Politicians?

QUEENIE: The hep guys ... hippos, who are smart enough to make it into the office. They get the best of it ... good grub, new shirts, and jeans, lightweight booties and special privileges ... extra gym, movie shows, and sometimes even tailor-made cigarettes. Like to get in on that?

SMITTY: I don't smoke.

QUEENIE: Well for cripes' sake don't tell them. Take your deck of weed and give it to your mother.

SMITTY: My ...

QUEENIE: Me, honey! Who else!

SMITTY: Oh! Okay!

MONA: Tailor-made cigarettes are contraband, but your package of tobacco is handed out with a folder of cigarette papers and a razor blade when you go for clothing change once a week ... it's sort of a payday!

ROCKY: Listen to our little working girl. She works in the gashouse sewing pants together for the guys to wear. Her only complaint is there's nothing in 'em when they're finished.

SMITTY: Is that what I'll be doing ...?

QUEENIE: No baby, you won't. The tailor shop and the laundry are especially for us girls. They can make sure, that way, we don't stray behind a bush. But I like the laundry since they made me forelady. It's a sweet act of fate because it's the only place in the joint where I can get Javex – to keep myself a natural blonde.

ROCKY: And it's easier to show your ass bending over a tub, than under a sewing machine or a wheelbarrow.

QUEENIE: You've got a one-track mind, and it's all dirt.

ROCKY: My shovel's clean.

QUEENIE: I don't know how. Every time you get in a shower, you've got it in somebody's ditch.

ROCKY: Don't be jealous. I'll get around to shovelling in yours.

QUEENIE: Be sure you can fill it with diamonds when you come callin'.

ROCKY: You'd be happy with a fistful of chocolates.

QUEENIE: Feed the Lauras to your chickens at jug-up, eh Smitty?

SMITTY: Jug-up?

QUEENIE: Meals! Didn't they yell jug-up at you before you ate today?

SMITTY: I wasn't hungry. I thought the food would be the same as at the city jail, and it always made me sick after.

QUEENIE: Don't remind me of that sewage dump on the River. I think they bought that bloody old baloney and those withered wieners once a year ... and you could put up wallpaper forever with that goddam porridge. Don't worry ... the pigs they keep here are fed better than that.

MONA: Yes, the meals are good, Smitty. This place has its own farm, so the animals and vegetables are all raised by the prisoners.

SMITTY: I once worked on a farm, between school terms. I

wouldn't mind if they put me on that . . . the time would go fast.

QUEENIE: That's the idea, honey! I'll try to wangle you a good go so you don't hafta do hard time. I got some pull in the office.

ROCKY: You'll have to serve a little keester to the politicians who wanna put you in the barn.

SMITTY: What?

ROCKY: But I guess you been in the hay before. Queenie's all for fixin' you up with an old man. You're ripe for tomato season.

QUEENIE: One thing about it, Rockhead. It'll be a hippy who's got it made, and no crap disturber like you that picks him off my vine.

SMITTY: I don't want to hurt anybody's feelings, but I'm not . . . queer. I've got a girl friend : she even came to court.

ROCKY: You shoulda brought her with you. I'da shared my bunk with her.

SMITTY: You don't understand, she's not that kind of . . .

MONA: It's all right, Smitty; he's just teasing you. Life inside is different, but you still don't have to do anything you don't want to, not if you –

QUEENIE: I'm tryin' to smarten him up, Mona, and you try to queer the play. Has sittin' outside the fence got you anything? At jug-up some punk's always grabbin' the meat off your plate and you're scared to say boo.

MONA: I get enough to eat. If anybody's that hungry, I don't begrudge it.

QUEENIE: And look at your goddam rags. They give you that junk on purpose, to make a bloody clown outa you. You ain't had a garment that fits since you come in.

MONA: I can fix them to look better at the shop when the guard's not looking.

QUEENIE: Well I like everything new. I can't feel sexy in rags.

MONA: I don't really care what I look like here.

QUEENIE [*sigh of despair*] : See, Smitty! I try to sharpen the girls I like and she don't listen to a screwin' word I say. I coulda got her a real good old man, but she told him she liked her 'independence' if you can picture it.

SMITTY: I can understand that.

QUEENIE: Yeah? So what happens? One day in the gym a bunch of hippos con her into the storeroom to get something for the game, and teach her another one instead. They make up the team, but she's the only basket. They all took a whack, now she's public property. You can't say no around here unless you got somebody behind you. Take it from your mother ... I know the score.

SMITTY: I'll have to think about it.

QUEENIE: Well don't wait until they give you a gang splash in the storeroom. Mona had to hold on to the wall to walk, for a week.

Austin C. Clarke

A WEDDING IN TORONTO

'A police coming in a man's house, and at a wedding reception, to boot! and breaking up a party? Merely because some old can't-sleep bitch next door, or down-below can't find a man, or something? What kind o' place, what sort o' country is this? It never happened in Barbados, and it never could. Imagine a police in Barbados, coming into a man's house, during a party, and a wedding party at that, to tell that man he is making too much noise! Man, that policeman's arse would be so stiff with lashes, he would never do that again! A police coming into a man's apartment, and breaking up a wedding reception because some old bitch who can't sleep, complained?' Boysie never got over the shock of seeing the policeman at the door, standing like a monument to something, with an untranslatable expression on his face, with one hand resting perhaps absent-mindedly on the holster of his gun, and the other, raised and caught in the slow-motion paralysis of knocking on the apartment again. It was a loud, firm knock of authority. The wedding guests were, at that time, in the middle of the speeches; and Boysie, who was the master of ceremonies, had been saying some amusing things about marriage. It was at the point when he was saying, *Ecce homo*, over and over again, (using his best stentorian, oratorical Barbadian dialect), exhorting them, as: 'La-dies and gentlemen! ladies and gentlemen too! greetings and salutations, because on this most auspicious of evenings, on the aurora of long and felicitous matrimony, I say to you, to you, ladies and gentlemen, I say, *ecce homo*, behold the man! *ecce homo*, here I stand!' (Freeness, dressed to kill, in a three-piece suit; Matthew Woods, spic and span; Estelle, beautiful as a virgin, as a star; and many others, crammed into the happy apartment, screamed for joy, when Boysie began this speech, his fifth for the afternoon's festivities. Each wedding guest including Agatha, the bride and Henry, the bridegroom, had made a speech. Some had made two speeches. Boysie had made his first, about an hour after the wedding party returned to the apartment. It was five o'clock then. Now, after many toasts and speeches and eats and drinks, Boysie was captivating his audience again. The time was midnight. The guests liked it; and they bawled and told Boysie they liked it. Henry, sober and married; Agatha, turning red, and flushed, and happy, and drunk as Dots, Boysie's wife, was, held her head back and exposed her silver cavities filled with silver, and said, 'I could have another wedding reception like this, tomorrow! One like this every month!') 'I say to you, ladies and gentlemen, I say, *ecce homo*, behold the man! *ecce homo*, here I stand! Here I stand, ladies and gentlemen, with a glass of drink in my hand, wherewithal for to mitigate the aridity of my thirst. And as I have arisen from my esteemed seat this fifth time, and as I have quoth to you, *bon swarr*, or goodevening, to the ladies and to the gentlemen of this nocturnal congregation of celebrating wedding guests, I say it again, for its sincerity can bear much repetition, *bon swarr*, my dear Agaffa, goodevening, Henry, you lucky old Bajan bastard!' And it was here, in the roar of acceptance by each person in the room, when they held their glasses up, and Boysie's glass was held right there, at the correct angle, that the knock brutalized the apartment. Its suddenness made them notice it. But they had no suspicions. Boysie said, with his glass still raised, 'Perhaps, ladies and gentlemen, it is some poor suppliant wanting warmth of this nocturnal congregation.' And he moved away, towards the door, his drink still in his shaking hands, to invite the person inside to partake of the hospitality. Bernice went to Agatha to fix the veil on her dress, and therefore, fortunately, blocked her vision of the police officer at the door, with his hand on his holster. Boysie didn't lose his aplomb. The police officer was very polite to him. 'Break it up, soon, buddy. It's past midnight, and the neighbours're complaining about the noise.'

Boysie was going to offer the officer a drink, but he changed his mind.

'Don't let me get another report that you making noise, eh? Break it up, soon, buddy.'

Boysie did not move from the door until the officer of the law walked back to the elevator; and he did not move until he saw him get into it; and Dots, who by this time had put a record on the machine the moment she heard the officer's voice, was now standing beside Boysie, like a real wife, supportingly.

'And the poor girl's enjoying herself so much! And on her wedding day? Jesus Christ, these people is savages; man, they're damn uncivilized! You mean to tell me, on the girl's wedding day?' Boysie put his arm round Dots's new, shiny, almost bare shoulder, and he squeezed her a little bit, and said, 'We going party till that bitch come back!' Boysie left her, and went to Bernice and whispered in her ear, 'The police!' Bernice grew tense. 'But only me, and now you, and Dots know. So keep it dark. Keep it dark. We got to go on. How the hell could we ask the people to leave? How would Agaffa feel? How would Henry feel, on his wedding night, to boot?'

But Boysie and Dots and Bernice made certain not to make Agatha and Henry feel the tension that had begun to creep into the party. It was impossible to recapture the gaiety and the enjoyment that was present before the policeman knocked on the door. Dots would have had the guests leave immediately; after a respectable drink; she would have insisted upon it, because Agatha and Henry had to go on their honeymoon, to Niagara Falls. But Boysie said no. 'This is a wedding. Not any old damn party with beatniks.' And he left Dots standing there, arguing the wisdom of his suggestion with Bernice; and he went to the record player; (this record player had arrived from Eaton's department store two hours before the wedding reception began; delivered on a hire-purchase, the monthly payments of which were fifty-five dollars and twenty-five cents; and which Dots did not know how she would meet; but the sound was high and high-fidelity and stereophonic too, and the beauty and the loudness of the sound allayed their fears of having the machine repossessed. 'Man, let we play the thing for today, then; and enjoy it, and then see what happen, man!' And Boysie agreed to that; although before Dots said so, he had already agreed, in his mind, to keep the record player). Boysie now selected a calypso by the Mighty Sparrow, *Shanty Town People*: in which

Sparrow was complaining of having to move out of his comfortable apartment, in Trinidad, because people from the slums had encroached on his location on the hill. The music raged, as the spirits in the guests and in the drinks raged. Estelle was beautiful in her wedding-party dress. She was thinking of the closeness she herself had come to marriage. And more than once, during the hectic afternoon and night, she wondered where the hell her man, Sam Burrmann, was, at this happy time. But by now, she had put him out of her mind, and she devoted all her body and energy to Matthew Woods, who shook his body in dance, as if he was in some mad trance. *Sunday morning, they fighting, they drinking, they beating pan . . . send for the police, still the bacchanal won't cease.* It was a royal time: it was an ironic time, to have a calypso reproduce the exact conditions of a party at which the police had come. And judging by the hour hand, it was Sunday morning too! But no one cared for Toronto, or police, or the neighbours: this was a wedding; and as Dots said, 'A person can only get married one time. Even if he divorce and marry a second time, the second time don't seem to be like the first time! So the first time *is* the time!' Boysie was dancing with her. Brigitte had held on to Freeness the whole day, probably by design; probably by the suggestion of Boysie (whose woman she was); Boysie, who, now in the castle of skin and pride, in his briar patch of host and wedding-giver, had no time for outside-women); and Bernice was dancing with a man who nobody knew, who nobody invited, but who was treated with the same courtesy and hospitality as the bridegroom, as if he was the bride's father. Agatha's father hadn't arrived yet. Agatha's mother hadn't arrived yet. Agatha's friends, Agatha's many friends from the university, and her lawyer-friend (all of whom had been sent invitations – that was Boysie's personal gift to the couple) hadn't arrived yet. It was a sorrowful sight, at the church, when it was found out that no one was sitting on the bride's side of witness and evidence. Dots quickly saw the situation developing, and quickly saw the embarrassment it would cause to Agatha when she arrived sweet and young, virginal and white, in her long dress, to glance over the wide expanse of the desert of her friends. And Dots ushered and re-ushered half of the church over to Agatha's side. When the organ roared and snorted through the Wedding March, everybody was laughing, even Agatha. Reverend Markham was happy. The choir was in good voice, loud when it was supposed to be loud, soft when the organist breathed with the organ, and whispered that the choir be like a piano, pianissimo. But when they were in the office, signing away their lives and their promises to one another, Dots stood like a mother-hen on the top steps of the church, directing the people (those who didn't have cars) to cars, and warning the photographer who had arrived late, 'Look here! don't take the whole day, hear? We have things waiting at the wedding reception.' And after that, she whispered in Bernice's ears, 'It's a shame, a great burning shame that that bastard, Agatha's father, thinks he is too great and too proud to come and witness his own daughter on her wedding day. A person does only have one wedding day in her life, and that bastard didn't even come. He didn't come.'

'And the mother ain't turned up yet, neither.'

'Bernice, gal, you are seeing the ways o' white people this lovely autumn day. The ways o' white people. They would kill their own flesh-and-blood just to prove a point.'

'It is sad, though.'

Estelle had overheard, and she said, 'They love one another, though, Agatha and Henry. And they won't be living at the parents.'

'Still a blasted shame!'

And now, at the reception, nobody apparently tired, after so many hours of eating and drinking and dancing, with the problems of *Shanty Town People* being reproduced for them, by the visit of the policeman, and by the record itself, these West Indians and one white woman, ('She's a Wessindian now, gal! We claim her now that her people and her parents let her down. Gorblummuh, we is one people who don't reject nobody through prejudice.'): ... *I tired and I disgust* ... *big Sunday evening, they cussing, they fighting, they gambling, they beating pan and bup-bup!-iron bolt, and stone pelting, send for the police, still the bacchanal won't cease.* ... There were fifty people invited to the reception. They were fifty people in the two-bedroom apartment from five o'clock.

They are fifty-one people (with the un-invited man), in the apartment now, at one-thirty, Sunday morning. Boysie has his arms in the air, and is dancing as if his body has been seized by some voodoo, or St Vitus dance mood; Dots has thrown one brocaded expensive slipper somewhere in a corner, and she is jumping up. The record, a favourite with everybody in the room, is put on again. It is put on three times, four times, five times, six times; and Boysie says, on the seventh time, 'Man, play that thing a next time, do!' And it is put on the eighth time. . . . *and big Sunday morning, they cussing they fighting they gambling; they beating pan and bup-bup!-iron bolt and stone pelting, send for the police, still the bacchanal won't cease, so they violent so they fast, they better go back to their mansion on the Labasse.* . . . A smudge of fatigue and sweat walked imperceptibly from under Estelle's hairy armpits. Bernice noticed it; and she took Estelle into Dots's bedroom, and rubbed some of Dots's under-arm deodorant, 'Ban', on the story-telling odour. Estelle smiles, and dashes back out to dance. Agatha, with the first signs of marriedhood and possessiveness, sits and watches Henry dance with Pricilla, the nurse ('But who the hell invited that whore? Who invited Pricilla in here, in my decent place, eh? Boysie you invited Pricilla?'); and Agatha watches him, and she watches Pricilla's sterilized nurse's hips, as they do things with the rhythm that she herself, legal and wedded to Henry for better and for worse, cannot do. Some men are in the kitchen, eating, as they have been doing since five o'clock in the afternoon. There is a big argument going on, about cricket. None of these men has seen a cricket match, in five years, not since they left their islands. But they are arguing about Sir Frank Worrell, and the cover drive he made off Alec Bedser at Lords in 1950, many many years ago. One man says, 'The English think they great? They playing they're great? But be-Jesus Chroist, when Worrell, when Sir Frank leaned into that outswinging from Bedser hand, gorblummuh, like lightning it went to the fucking bound'ry for four. Right offa Worrell's wrist; and you-all know, Worrell, Sir Frank, is one man with more wrist than, than – than Boysie in there, have stones in his underwears!' And like a contagion, everybody bawled, and poured himself another,

larger rum. The record is changed. Sparrow is talking about his boy-
hood. The men dropped their glasses and ran for the women. They
reached out their hands, and lifted the dripping, shining, shiningly-
dressed, rouged-and-perfumed-smelling tired women off their chairs.
Boysie is dancing with Dots, as if they are lovers : close. His bril-
liantined head, which had sweated four hours, for hours, under his
stocking-top, is sleeked down and shining; and Dots's hairdo, done
amidst pain and time, talk and gossip in Azan's beauty parlour, the
previous Thursday, when the shop was noisy and filled with domes-
tics and talk about 'this rich-rich Jewish girl who is marrieding
with some Bajan bastard, by the name of Henry-something, Christ
I wonder if she really have rocks inside her head ! She couldn' find
nobody better?' Dots had listened, and had held her peace : they
did not really know the facts. Now, *I am a rebel, I seeking my
revenge any kind o' way, I'm a devil. I don't laugh, I don't smile I
don't play.* ... Boysie is not smiling. He is holding Dots so close
that she can feel something stiff in his trousers legs : but she is his
wife and he, her husband. ... *Anytime we meet, man-to-man, it's
blood and sand!* (Estelle thinks of the time when Bernice and Dots
and Boysie had come to the room on Bedford Road, and had found
her delirious with fever and misery and thoughts that could not be
achieved; and how they dressed her; how they paid the landlord
the rent owing, which Matthew Woods had sworn he wanted to
pay for her, but which she told him not to pay, because she didn't
want to be obligated to another man; and how they had driven her
back to Boysie's and Dots's apartment and here, she had slept, the
first good night's rest in such a long time. She is thinking of Bernice, her dear sister, and of her bad luck : 'that woman, Mrs Burrmann thinks she can solve anything by treating my sister so rotten?
But let her wait till I get more strength, till I have this baby, well,
be-Christ, if I don't go right up there in Forest Hill for her arse !
Her husband, Sam Burrmann could breed me, and then she could
fire my sister from her job !' And Estelle thinks too of the future:
hers and Bernice's. 'What is my sister going to do? I left Barbados,
and come all the way up here, and spoil things for that girl !' And
she thinks of the present. There is a man standing before her. He is
the man who nobody invited. He is standing in front of her like a

threat, like a challenge. He wants to dance with 'the prettiest lady in this place'. The compliment is sincere, and Estelle stands up, just as Sparrow says, *They treat me like a savage, of me they took advantage; when I was young and growing up in town, all o' them bad-johns used to knock me down.* . . . A tear is crawling like perspiration down Estelle's face. The man does not notice. He has his mind on other parts of her anatomy.

It was then, that the second knocking was heard, on the apartment door. Boysie went to the door. The same policeman, plus another, were standing there. 'I told ya,' the first policeman said. There was no anger in his voice. He seemed peeved that someone would report noise twice in one night; he seemed as if he had been awakened from his slumbers in some dark alley in the dark city; as if he had been roused from a poker game; as if, and it could be (his fly was still open) he had been disturbed from the pants of some woman, somewhere down in the jungle of apartments near by. Boysie knew what to do. The guests began leaving right away. Everybody except those who were staying for the night, those who lived there : Boysie and Dots and Bernice and Estelle. Henry looked at the policemen and said things in his heart, which if they were audible would have given him a beating and then a long jail term. Agatha was crying. She was still in her wedding gown; Henry in his formal morning suit. The policemen waited until every one of the guests left. As Agatha, walking beside Henry, along the long corridor, as if she was still walking that interminable aisle up the aisle to face the altar and the cross and the Maker and Reverend Markham, women with curlers in their hair, peeped through open doors; and just as the policemen entered and went down into the half-awake apartment building, in the elevator going out, one white woman, in a torn pink nightgown, which showed the blackness between her thighs, sneered, 'You white bitch ! You white trash !' and slammed her apartment door. The others, among the onlooking guard of honour and dishonour, shook their heads, and did not slam their doors : but nobody knew what they were saying in their hearts, behind their closed doors. In all the confusion, in all the disappointment and crying (Dots and Bernice and Estelle remained sitting on the large, new couch, crying for Agatha's sake; and Agatha herself, in tears, had just wet their cheeks with the tears of her kisses), the record player was still commenting: *They treat me like a savage ... they treat me like a savage ... they treat me like a savage ... they treat me like a savage ... they treat me like a savage....* The needle was stuck in a groove of the record.

George Bowering

30 BELOW

In Alberta the antelope
are dying on the C.P.R. tracks
at 30 below zero.

Their frozen bodies
lie beside the tracks,
feet pointing
at the passenger train going by.

This summer
the hunters will walk
far north
looking for game.

Chief Charley Horse says
Manitou brought the ice
to punish white hunters
who leave their dead ducks & rabbits
by the side of the road.

But the animals are frozen
carcasses now by every road,

the hunters are warm in lodges
waiting for the big thaw.

They know Manitou
doesn't hold his breath
all winter.

Adèle Wiseman

FROM CRACKPOT

Hoda had never got over her mistrust of the downtown trade, where a girl really needed protection, and even so, with all her protection, look what had happened to Seraphina. That's just it, what had happened to Seraphina? Nobody knew. Several times Hoda had tried, after a long time had passed and Seraphina hadn't been around, to try to contact her somehow, but Seraphina, and her pimp too, the flashy Les Less more more, had simply dropped out of sight a couple of years ago. Seraphina's mother didn't know where she was, and was pretty rude about it when Hoda came, with the friendliest intentions, to inquire. And one or two other people Hoda tried to inquire through also didn't know, and didn't seem to care, either, enough to let her disappearance worry them. Maybe Les had got restless and taken his girls, like he had always promised he would, out East and into the big time. Or maybe he was serving time, and the girls were scattered. But where? Hoda hoped that Seraphina really had made it out East in the big time, like Hymie had. But she doubted. She couldn't expect one from Hymie but Serry would have sent a card, at least. One time she ran into an old friend of Seraphina, one of her reform school pals, who told her that though she herself hadn't seen Serry for years and years, last she had heard, Serry wasn't even with Les anymore. Someone had seen Les and asked after her and Les had said he couldn't afford to support a sick pig, coughing and puking blood all over his customers. Put that together with what Seraphina had told her towards the end, that Les was bribing her with little extras to take on specialty tricks and let them beat her up, and Hoda didn't like it at all. She told Seraphina she was crazy to do it, but Serry had laughed a funny, frightened laugh, and said what could you do if those were all the customers he got for you nowadays, and maybe all you were good for anymore like he said, and a girl had to eat, and you know what a temper Les had; if you're going to get beaten up anyway it might as well be on a full stomach. It's unnatural to puke on an empty one; the doctors don't like it.

Hoda had got mad and stormed at her and tush tushed the way she was running herself down. 'You don't need him! Why don't you leave him and go to a house like you always said?'

But Serry, poor dimwit though she was, explained that Les was her only security, and nowadays she didn't seem to look so good to the brothel keepers either, and anyway, she didn't mind the beatings so much; they always stopped sometimes, and then you felt better, and besides, she couldn't run out on poor Les. 'I'd worry how he was getting on. You get set in your ways, Hoda.'

Well, Seraphina might, but Hoda wouldn't; that she promised herself. Nobody was going to call her a sick pig and abandon her. Where? Hoda had written letters to the T.B. Sanitarium and to the contagious diseases hospital in town, and she had called up the other chronic sickness hospitals, but they didn't have any Seraphina, so all she could do now was hope that her old friend might just turn up again like she always had. As for Les, she hoped he was doing time, that's what she hoped. Even if a guy was a pimp he should have a sense of responsibility. But when she caught herself thinking something like that, say about somebody like Les, Hoda laughed at herself, because actually, she did know better, though it still griped her, the way things were, the way people were, the way everything was.

Look, even the way the City Hall was; should things be like that right in the very centre of the city where you belonged? Concerned as Hoda was with very personal things on the one hand, and with large, universal political and humanitarian concepts on the other, she always felt when she thought of the City Hall that this should be the place where everybody would feel the same concern for everybody else. But instead, it was from the top of the stone staircases out front of the City Hall that the mayor had read the riot act and given the order for the militia to charge on the workers in the general strike. And it was here that she herself came, fearfully, to perform her regular personal errand and got a sinking feeling every time she caught sight of things she really liked to see, like the old trees, the landscaped lawn, and the pretty flower beds. She stood and looked at the large statue of the heroic soldier going out to get shot, and she knew that though she felt ever so close to them and sorry for them and everything, she would get little sympathy herself even from the old soldier bums and cripples who hung around here, if she were so far to forget herself as to ask for it, that is. What did she expect? If you're going to peddle your ass you can expect to get sold sometimes, so why should they sympathize? And yet she sympathized with them, didn't she, with all these listless figures of crippled and jobless old soldiers and down and outs who leaned against the City Hall fence and watched the pigeons and hardly ever looked up at the fine old dark metallic figure in full battle dress and pigeon shit, that stood for what they themselves had been like before gunshot and gas and government had brought them back to hang about the City Hall and the welfare offices because there was nothing else for them to do, good old soldiers who knew better than to disobey the green and white wooden signs that said 'Please don't walk on the grass'. They'd peddled their asses too, hadn't they? and cheap. And had they known any more what it was all about than Hoda had, when she had thrown all her innocent goodwill into pleasing and being pleased? Oh, Hoda was not afraid to say what she thought about it all, and she said it, too, inside, when she was waiting her turn. That was probably another reason why they rushed her out so fast, which was all right by her, better than being kept waiting all day, like they'd probably start doing to her again, if she gave them half a chance.

Not that Hoda minded the City Hall itself. In a way she liked being somehow connected to a nice, big, ugly old building, and this one was maybe as big as a palace, the crazy, haunted kind you used to see drawings of when you were a kid, kind of gloomy but impressive, the way those broad, double armed stairways led up to the front entrance, and all those bumps and protrusions and separate cockeyed little constructions rising up and up all over the place, with hundreds of little windows set into masses of stale old genital coloured brick. Once you got in there you were lost right from the start, unless you happened to be familiar with all the little crooked byways of government. That much Hoda knew from experience.

She didn't often look in at that entrance nowadays, only sometimes when they wanted to warm up after a rally maybe she and one of the comrades would slip in for a few minutes and pretend they were tourists. She was now far from the naïve young girl who had first climbed up the staircase and tugged open the massive door and wandered about among unfamiliar musty smells and huge, dark paintings, and broad stairways, looking for the mayor or an alderman or school trustee or some other official who would lead her to where she was going. It was funny, no matter how much a person thought she had learned, tomorrow, when she looked back at the person she'd been yesterday, she'd still be amazed at how dumb or how innocent or how naïve she was then.

Well, naïve or not, she hadn't liked the treatment from the start. At first she had thought the people she stopped to ask just didn't understand the question, and you had to persist until you got hold of the mayor himself who must be the only one who knew anything around here. And since she was still pretty young at the time, she had felt called on to explain her perfectly simple errand confidentially to each one she asked, repeating painstakingly over and over again, and it wasn't so hard after the first time, because she was getting so exasperated, that she had been told that if you went to the City Hall, they would give you a free checkup to see if you had caught a dose or anything. All she wanted was to be directed to the room where the doctor was. After a while she realized that maybe they had understood her after all. The way they looked at her, you'd think they were afraid they'd catch something from just talking to her ! And the way they answered, you'd think it was a sin to be caught just knowing where the clinic was. Finally, when they sent the guard after her that time, and he had directed her curtly out the front entrance again and right around back to a mean little door that led into a cellar, and had a sign over it that said 'Public Health', she'd thought that here at least the people knew what they were being paid for and would treat her like any other patient. Well, they didn't. They acted as if she was something at the other end of a long stick. They kept her waiting for hours, and were a lot more polite to people who came in after her, and didn't keep them waiting nearly as long either. Sometimes they even made her come back in the afternoon, and kept her waiting then too.

Sure, and Mr Polonick agreed with her; that's how they treat you when you're a charity patient. And they probably thought they could treat Hoda with special contempt because of the nature of her errand. They wouldn't keep a society lady waiting if she was afraid she had a social disease, but someone who had to earn her living and didn't really want to spread anything bad around, like Hoda, her time could be wasted. Hoda bitterly resented their attitude, but at first she didn't know what to do about it. If she made a fuss like she felt like doing, they might call in a cop or a guard and start investigating and who knows what trouble they could get her into, if they wanted to, those cops. So she told herself, 'Look, so they're mean, so what are you going to do, stop coming?' – Boy how I'd like to, and to hell with them ! – 'So you stop coming and you catch something and spread it around and make other people sick and get sick yourself too, so you end up acting as rotten as they do. Remember what Mr Polonick says, they may be doctors and nurses and educated goyem, but they're still public servants, and you're the public, and they're at your service, no matter if they think they can put on airs. Treat them nicely, even if they have no manners, like you'd treat any other servant.' So she did; she ignored their frigid manners and their cold faces, and she chatted and joked at them, and during the time she spent in the waiting room, she entertained herself and whoever else happened to be waiting, with conversation and jokes, and in general tried to cheer up the drab little anteroom. Sometimes it got pretty busy, and she met all kinds of interesting people. It turned out this place wasn't only for checking against the dose; it was for pre-maritals, and vaccinations of all kinds, and other odds and ends of public medical service. Sometimes when there was a good natured bunch happened to get together in there they had a very good time. Hoda, once she got going, could keep them in stitches for hours. The audience in the waiting room was usually fun to kibitz with, because they were all a little anxious about one thing or another, whether they were worried they might have got the clap, or thought they might be a little bit pregnant, or simply didn't look forward to having needles stuck in them. So they laughed with a nervous readiness, an almost pathetic willingness to have their jitters turned to hilarity. Hoda actually began to enjoy these visits to the Public Health, at least the chatty waiting part.

Then she realized that they were suddenly rushing her through practically the minute she arrived, taking her first, interrupting her conversations just as they got started, pushing her tests through the lab, dismissing her before she hardly had a chance to open an acquaintanceship with anyone. It dawned on her then that there was something the staff didn't like about her conversation. The minute they heard her voice, they couldn't get her out quickly enough. That's when she really began to get some enjoyment out of the game. 'Hi there!' she'd call out innocently to a young couple who sat facing her on the opposite bench, that you could see from miles away were green little pre-maritals, probably waiting to get vaccinated for their honeymoon trip. 'You two been playing around?' Or else she'd fix the young man with a bright grey eye and say tenderly, all the while sloshing her yellowed retort gently to and fro, 'Don't I know you from some place?' Other times she teased and joked suggestively with the young louts who sat sheepishly clutching their own specimen bottles. She developed, over the years, a kind of sophistication, a public attitude, a way of outfacing whoever faced her. Deliberately she would introduce a round of questions, 'What do you do for a living?' so that when her fellow patients asked her in turn what she did for a living, she could reply, still sloshing her specimen innocently, 'Oh I make ends meet,' and her wicked chuckle would bust out of her and she could just feel the doctor and nurse squirming in the examination room, and imagine them muttering, 'For God's sake get her out of here!' Or she would say brightly, when she saw the expression on the young doctor's face when she appeared again, 'Just keeping clean like you want me to, Doc.' And she was amused because, rush though they might, it still took them a little time to process her business, and it eased her own nervousness to know they didn't have things all their own way.

All that had been in the early years. Now Hoda had been coming so long that she even had, as she jokingly put it, seniority over the doctor. Several young men and women had taken their turns in looking after her urine. She had even picked up the odd bit of biographical information about some of them, past and present, and could tell you where this one who used to be here now had his private practice, or what hospital that other one worked at, and how his nurse had followed him there soon after, though his wife probably didn't know it. She was free with these little bits of information, out of a kindly impulse, a desire to soothe her companions, because she saw that the more nervous patients found it soothing to be given a feeling of homey familiarity with the cold little office. It was somehow comforting, too, to know that doctors as well as patients come and go, though it was hard to believe when you faced them. Sometimes a very young and inexperienced staff member, hearing from Hoda's lips some item of personal information about a predecessor, something that no patient should know, and that was being cheerfully disseminated about the waiting-room benches, cringed to think that somehow some odd little intimate fact about himself might find its way out of that great mouth and strip the cool white coat away from between himself and his patients. And regrettably, it happened occasionally, that a patient was jabbed with unnecessary force, as a direct result of the fact that Hoda's voice was coming through loud and clear in the examining room, and the patient went off convinced that the Public Health had the heaviest handed doctors because, as the fat girl said, the city didn't care about you if you couldn't afford to pay.

As time passed, though Hoda still loved a cheerful bit of a chat and a kibitz with strangers that she met there, her conversation began to reflect the increase of restless bafflement that she felt about everything. The sentences she puzzled together lost some of their youthful clarity and certainty, and gained a little more of the disturbing resonance of ambiguity, took on, in fact, something of a rudely philosophical cast. Oh she still joked, but her jokes had an acidic, even faintly seditious tone that sometimes made her audience a little uneasy. She would get started on the condition of the water fountain, for instance, out front there, with the pigeons and the lounging bums, and how she wouldn't take a drink out of it if you paid her. What did the mayor think, she wanted to catch a social disease or something? But then, after a brief guffaw, she would go on more moodily, to the dirt and the spit, and remark on how people could hardly wait to get to the City Hall to clear the disgust from their throats. What could those strangers think when they came to town, all those visitors they had the 'Welcome Visitors' sign up front for, whoever they were; for her part Hoda never saw anyone but down and outs and the occasional farmer bringing his wife to show her things weren't good in the city either.

And Hoda would ramble on about things she had half-mulled over in her head, making sure she interspersed her comments with jokes, so her fellow patients wouldn't begin to get restless and turn their haunches away from her. But sometimes she gave way to the pressure of her thoughts, and went off, after a light hearted beginning, into long, discursive monologues, noting the restiveness of her captive audience after a while, but unable to stop herself just yet from trying to hunt down and capture the truth towards which her unwinding words seemed to beckon, perennially teasing her to a perennially incomplete revelation.

'Have you ever noticed that motto up front? I mean what's written up on that big fancy shield, right in the centre of the building, up over the front doors. You know, like, our city motto. You don't even know your own city motto? What kind of citizen are you? I know it all right. I ought to. It says : "Commerce, Prudence, Industry." That's my motto too, in fact. I figure if it's good enough for my home town, it's good enough for me. Commerce? Any time you like. Prudence? What do you think I'm doing here with the bottle? Industry? Hell, I ain't had no complaints yet. I figure I'm a model citizen. What I want to know is where does it get me? Ten-twelve years ago, believe it or not, I was sitting here just like this, holding my sample and waiting for the doctor to tell me what a beautiful specimen I got. And here I am still sitting with the bottle. Instead of those pictures they have on that shield up there, that nobody looks at anyway, you know, the sheaf of wheat and the buffalo and stuff, they should pay me to go sit up there, just like I am now, or maybe in my bare skin, on a bench, holding the bottle in my lap. People would look then all right. Yeh. What a way to live.

'Mind you sometimes it pays off. I know a guy it paid off for, in a big way, too. He went into foreign commerce. There's money in that, if you've got the right product. Of course he started small. He was only a driver when he got into the business. Would you believe it, he actually asked my advice whether he should go into it or not. You'd be surprised how many people ask my advice, tell me their troubles. Yeh, their wives would be surprised too, hah! But my friend Hymie, he's a millionaire today because he didn't take my advice.' Hoda chuckled. She always got a good laugh out of remembering how she had advised Hymie to stay away from the booze pipeline people.

'You see what happened, in those days, not so long ago either, just yesterday in fact, when the Americans weren't supposed to be able to get hold of any liquor, my friend was sniffing around for contacts, because he wanted to build up a really classy floating crap game here in town, with good bootleg stuff to bring in the big money types. First thing he knows he gets offered a job, hauling the whiskey around. "Should I take it, Hoda?" he asks me. "It's good money." "What's so good about it?" I says. "Gambling's one thing," I tell him. "You can run a pretty clean game. But bootlegging? It isn't honest! Crooks and murderers and racketeers," I says. I don't mean the friendly-house kind of bootlegging we got here,' Hoda caught herself up quickly. 'If the government's crazy you can't blame anyone for doing a little under the counter finagling. I don't ask where every drink somebody offers me came from myself, and I don't think anyone has the right to tell me I should drink or I shouldn't, either, or where I can and where I can't.' Hoda smiled genially at her audience. In a place like this you never knew, you could be talking to bootleggers, and she wasn't out to hurt any feelings.

'But big time bootlegging, international commerce, stuff like that, you know yourself who gets into that. You see it in the movies. Crooks and murderers and racketeers. "That's no job for a nice Jewish boy," I says to him, "And besides it's too risky. In those rackets it's the small fry that always get caught. The big shots grease their way out of trouble. You want your mother to have to live through it, all the neighbours should know she has a son sitting in jail?"

'So he says, "Listen, she complains anyway because I just sit around without a job. This way at least if I'm in jail I don't have to listen to her. Anyway, I don't have to be a racketeer or a murderer. It's just a job for me, a job with a few risks, so what? Instead of just sitting on my arse I'll risk it for a change, and if I lose I'll sit on it again and let the government take care of me."

'That's what he said when he went into it. We used to have arguments all the time about it. He still thought once he'd got in right he'd be able to work a deal and get his gambling game going. But he never did. Do you know why he never did?' Hoda stopped and beamed around challengingly at the uneasy, inquiring faces. She loved it when she came to the fairy-tale part of Hymie's story. Who would have thought that it would happen to Hymie, after all, Hymie whose imagination had never dared soar beyond the vision of himself as the brains of a thriving floating crap and poker game, with three or four hand-picked alternate locations, a smoothly organized pickup system, a cheap source of good bootleg booze, to attract the better clientele, and Hoda, all girded about in spangles, to give the deal class and provide the sundries. But who got the glass slipper after all? All those early dreams must look like pretty penny ante stuff to him now.

'That's what he always used to say to me.' Hoda, once she was sure of the continued interest of her audience, for so she interpreted what was often closer to astonishment, felt she could afford to keep them waiting. 'It's my arse I'm risking, Hoda!' She liked to repeat some of her more pungent bits of dialogue, particularly when she encountered faces like these. 'Well, when a guy says that, what can you answer? So I said "All right, it's your arse, risk it then!" So he went right ahead and he risked it, see? And you know what? Everybody's kissing it now. He's some kind of hero like. That's what they call a happy up-ending.' Hoda broke off to lead what did not turn out to be an enthusiastic round of appreciation of her wit. People are slow. 'You want to know how come he make out so well? I'll tell you. Like I say he went into foreign commerce, peddling bootleg booze to the Americans. But he was small fry in the organization until one of his boss's daughters happened to notice him; he was a big, healthy looking boy. I don't know, maybe he was lifting a case or something; anyway, whatever she saw, she liked it. And he was prudent too, you see? He had enough prudence for a change, not to knock her up before her daddy proposed to him. These big-time bootleggers are fussy about how you fool around with their kids. And now, since the big-time booze business has folded up and everybody's going legitimate, Hymie's moved down East too, and he's gone into big industry, and he's a big shot millionaire today. How do you like that?'

Hoda didn't expect an answer to her strictly rhetorical question. She didn't leave time for one, but went right on triumphantly to the moral of her story. 'So don't you ever be ashamed of your city motto, is all I can say. You take those three words, plus a little bit of this and a little bit of that, and you can end up where you won't ever have to worry about commerce, prudence and industry again, because when you're up there that high, anything you do or don't do is all right by everyone all over. And I'm the dumb bunny who tried to tell him it wasn't honest!' Again she chuckled, solo laughter, shaking her head at her own stupidity. Honest! So what? Pretty soon his grandchildren will be saying, 'My great granpaw, the old crook, he built the family fortune!' And they'll be proud of it, see? Show there was guts in the family once. Come to think of it, maybe they should change our motto up there altogether. Instead of those three words and those pictures, they should have a big, naked arse, and underneath it just two words, 'RISK IT!' Hoda laughed so hard even those of her fellow patients who were profoundly shocked, particularly the two school teachers at whom she had, by some perverse intuition, aimed most of her monologue, and who had not expected to encounter anything like this when they came to get vaccinated before their holiday trips abroad, couldn't help the momentary flutter of guilty smiles. Later, they would assure each other most emphatically that they were laughing at, not with, the degraded creature; no, not at; one is not supposed to laugh at. They hadn't actually laughed, just expressed their astonishment involuntarily. They were too horrified to laugh. No wonder one had to take one's holiday abroad. The types that one found in one's own country nowadays! It really was too bad.

'Honest, that's really what happened,' Hoda assured them earnestly. 'You don't have to believe me, but if I named names you'd believe me all right. I don't know, of course I've never been interested in anything like the bootleg racket myself, but sometimes I feel like I'll go on sitting here all my life, without anything ever happening, really, without ever getting the chance, I don't know, to risk anything, to bring me close to anything that will get me to understand something.' Hoda trailed off rather lamely, because when she tried to step outside of the confines of her story she bogged down in a shapeless mire. And yet when she told about Hymie it all seemed so simple, so full of meaning, as though it was really going to lead her somewhere. Did she envy him? She still didn't think bootlegging was honest, or really maybe worth it, which was silly. Millions of dollars and the power to thumb your nose at the world, that must be worth it. But what if Hymie had risked his arse without finding out, any more than that? Well, what did she expect him to find out, except maybe how to smoke fat cigars and take his women to fancy hotels. She wouldn't put that past Hymie, rich wife or no. What the hell more did he want? All right, so maybe she was a little jealous, and she wasn't going to pretend to herself that she wasn't. Sure, everybody cared about millions. She just hoped he remembered what he used to say when she used to try to get him and Limpy Letz to think about something else besides gambling and hanging around and hoping for the breaks to come their way, for a change. She used to try to get them to become more aware of political things, and helping other poor people, and the fight against the capitalist jackals. But Hymie just wouldn't get interested. 'When I'm rich I'll worry about helping the poor,' he used to say. 'While I'm poor I'll worry about what all the other poor people worry about, how to get rich.' Well, she just hoped that now he was rich he wasn't forgetting that promise, that was what she hoped.

When she told a story like that one about Hymie, in a place like this, she worried a little afterwards that the goyem might think that all Jews were bootleggers and millionaires. Well, to hell with them. They could see she was poor and honest, couldn't they? And anyway, whatever you said they'd think what they wanted to. She could see that when she got into arguments with them in the square. Maybe Hymie was a bootlegger, but those hadn't been Jews who'd stolen all those millions that were supposed to go into building the Provincial Parliament Buildings down town, when she was a kid; they were big shot gentiles, practising their own variety of commerce, prudence and industry. Let anyone make a crack and Hoda knew what to come back with all right, for all the good it did.

David Wevill

THE SOUNDING

Thirty-three years ago today
Hart Crane thought twice, and chose the sea.
It was a moment. Something,
A gull, a porpoise, a dory or shark
Must have seen it happen –
Something is always watching,
Though it may not understand.

Or what it understands is what it sees,
And this, too, is life –
To be known for what you are not,
A shirt-tail flare in the wind, a child's
Delight in accident : the high-wire scream.

This too is the reason it happened;
For the accumulation of alien eyes
Makes every man a stranger to himself,
Both Christ and tempter. Invoke the one,
The other's face will smack you, blind as the sea ...

You cannot have both.
You cannot *begin* again.

DEATH OF A SALESMAN

By the big Shell sign I turned left
Around the cloverleaf, and drove out north
Across the boundary river into Quebec.
Beside me a boy on a bicycle raced
Abreast of me, level with my door –

I could feel the beat of his heart against the wind
And whirl of his knees spinning against my
Engine, straining to lose
Not a foot, as I pushed the car faster.

But where the road forked
Right, into Hull, I lost him; looked back to see if he'd stopped,
Fallen, or gone in another direction.
Nowhere in sight . . . I waited a moment,
Smoked, reflected : thinking I'd betrayed him,
Not given him a chance,
All that effort lost in the wind –
Game I used to play myself to win.

But now on this road, not exulting, what had happened?
Between those tall dreaming elms at the intersection
He'd given it up, as he knew he must,
Though his heart thumped faster still, ahead of him, hot to outrace
   me.

In the mirror I see
Just the empty road behind me,
The vanished boy, and the wheels loitering back slowly . . .

And the whipped heart retreats to pride, my loss.
His victory will come when he owns a car.
His loss will follow when he wins this race.

Jack Ludwig

EINSTEIN AND THIS ADMIRER

Spiral, silver, sleek, a triumphant sunglittering worm, the diesel cleared the masking evergreens and ran free, like crystalcold water. Black pines scuttled away in the wake of the engine's progress. The dark forest fell back like a repulsed invader. The valley below the tracks revolved slowly, receding into mists and heat shimmer which transformed distant villages mysteriously, magically, as if they were at the bottom of a grey pool.

Space, Owen thought with a shake of his head, *his* space. Imagine him, in this of all centuries, retiring from the world to *contemplate light*. A lovely man. A beautiful man. Who buttoned him into that sweater? Who combed his straggly moustache straight? Those ancient glittering eyes are gay. Old man, old man, what see you in the distance? What is it about us that can make you still smile? Thou art shaggy of head and steelsharp of brain. Happy birthday, Dr Einstein. A blessing for each of your seventy-four years. Let it be written on my epitaph that I lived when you did. In the midst of this madness my life. I bow my head in awe, in worship. Ten seconds I render unto truth. Then, once more the circus.

The cigarette's long ash fell into dust on his blue serge lapel. Smudge upon smudge. A palimpsest of dying moments. His blue tie was twisted from frequent retyings into a limp straw – *but first, darlint, I must my cravat remove; and while I do that, and more, tell me, sweet, your name.* Trousers bagged to clown pantaloons. A buffoon's belly boiled over at the belt like a pudding.

'Paunch,' Owen hammed in full vibrato, 'hast turned gentle Hamlet into oxish Falstaff. Swell Valentino is but swollen Laughton. Thou art a gross intrusion on Einstein's space. Solid state beer. Clay. Yesternight I drank me twice ten spadesful. Mine own gravedigger. I did promise mother, Paunch, I'd not drink my way to the grave; crafty, I said nought about drinking the grave on to me.'

How many miles to Princeton town where my idol, Einstein, thrives?

*

What was that fine thing Kafka said about Abraham and Isaac? When God called him to the sacrifice he answered *yes, but first I must put my house in order.* And he put his house in order, and put his house in order, and never did keep his appointment with God. Princeton will come in its time; but first there is Albany, the last stop on this – if it please Thee, Sire – last tour. Only one lone versifying Cham, and a coliseumful of badgering Boswells.

Oh, the girlies will marvel, and their eyes will say it all: 'I thought you the one pictured in those first books – a Chatterton of a Keats of a Rimbaud. Jowls? Flab? A gut like a knapsack? Bloom's eyes, *poached eggs on ghost?*'

'Giving way to time, darlint, was never original with me. For m'self I would have stayed as I was early imaged. Having exemption yourself, be grateful.'

Call the roll!

Arthur Acne.

Arthur would of course be in Albany. Lank Arthur, bifocals and cheek of down: 'Sir, I hear you can be terribly insulting. Would you say something terribly insulting for us?'

Belinda Blight.

A slim volume clutched close to her slimmer bosom – perhaps something will pass from one to t'other. Belinda always seeks inscription – *wouldst be inscribed on book or bosom, Belinda?* Belinda is a librarian, her husband a pipesmoker anod with understanding. *He would understand thee, Belinda, to a bellyful.*

Clytemnestra Candor.

What seek you, Clytie, to crush or sever? She wishes only to further her lad, Narcissus, introduce her uncle, Polonius, and provide me passionate poet-tasting Natasha and goldenhaired Alice. 'To comfort you, Mr Owen, and make you feel warm.'

Zuleika Zipper.

Wool on top, promise below. Long black hair atwist to her slim lovely waist. 'I guess there's just nothing in this world I'm afraid of

doing, Idris.' *You, Zuleika, I'll love to my dying day. I'm at my best
with impossibility.*

Questioners, come, like archers. The archetype bore will shoot the
first Albany arrow.

'Mr Owen, do you think Pound is our greatest poet?'
Pence is good, Shilling is better; Pound, if not greatest, is best.
'Sir, was your early poetry influenced by Shakespeare?'
As the earth, sweet, was influenced by rain.
'Are you working on anything at this time, sir?'
Self-preservation, darlint. Fulltime.

Later, the reception. Whispers. Throats clearing. Popping corks.
Clinking glass. A swoon of blacklegged bluestockings like dreamed-
of mermaids at his feet. Sip suds and spot tonight's Thersites. One
lunatic a night was normal though excessive. Pale-eyed, unseeing,
his act rehearsed to sound spontaneous. In Syracuse Thersites had
a plantation owner's drawl – massive, curly-haired, tweeded and
unpressed. In Rochester he was stage-Irish. Thersites-Iago, stalking
to kill. Cleveland, he turned up Germanic, standing at attention, a
gymnasium student. In Chicago a wall-eyed little man in a child's
red vest, lisping ideas, suggesting all British poets were anti-semitic.

When two exhibitionists converged, a gala night. 'I could not
hate thee less, Owen, did I not hate my rival more.' Smith, Benning-
ton, Sarah Lawrence brought him out, surrounded by the long-
haired ladies of the court, pliant lovelies attuned to his fearlessness,
friendliness, frankness. Sometimes he was a painter, or a composer
of *Homage to Hiroshima*, cantata for croaking voices, viola de
gamba, jews' harp and hissing gas. Or a 'new poet' full of typo-
graphical devices, handmade papers, woodcuts, and a tin ear. Time
might mark off a day, and space a city, but a tour was continuous,
like an unbroken dream. Food superimposed on food – *The L.A.
shrimp are sweeter but the Texas shrimp need batter, and so we
thought it meeter to serve you up the latter.*

'Mr Owen,' says Mrs President-Dean-Chairman of the Department, 'we are so glad to have you.'

That, dear grey lady, is not in my contract.

And the sincere one:

'My wife and I read you long before this country took you up.'

One of each in every hamlet.

Owen stood up in the swaying car :

'Paunch,' he said with a sharp pat to his belly, 'wert thou less prominent these bones and sinews might dream up crucifixion. Silver I took from them, though my integritous heart broke even by crushing cigarette butts in their hubristic meringues. I have played both duke and king queasy-kneed from coat-to-coast, and when I return all London shall thorn me martyr. Saint Idris the Fat, who charmed the snakes out from under their rocks.'

Who paid whom?

'Fie, fie, conscience,' Owen said with a stretch and a yawn, 'a pox on thee and thy existential questioning.'

*

A blonde girl, beautiful head to one side, legs crossed, soft in blue silk flowers, long wrists and fingers, a posh woman's magazine propped on a knee. Twice she looked up, twice glanced back quickly at his picture covering the page. Her recognizing look was shy, and lovely.

An all-business photo. Shirt open at the neck, suspenders and belt tugging paunch into good behaviour like a leash on an unruly pup. The long ash on the cigarette. A curled nimbus round his head. Elsa Lanchester's eyes and mouth, hubby Laughton's everything else.

Am I as I am imaged?

Imaged. I'm aged.

Language has its own jokes. Joyce found it out. Some funny. Some cruel.

The blonde was uncomfortable. Owen realized he had been staring.

Years ago, if he had seen her, perhaps they would have flown the train before Albany. *Come into the unknown country, sweet. Our destinations cannot but be paltry.*

The train slowed. Smalltown America. Abandoned freightcars rotting on side spurs, greychalky red. Unhitched paintless wagons piled with dullsilver milkcans. Collapsed mailsacks. Peeled paint on pounded metal trunks – loveless green, grudging blue. Planks sagging on platform, a duncoloured waitingroom faded to smog, its placename gone with it. On the streets two no-colour bars with sick neon beer signs, a candle to light ways for the lone and lonely. Out of the smoky swirl of Einstein's space they rose, town after town, then whisked off into haze and distance; a dream, everything running together; his tour, stop start stop start; introduce, colourless; read, speak, joke; applaud; move; *goodbye Mrs X and tell President X I'm sorry he couldn't make it, and I will try to return to X on Xless day in the morning.*

Every poet has been a bit in advertising since old Walt first sang himself.

*

The train speeded up. A rush of red barn and its even quicker retreat. An empty silo. Steam over a pond. Dark treetops sprang up like soldiers out of trenches, then down, gone.

The blonde girl was smiling shyly.

Sweet, let's begin life. I am half in love and have yet to hear you speak.

Owen bent over her upturned face. Soft grey green eyes.

'You are Idris Owen?'

'Yes I am.'

'I'm glad we're on this train.'

'I'm glad too.'

His gentleness surprised her; him more. A hundred times before he had heard 'I have your records,' 'I've listened to you read.' His response was always harsh, rude.

Not with thee, sweet. Surely 'tis elde. No, it's almost-believed-in love.

'My husband would love to meet you. He *thought* it was you. I wasn't sure. He's in the bar car. Come join us.'

I could not share you with another, sweet. Even this short space to Albany.

'Run on ahead, dear. I've a thing or two to do.'

'You will join us. Promise.'

'I will join you.'

He offered his hand to steady her as she rose, a strand of hair falling forward on her brow. Tall, a dancer's leg and walk, toes forward. The blue silk trailed her in a puff. At the door she flashed a turn, a smile, pulled the door open, slipped out in a sway of blue.

Owen for the first time in his life experienced jilt.

Slowly he made it back to his seat.

'I shall die of the milligrubs and the sullens. Father Einstein, what say you when such creatures rise up out of space? Who would contemplate light now? Is bend or curve of time relative to this my not-my lady?'

Einstein's birthday photograph shone out from the drabness of newsprint.

'I must confess mortal weakness, sir. If my sweet were free, I would follow, and never make pilgrimage to Princeton town.'

The shaggy head and crinkly eyes were unperturbed.

Owen stood up quickly and almost ran to the bar car.

*

The blonde girl waved from the far end of the coach; the suburban man beside her inclined his head in friendly greeting. The train swung sharply round a corner. Owen lurched to one side, almost fell. A hand closed round his wrist, tugged. He fell with a slam into an empty chair.

'Glad to have you aboard, pal. What'll it be? Name's Bird – Melville – Mel.'

The blonde and her husband looked startled. Owen tried to get up again. The hand was still on his wrist.

'You ain't buttin' in, buddy boy. I ain't in a party. You wanna join your friends? They got only one place. Have a drink first. On me. My vacation. I work for this lousy railroad.'

Bird's face was pointy, not a bird's, a weasel's, eyes close together, red-rimmed, redbrown. Everything he wore was too large. Shirt gaped back from a thin ridged neck; his too-wide shoulders humped behind him like a monk's cowl.

'I spot a guy out for kicks every time. You, buddy boy. A drinker's face – I study types. You go for Schaeffer's? It's the best we got in the state – real pale, dry –'

'I'll have a short one, Mel. Budweiser –'

'Sure – hey, you're foreign, ain't you? Or from Boston. What's your name?'

'Idris Owen.'

'I married a foreigner – put 'er there, pal. Annie's from Scotland. She hates American beer. You hate American beer? Budweiser ain't really American. Eastern beer – every guy's entitled to his own opinion, eh Idris? Hey, waiter – boy – here – a Schaeffer, a Bud.'

Owen telegraphed a shrug the length of the car. The blonde girl and her husband broke out of a frown and smiled back their understanding.

Not till the waiter brought the beer did Bird let go of Owen's wrist. He fumbled two bills out of a tooled Indian-headed wallet.

'Keep the change, boy. You wonderin' about this billfold, Idris. Heather made it. Two years ago. My kid. Beautiful. Don't look like me or Annie. Well, never mind all that – here's how.'

Owen hoisted his glass toward the blonde girl and her husband.

'Aw, come on, Ide. You're drinkin' with me. You'll join them – friends of yours? Quite a piece. Get her to shake her husband. They all will. Come, clink glasses on it, buddy boy.'

Bird turned his pointy nose up, sniffed craftily, broke into a grin. If this is Einstein's universe, Owen thought, Bird is his revenge for my fickle heart.

'Your glass didn't touch mine, Ide. That's better. Chugalug. To kicks!'

Owen tried to down his in one gulp. Haste sloshed beer over his chin, droplets beaded his ash-smudged lapel.

'Take your time, Ide. Am I so lousy company you gotta rush over to them? I could understand if blondie was by her lonesome. Listen, buddy boy – what do you do for a livin'?'

'I write –'

'Honest? For what paper?'

Bird didn't wait for an answer. His chin dropped, his voice fell with it.

'Boy, you wouldn' believe it – my life, Ide. Me just a railroad workin' stiff. Not just a story. A book. Ide, you wanna see somethin'? Look.'

He shot his cuffs, shoved his wrists free of shirt. Welts, dozens of them, brown, like huge freckles, then redder circles, inflamed, and in among the red and brown, pale faded blotches. Bird brandished his fisted hands, showing off the strange markings as if Owen should read the story there.

'Annie's revenge, Ide. You married?'

'Yes.'

'To a ugly woman?'

Owen shook his head.

'Then you don't know. Drunk. To go home I got to get drunk, Ide. That's how ugly sloppy – hey, waiter, another Schaeffer – how come you ain't ready for another Bud, Idris? Waiter! A Schaeffer! Ugly, Idris. My kid's mother. I got to climb in bed. She knows I been out for kicks. Beer and barmaids. Every payday. I come home blind so's I can't see her kisser. It's dark, see, Ide. I sneak in. I figure I'm in free. Never!'

Bird's words broke into a cry.

'Never! I see the tip of her burning cigarette – too late, Ide. She's got me. Always the wrist! Bloody ugly woman – how come I ain't smashed her face in, Ide? How come I let her torture me with a burning butt?'

Owen felt his stomach heave. Bird pulled his arms back, covered each wrist carefully, as if he were applying a dressing.

'You ever been burned by fire, buddy boy?'

Over Bird's head Owen watched the blonde girl huddle with her husband. This is what hell will be, he thought: she at the other end of the car, and married: I here with Melville Bird and his Annie's mementoes. Darkening space between us unfolding – this distance, all distance. The chasm, the abyss.

'I scare you pretty good, Idris? Sorry, pal. I get carried away. Got to tell. Pretty dumb, eh, unloadin' like this on a stranger – not even an American. Can't help it. It ain't all Annie's fault, Ide. I wouldn't want you to think that. What woman could stand bein' married to Mel Bird? A angel would end up with burnin' cigarettes.'

Again it came to Owen that this tour was continuous, in space, in time. In the San Remo it began, weeks, months earlier, then washed back by the California Pacific, riding untriumphantly on lowsweeping foam, almost all the way to the San Remo where the first darkness unfolded, the woman who licked her lower lip, swooned with her eyes, now Sophia, now Gina, now Marilyn's swushin' walk – a scrapbook of a woman. Malice. Gratuitous. Her husband and two other chaps she did in that night. Better Arthur Acne and Belinda Blight anyday.

'You listenin', Idris? That jigaboo ain't brung me my beer. Half a buck tip – ain't that plenty? For a workin' stiff. That friend of yours there – the business type – musta tipped big. The jigs go to tippers like flies to sugar.'

Owen tried to drink down the beer. It tasted metallic. *Einstein, sire – hast bewizarded e'en my brew?*

The tour, the tour, it was all part of the tour. For what, money? Not all the ingots in Fort Knox could atone.

That London stripper, old, so fat, so Cockney, panting, perspiring, under pitiless lights and before pitiless voyeurs. Grunting free of a girdle, unhitching a massive damp brassiere, catching Owen's pitying eye, bending toward him from the stage, a sad wink, and a whisper.

'*'Tain't funny, ducky. But it's a livin'.*'

Her motto, his.

*

Owen tried to get to his feet. The blonde girl shook her husband's arm; across the car they both smiled 'welcome'.

'You can't go now, buddy boy. I ain't told you yet. The big story. You'll write about it some day. Not just a newspaper piece, I bet – something long. Maybe a whole book. A ball. The biggest kicks ever. Come on – just finish your beer, Ide. They'll wait. See them talkin' t'each other head to head. You wanna butt in on that, pal?'

Again Bird ducked down his head and fell into a mumble.

'I tol' you how fat Annie is, Idris. Summer kills her. Blood pressure boils her up inside. She can't catch her breath in the city. Keeps crying she wants to go to the mountains. Her old man in Scotland

took them to some kinda retreat every summer. Drunk in pubs with
her from the time she was sixteen. But it's the summer – in Albany,
buddy boy. I tell Annie no vacation this summer because I got to
work out of Chicago. Durin' the war – maybe England was like this
too. Hundreds of beautiful girls and women. Dyin' for a nice word.
Do anythin', Ide, anythin'. I don't work no Chicago, not your
buddy Mel – I go to the mountains, me and a seventeen-year-old
bride with her soldierboy on a Jap island. Annie's sweatin' puppies
in Albany and me – kicks – three weeks!'

Bird grabbed at the beer the waiter brought, gulped quickly. The
laugh starting up in him never got out. He coughed.

'Once I felt a hell of a lot better about that. You understand
it, eh buddy? How old are you? Not many years beyond me, I
bet.'

Owen shook his head in shock. Bird was probably right. Yet when
Owen first looked at the weasel face he thought, 'an ageing man'.
Younger than I am!

'It's Heather I mean to tell about – you'll know, Idris. Do you
have kids? They on to you? Heather ain't like Annie or me – not
just looks, Idris – everything – brains, class. I see it in her eyes. She
knows her old man stinks. Maybe she guessed first. But now...!'

The tour. The blonde girl. Einstein. Melville Bird. The universe
was without a handle. Owen felt the train slipping beneath his
heavy feet. The blonde girl was receding into the evening light
masking the bar car windows. A common greyness silvers everything. Soon the particles of space will crowd together into darkness
and no forms. The blonde girl's blue print flowers were colourless
in shadow, her lovely hair a black-and-white print. Face to face, she
and her husband had given up on Owen.

'Don't look there, Idris. Look here. I'm telling it to you now. The
real thing. The rest was jazz. Heather took the kicks out of kicks
– forever, buddy. Forever.'

His face in the shadows was broken. Picasso's head. The broken
cheeks of Melville Bird. The hollow eyes.

'Summer wrecked me – last summer – wrecked me, hexed me,
you lived by kicks – you know what it is, Idris? This summer I was
a nice guy, see? I sent Annie and Heather to the mountains. It was

all arranged. Heather's best girl friend, Mary – like Bardot – not particular – lies to her ma – says she's goin' to the mountains with Heather. We shack up in my place, Idris. The kid's crazy. I'm livin'. Only there's a cold spell in the mountains.'

In the greyness his small eyes showed a strange yellowness – an animal's hurt. His voice was in a whisper, but weighty, sounding in Owen's ears louder than Bird's insisting whine.

'In the middle of the night, dark, Mary and me sleeping, Annie and Heather come back – got a lift – the light goes on – Annie sees, drops her suitcase – sits down on the floor, but Heather, buddy, Heather,' Bird's fingers wrapped tightly round Owen's wrist, pressing, shaking, 'Heather sat on her ma's bag in the middle of the room, I could hardly hear her – like a baby whimperin' – "Mummy, mummy, oh oh, mummy." Not at Mary who's dressin' and beats it out the door, not at her old man who's wrapped in a sheet and pleadin', "Come on, Annie, be a good sport. Be broadminded, Annie. Yell, Annie. Burn me good, Annie. I just got lonesome, Annie." Heather, can you hear that big girl – can you see her in the bright light, Idris – on that suitcase, saying like she was a baby, "Mummy, mummy, oh – mum" – Idris, don't chicken out on me – you gotta tell me – anything – I'll take it – Annie like stone and Heather cryin' "Mummy, mummy. . ."'

Owen stood up. The blonde and her husband rose to meet him. He turned quickly to the door.

'Idris, buddy, don't go. God, man, don't go!'

The door swung open. Owen tumbled through, Bird's voice pursuing, beneath it, repeating her cry, Heather's, piping, exhausted, 'Mummy, mummy, oh, oh . . .'

*

Albany.

The tour.

The train slowed. The blonde and her husband got up out of their seats, looked Owen's way without expression. The magazine with his picture slid to the floor. They did not pick it up.

On the train platform Mel Bird alighted, the train not yet stopped; he rushed bareheaded into a swallowing crowd.

'I, sir,' Owen said to Einstein rolled up in *The Times*, 'I here shall be faithful.'

Eager, friendly faces looked up. Hands waved. The tour took over. He waved back Einstein's photo, but as he stepped into the crowd it was St Joan who flamed into his head – 'Where, where shall I lay my head this night?'

Mavis Gallant

THE ACCIDENT

I

I was tired and did not always understand what they were asking me. I borrowed a pencil and wrote:

PETER HIGGINS

CALGARY 1935 – ITALY 1956

But there was room for more on the stone, and the English clergyman in this Italian town who was doing all he could for me said, 'Is there nothing else, child?' Hadn't Pete been my husband, somebody's son? That was what he was asking. It seemed enough. Pete had renounced us, left us behind. His life-span might matter, if anyone cared, but I must have sensed even then that no one would ever ask me what he had been like. His father once asked me to write down what I remembered. He wanted to compose a memorial booklet and distribute it at Christmas, but then his wife died, too, and he became prudent about recollections. Even if I had wanted to, I couldn't have told much – just one or two things about the way Pete died. His mother had some information about him, and I had some, but never enough to describe a life. She had the complete knowledge that puts parents at a loss, finally: she knew all about him except his opinion of her and how he was with me. They were never equals. She was a grown person with part of a life lived and the habit of secrets before he was conscious of her. She said, later, that she and Pete had been friends. How can you be someone's friend if you have had twenty years' authority over him and he has never had one second's authority over you?

He didn't look like his mother. He looked like me. In Italy, on our wedding trip, we were often taken for brother and sister. Our height, our glasses, our soft myopic stares, our assurance, our sloppy

comfortable clothes made us seem to the Italians related and somehow unplaceable. Only a North American could have guessed what
our families were, what our education amounted to, and where we
had got the money to spend on travelling. Most of the time we were
just pie-faces, like the tourists in ads – though we were not as clean
as those couples, and not quite as grown-up. We didn't seem to be
married: the honeymoon in hotels, in strange beds, the meals we
shared in cheap, bright little restaurants prolonged the clandestine
quality of love before. It was still a game, but now we had infinite
time. I became bold, and I dismissed the universe: 'It was a rotten
little experiment,' I said, 'and we were given up long ago.' I had
been brought up by a forcible, pessimistic, widowed mother, and to
be able to say aloud 'we were given up' shows how far I had come.
Pete's assurance was natural, but mine was fragile, and recent, and
had grown out of love. Travelling from another direction, he was
much more interested in his parents than in God. There was a
glorious treason in all our conversations now. Pete wondered about
his parents, but I felt safer belittling Creation. My mother had let
me know about the strength of the righteous; I still thought the
skies would fall if I said too much.

What struck me about these secret exchanges was how we judged
our parents from a distance now, as if they were people we had
known on a visit. The idea that he and I could be natural siblings
crossed my mind. What if I, or Pete, or both, had been adopted? We
had been raised in different parts of Canada, but we were only children, and neither of us resembled our supposed parents. Watching
him, trapping him almost in mannerisms I could claim, I saw my
habit of sprawling, of spreading maps and newspapers on the
ground. He had a vast appetite for bread and pastries and sweet
desserts. He was easily drunk and easily sick. Yes, we were alike. We
talked in hotel rooms, while we drank the drink of the place, the
grappa or wine or whatever we were given, prone across the bed,
the bottle and glasses and the ashtray on the floor. We agreed to
live openly, without secrets, though neither of us knew what a
secret was. I admired him as I could never have admired myself. I
remembered how my mother, the keeper of the castle until now,
had said that one day – one treeless, sunless day – real life would

overtake me, and then I would realize how spoiled and silly I had always been.

The longest time he and I spent together in one place was three days, in a village up behind the Ligurian coast. I thought that the only success of my life, my sole achievement, would be this marriage. In a dream he came to me with the plans for a house. I saw the white lines on the blue paper, and he showed me the sunny Italian-style loggia that would be built. 'It is not quite what we want,' he said, 'but better than anything we have now.' 'But we can't afford it, we haven't got the capital,' I cried, and I panicked, and woke: woke safe, in a room of which the details were dawn, window, sky, first birds of morning, and Pete still sleeping, still in the dark.

II

The last Italian town of our journey was nothing – just a black beach with sand like soot, and houses shut and dormant because it was the middle of the afternoon. We had come here from our village only to change trains. We were on our way to Nice, then Paris, then home. We left our luggage at the station, with a porter looking after it, and we drifted through empty, baking streets, using up the rest of a roll of film. By now we must have had hundreds of pictures of each other in market squares, next to oleanders, cut in two by broomstick shade, or backed up, squinting, against scaly noonday shutters. Peter now chose to photograph a hotel with a cat on the step, a policeman, and a souvenir stand, as if he had never seen such things in Canada – as if they were monuments. I never once heard him say anything was ugly or dull; for if it was, what were we doing with it? We were often stared at, for we were out of our own background and did not fit into the new. That day, I was eyed more than he was. I was watched by men talking in dark doorways, leaning against the façades of inhospitable shops. I was travelling in shorts and a shirt and rope-soled shoes. I know now that this costume was resented, but I don't know why. There was nothing indecent about my clothes. They were very like Pete's.

He may not have noticed the men. He was always on the lookout for something to photograph, or something to do, and sometimes he missed people's faces. On the steep street that led back to the rail-way station, he took a careful picture of a bakery, and he bought crescent-shaped bread with a soft, pale crust, and ate it there, on the street. He wasn't hungry; it was a question of using time. Now the closed shutters broke out in the afternoon, and girls appeared – girls with thick hair, smelling of jasmine and honeysuckle. They strolled hand in hand, in light stockings and clean white shoes. Their dresses – blue, lemon, the palest peach – bloomed over rustling petticoats. At home I'd have called them cheap, and made a face at their cheap perfume, but here, in their own place, they were enravishing, and I thought Pete would look at them and at me and compare; but all he remarked was 'How do they stand those clothes on a day like this?' So real life, the grey noon with no limits, had not yet begun. I distrusted real life, for I knew nothing about it. It was the middle-aged world without feeling, where no one was loved.

Bored with his bread, he tossed it away and laid his hands on a white Lambretta propped against the curb. He pulled it upright, examining it. He committed two crimes in a second : wasted bread and touched an adored mechanical object belonging to someone else. I knew these were crimes later, when it was no use knowing, no good to either of us. The steering of the Lambretta was locked. He saw a bicycle then, belonging, he thought, to an old man who was sitting in a kitchen chair out on the pavement. 'This all right with you?' Pete pointed to the bike, then himself, then down the hill. With a swoop of his hand he tried to show he would come straight back. His pantomime also meant that there was still time before we had to be on the train, that up at the station there was nothing to do, that eating bread, taking pictures of shops, riding a bike downhill and walking it back were all doing, using up your life; yes, it was a matter of living.

The idling old man Peter had spoken to bared his gums. Pete must have taken this for a smile. Later, the old man, who was not the owner of the bike or of anything except the fat sick dog at his feet, said he had cried 'Thief!' but I never heard him. Pete tossed me his camera and I saw him glide, then rush away, past the girls who smelled of jasmine, past the bakery, down to the corner, where a policeman in white, under a parasol, spread out one arm and flexed the other and blew hard on a whistle. Peter was standing, as if he were trying to coast to a stop. I saw things meaningless now – for instance that the sun was sifted through leaves. There were trees we hadn't noticed. Under the leaves he seemed under water. A black car, a submarine with Belgian plates, parked at an angle, stirred to life. I saw sunlight deflected from six points on the paint. My view became discomposed, as if the sea were suddenly black and opaque and had splashed up over the policeman and the road, and I screamed, 'He's going to open the door!' Everyone said later that I was mistaken, for why would the Belgian have started the motor, pulled out, and *then* flung open the door? He had stopped near a change office perhaps; he had forgotten his sunglasses, or a receipt. He started, stopped abruptly, hurled back the door. I saw that, and then I saw him driving away. No one had taken his number.

Strangers made Pete kneel and then stand, and they dusted the bicycle. They forced him to walk – where? Nobody wanted him. Into a pharmacy, finally. In a parrot's voice he said to the policeman, 'Don't touch my elbow.' The pharmacist said, 'He can't stay here,' for Pete was vomiting, but weakly – a weak coughing, like an infant's. I was in a crowd of about twenty people, a spectator with two cameras round my neck. In kind somebody's living-room, Pete was placed on a couch with a cushion under his head and another under his dangling arm. The toothless old man turned up now, panting, with his waddling dog, and cried that we had a common thief there before us, and everyone listened and marvelled until the old man spat on the carpet and was turned out.

When I timidly touched Pete, trying to wipe his face with a crumpled Kleenex (all I had), he thought I was one of the strangers. His mouth was a purple colour, as if he had been in icy water. His eyes looked at me, but he was not looking out.

'Ambulance,' said a doctor who had been fetched by the policeman. He spoke loudly and slowly, dealing with idiots.

'Yes,' I heard, in English. 'We must have an ambulance.'

Everyone now inspected me. I was, plainly, responsible for something. For walking around the streets in shorts? Wasting bread? Conscious of my sweaty hair, my bare legs, my lack of Italian – my nakedness – I began explaining the true error of the day : 'The train has gone, and all our things are on it. Our luggage. We've been staying up in that village – oh, what's the name of it, now? Where they make the white wine. I can't remember, no, I can't remember where we've been. I could find it, I could take you there; I've just forgotten what it's called. We were down here waiting for the train. To Nice. We had lots of time. The porter took our things and said he'd put them on the train for us. He said the train would wait here, at the border, that it waited a long time. He was supposed to meet us at the place where you show your ticket. I guess for an extra tip. The train must have gone now. My purse is in the duffel-bag up at the the. ... I'll look in my husband's wallet. Of course that is my husband! Our passports must be on the train, too. Our traveller's checks are in our luggage, his and mine. We were just walking round taking pictures instead of sitting up there in the station. Anyway, there was no place to sit – only the bar, and it was smelly and dark.'

No one believed a word of this, of course. Would you give your clothes, your passport, your traveller's checks to a porter? A man you had never seen in your life before? A bandit disguised as a porter, with a stolen cap on his head?

'You could not have taken that train without showing your passport,' a careful foreign voice objected.

'What are you two, anyway?' said the man from the change office. His was a tough, old-fashioned movie-American accent. He was puffy-eyed and small, but he seemed superior to us, as he wore an impeccable shirt. Pete, on the sofa, looked as if he had been poisoned, or stepped on. 'What are you?' the man from the change office said again. 'Students? Americans? No? What, then? Swedes?'

I saw what the doctor had been trying to screen from me: a statue's marble eye.

The tourist who spoke the careful foreign English said, 'Be careful of the pillows.'

'What? What?' screamed the put-upon person who owned them.

'Blood is coming out of his ears,' said the tourist, halting between words. 'That is a bad sign.' He seemed to search his memory for a better English word. 'An *unfortunate* sign,' he said, and put his hand over his mouth.

III

Pete's father and mother flew from Calgary when they had my cable. They made flawless arrangements by telephone, and knew exactly what to bring. They had a sunny room looking on to rusty palms and a strip of beach about a mile from where the accident had been. I sat against one of the windows and told them what I thought I remembered. I looked at the white walls, the white satin bedspreads, at Mrs Higgins's spotless dressing case, and finally down at my hands.

His parents had not understood, until now, that ten days had gone by since Pete's death.

'What have you been doing, dear, all alone?' said Mrs Higgins, gently.

'Just waiting, after I cabled you.' They seemed to be expecting more. 'I've been to the movies,' I said.

From this room we could hear the shrieks of children playing on the sand.

'Are they orphans?' asked Mrs Higgins, for they were little girls, dressed alike, with soft pink sun hats covering their heads.

'It seems to be a kind of summer camp,' I said. 'I was wondering about them, too.'

'It would make an attractive picture,' said Pete's mother, after a pause. 'The blue sea, and the nuns, and all those bright hats. It would look nice in a dining-room.'

They were too sick to reproach me. My excuse for not having told them sooner was that I hadn't been thinking, and they didn't ask me for it. I could only repeat what seemed important now. 'I don't want to go back home just yet' was an example. I was already in the future, which must have hurt them. 'I have a girl friend in the Embassy in Paris. I can stay with her.' I scarcely moved my lips. They had to strain to hear. I held still, looking down at my fingers. I was very brown, sun streaks in my hair, more graceful than at my wedding, where I knew they had found me maladroit – a great lump of a Camp Fire Girl. That was how I had seen myself in my father-in-law's eyes. Extremes of shock had brought me near some ideal they had of prettiness. I appeared now much more the kind of girl they'd have wanted as Pete's wife.

So they had come for nothing. They were not to see him, or bury him, or fetch home his bride. All I had to show them was a still unlabelled grave.

When I dared look at them, I saw their way of being was not Pete's. Neither had his soft selective stare. Mr Higgins's eyes were a fanatic blue. He was thin and sunburned and unused to nonsense. Summer and winter he travelled with his wife in climates that were bad for her skin. She had the fair, papery colouring that requires constant vigilance. All this I knew because of Pete.

They saw his grave at the best time of day, in the late afternoon, with the light at a slant. The cemetery was in a valley between two plaster towns. A flash of the sea was visible, a corner of ultramarine. They saw a stone wall covered with roses, pink and white and near-white, open, without secrets. The hiss of traffic on the road came to us, softer than rain; then true rain came down, and we ran to our waiting taxi through a summer storm. Later they saw the station where Pete had left our luggage but never come back. Like Pete – as Pete had intended to – they were travelling to Nice. Under a glass shelter before the station I paused and said, 'That was where it happened, down there.' I pointed with my white glove. I was not as elegant as Mrs Higgins, but I was not a source of embarrassment. I wore gloves, stockings, shoes.

The steep street under rain was black as oil. Everything was reflected upside down. The neon signs of the change office and the pharmacy swam deeply in the pavement.

'I'd like to thank the people who were so kind,' said Mrs Higgins. 'Is there time? Shirley, I suppose you got their names?'

'Nobody was kind,' I said.

'Shirley! We've met the doctor, and the minister, but you said there was a policeman, and a Dutch gentleman, and a lady – you were in this lady's living-room.'

'They were all there, but no one was kind.'

'The bike's paid for?' asked Mr Higgins suddenly.

'Yes. I paid. And I paid for having the sofa cushions cleaned.'

What sofa cushions? What was I talking about? They seemed petrified, under the glass shelter, out of the rain. They could not take their eyes away from the place I had said was *there*. They never blamed me, never a word or a hidden meaning. I had explained, more than once, how the porter that day had not put our bags on the train after all but had stood waiting at the customs barrier, wondering what had become of us. I told them how I had found everything intact – passports and checks and maps and sweaters and shoes. . . . They could not grasp the importance of it. They knew that Pete had chosen me, and gone away with me, and they never saw him again. An unreliable guide had taken them to a foreign graveyard and told them, without evidence, that now he was there.

'I still don't see how anyone could have thought Pete was stealing,' said his mother. 'What would Pete have wanted with someone's old bike?'

They were flying home from Nice. They loathed Italy now, and they had a special aversion to the sunny room where I had described Pete's death. We three sat in the restaurant at the airport, and they spoke quietly, considerately, because the people at the table next to ours were listening to a football match on a portable radio.

I closed my hand into a fist and let it rest on the table. I imagined myself at home, saying to my mother, 'All right, real life has begun. What's your next prophecy?'

I was not flying with them. I was seeing them off. Mrs Higgins sat poised and prepared in her linen coat, with her large handbag, and her cosmetics and airsickness tablets in her dressing case, and her diamond maple leaf so she wouldn't be mistaken for an American, and her passport ready to be shown to anyone. Pale gloves lay folded over the clasp of the dressing case. 'You'll want to go to your own people, I know,' she said. 'But you have a home with us. You mustn't forget it.' She paused. I said nothing, and so she continued, 'What are you going to do, dear? I mean, after you have visited your friend. You mustn't be lonely.'

I muttered whatever seemed sensible. 'I'll have to get a job. I've never had one and I don't know anything much. I can't even type – not properly.' Again they gave me this queer impression of expecting something more. What did they want? 'Pete said it was no good learning anything if you couldn't type. He said it was the only useful thing he could do.'

In the eyes of his parents was the same wound. I had told them something about him they hadn't known.

'Well, I understand,' said his mother, presently. 'At least, I think I do.'

They imagine I want to be near the grave, I supposed. They think that's why I'm staying on the same side of the world. Peter and I had been waiting for a train; now I had taken it without him. I was waiting again. Even if I were to visit the cemetery every day, he would never speak. His last words had not been for me but to a policeman. He would have said something to me, surely, if everyone hadn't been in such a hurry to get him out of the way. His mind was quenched, and his body out of sight. 'You don't love with your soul,' I had cried to the old clergyman at the funeral – an offensive remark, judging from the look on his face as he turned it aside. Now I was careful. The destination of a soul was of no interest. The death of a voice – now, that was real. The Dutchman suddenly covering his mouth was horror, and a broken elbow was true pain. But I was careful; I kept this to myself.

'You're our daughter now,' Pete's father said. 'I don't think I want you to have to worry about a job. Not yet.' Mr Higgins happened to know my family's exact status. My father had not left us well off, and my mother had given everything she owned to a sect that did not believe in blood transfusions. She expected the end of the world, and would not eat an egg unless she had first met the hen. That was Mr Higgins's view.

'Shirley must work if that's what she wants to do,' Mrs Higgins said softly.

'I do want to!' I imagined myself, that day, in a river of people pouring into subways.

'I'm fixing something up for you, just the same,' said Mr Higgins hurriedly, as if he would not be interrupted by women.

Mrs Higgins allowed her pale forehead to wrinkle, under her

beige veil. Was it not better to struggle and to work, she asked. Wasn't that real life? Would it not keep Shirley busy, take her mind off her loss, her disappointment, her tragedy, if you like (though 'tragedy' was not an acceptable way of looking at fate), if she had to think about her daily bread?

'The allowance I'm going to make her won't stop her from working,' he said. 'I was going to set something up for the kids anyway.'

She seemed to approve; she had questioned him only out of some prudent system of ethics.

He said to me, 'I always have to remember I could go any minute, just like that. I've got a heart.' He tapped it – tapped his light suit. 'Meantime you better start with this.' He gave me the envelope that had been close to his heart until now. He seemed diffident, made ashamed by money, and by death, but it was he and not his wife who had asked if there was a hope that Pete had left a child. No, I had told him. I had wondered, too, but now I was sure. 'Then Shirley is all we've got left,' he had said to his wife, and I thought they seemed bankrupt, having nothing but me.

'If that's a check on a bank at home, it might take too long to clear,' said his wife. 'After all Shirley's been through, she needs a fair-sized sum right away.'

'She's had that, Betty,' said Mr Higgins, smiling.

I had lived this : three round a table, the smiling parents. Pete had said, 'They smile, they go on talking. You wonder what goes on.'

'How you manage everything you do without a secretary with you all the time I just don't know,' said his wife, all at once admiring him.

'You've been saying that for twenty-two years,' he said.

'Twenty-three, now.'

With this the conversation came to an end and they sat staring, puzzled, not overcome by life but suddenly lost to it, out of touch. The photograph Pete carried of his mother, that was in his wallet when he died, had been taken before her marriage, with a felt hat all to one side, and an organdie collar, and Ginger Rogers hair. It was easier to imagine Mr Higgins young – a young Gary Cooper. My father-in-law's blue gaze rested on me now. Never in a million years would he have picked me as a daughter-in-law. I knew that;

I understood. Pete was part of him, and Pete, with all the girls he had to choose from, had chosen me. When Mr Higgins met my mother at the wedding, he thanked God, and was overheard being thankful, that the wedding was not in Calgary. Remembering my mother that day, with her glasses on her nose and a strange borrowed hat on her head, and recalling Mr Higgins's face, I thought of words that would keep me from laughing. I found, at random, 'threesome', 'smother', 'gambling', 'habeas corpus', 'sibling' . . .

'How is your mother, Shirley?' said Mrs Higgins.

'I had a letter. . . . She's working with a pendulum now.'

'A pendulum?'

'Yes. A weight on a string, sort of it makes a diagnosis – whether you've got something wrong with your stomach, if it's an ulcer, or what. She can use it to tell when you're pregnant and if the baby will be a girl or a boy. It depends whether it swings north-south or east-west.'

'Can the pendulum tell who the father is?' said Mr Higgins.

'They are useful for people who are afraid of doctors,' said Mrs Higgins, and she fingered her neat gloves, and smiled to herself. 'Someone who won't hear the truth from a doctor will listen to any story from a woman with a pendulum or a piece of crystal.'

'Or a stone that changes colour,' I said. 'My mother had one of those. When our spaniel had mastoids it turned violet.'

She glanced at me then, and caught in her breath, but her husband, by a certain amount of angry fidgeting, made us change the subject. That was the one moment she and I were close to each other – something to do with quirky female humour.

Mr Higgins did not die of a heart attack, as he had confidently expected, but a few months after this Mrs Higgins said to her maid in the kitchen, 'I've got a terrible pain in my head. I'd better lie down.' Pete's father wrote, 'She knew what the matter was, but she never said. Typical.' I inherited a legacy and some jewellery from her, and wondered why. I had been careless about writing. I could not write the kind of letters she seemed to want. How could I write to someone I hardly knew about someone else who did not exist? Mr Higgins married the widow of one of his closest friends – a woman six years older than he. They travelled to Europe for their wedding trip. I had a temporary job as an interpreter in a department store. When my father-in-law saw me in a neat suit, with his name, HIGGINS, fastened to my jacket, he seemed to approve. He was the only person then who did not say that I was wasting my life and my youth and ought to go home. The new Mrs Higgins asked to be taken to an English-speaking hairdresser, and there, under the roaring dryer, she yelled that Mr Higgins may not have been Pete's father. Perhaps he had been, perhaps he hadn't, but one thing he was, and that was a saint. She came out from under the helmet and said in a normal voice, 'Martin doesn't know I dye my hair.' I wondered if he had always wanted this short, fox-coloured woman. The new marriage might for years have been in the maquis of his mind, and of Mrs Higgins's life. She may have known it as she sat in the airport that day, smiling to herself, touching her unstained gloves. Mr Higgins had drawn up a new way of life, like a clean will with everyone he loved cut out. I was trying to draw up a will, too, but I was patient, waiting, waiting for someone to tell me what to write. He spoke of Pete conventionally, in a sentimental way that forbade any feeling. Talking that way was easier for both of us. We were both responsible for something – for surviving, perhaps. Once he turned to me and said defiantly, 'Well, she and Pete are together now, aren't they? And didn't they leave us here?'

John Newlove

INDIAN WOMEN

Saturday night
kamsack is
something
to lie about,

the streets full
of indians and
doukobours,
raw men and

fat women (watch
out for
the women people
said, all the men

do is drink
beer and play
pool but watch
out for those

indian women),
cars
driving up
and down the

main street
from the new
high school

building to
the cn
station and
back

again, paved
road where
the rest were
only oiled

gravel in
the good
old summer

time, in the good
old summertime,
son, when
everybody who

was nobody was
out on the street
with a belly

full talking
to beat
hell and
the heat.

Norman Levine

OTTAWA LOWER TOWN

From *Canada Made Me*

I like the lower towns, the place across the tracks, the poorer streets
not far from the river. They represent failure, and for me failure
here has a strong appeal. On my first day out I walked along St
Patrick Street. Slush, mud, streetcar tracks on the road. And slush
and snow and mud on the sidewalk. Between the sidewalk and the
road, low hard grey-black snowbanks. Every time a car or a truck
went by it splashed the dirty melted water from the road on to the
sidewalk. It was strangely quiet, flat, and drab. The only optimistic
patches were the large billboards standing on stilts in the vacant
lots with their doll faces and yard-long smiles advertising soft
drinks, cars, cigarettes, and shoe polish. Sometimes a large gaily-
painted car, or a truck, drove by, crunching the snow and the slush
and splashing water. Or a red streetcar, like a mechanical goose,
swayed along the tracks. Otherwise it looked like a cemetery; only
it was second-hand, washed out. And the drabness was heightened
by the intensity of the harsh light and the freshness of the air that
I could feel cold in my throat.

The houses were not built to last. The owners who lived away did
not trouble about repairs for the rents were too low. And those who
lived here and owned their houses had moved in too late. They were
run down, sinking in the ground. Solemn boxes with wooden
verandas. A dull brown dark green broken by a narrow yard that
widened as it skirted behind the house. Then another repetition of
wooden veranda and shabby box. I saw two houses in no worse
condition than those beside it being pulled down beside a filling
station to make room for a second-hand car market. There was no
outward sign of possession or pride. A few had their outside walls
painted so that the wood looked like imitation bricks. But the paint

had worn off. There was a bit of land, in front, separating the veranda from the sidewalk. Around this bit were the small green boiler pipes for railings. And inside the railings, an old boiler, part of its centre cut out for a flower box, rested on a pair of rough wooden trestles, all smothered in snow. Some houses had in their front rooms a grocery, a tailor, a laundry, a barber shop, Chez Maurice ('no free reading'). While in the back, behind the curtain, lived the family. You could tell these houses by the tin signs nailed to their sides or hanging on a piece of iron, creaking in the wind, giving the name of the owner and advertising Pepsi-Cola, Sweet Caporal, Alouette, Kik. Most of the signs were in French.

Towards the river. Down King Edward Avenue. Black trees in the middle, their branches dripping. Dirty snowbanks around the trees. The best place to walk was on the road. At the corner of Guigues there was a large three-storey red brick house, squatting, very ugly. A *Chambre à Louer* sign nailed to the outside door. The double windows were few and small so that the massiveness of the brick was exaggerated. It looked like a house afraid of the light. On a slope between the side of the house and the sidewalk were two tin-covered wooden doors lying flat on the ground. They lead to the cellar. I remembered how I used to slide on these doors in winter. And skate in between the trees of the Boulevard after a rain when it froze at night and the ice weighed the trees over until the branches touched the ground like enormous silver brooms; if a wind came along it set them crackling. Now I could hear only French around me. On another street a house was practically smothered by the snow. Newspapers covered up empty windows. Rocking chairs on the verandas were thawing out. And parked in front of these drab wooden shacks were the large bright cars with the huge back fins with three sets of tail lights.

By the small park, the sour tunnel, the Black Bridge, the river was frozen hard. Trees were black. The snow piled high in the park made the green benches small and sunken. All around the snow was thawing, losing its whiteness and its solidarity. The surface texture was that of a watermelon flesh, only black and dirty as if someone had blown coal dust across. Boys in windbreakers and flying boots walked by. Some children were playing with alleys in front of a veranda. Three others dressed warmly in winter helmets stood on the road. One of them was counting out

> My mother and your mother
> Were hanging out the clothes.
> My mother gave your mother
> A punch in the nose.
> What colour was the blood?

The finger pointed, a child replied. White.

> W-H-I-T-E spells white and you
> Are straight out of this here game.

Then I came back by the frozen river, passed the convent, the ice-yards, the Good Shepherd Laundry, water running from the roofs. Crossed over drab St Patrick Street, by the Catholic church, the French supermarket; and I was back to where one had grown up.

*

A *letter from Morocco*: You ask why I left Canada. Well, in the first place, I think I left for the sake of a change. As far as I can remember I intended to return and settle, and then I gradually forgot about it. Any emotional feelings or ties I had to Canada were to various small regions, but I had become attached to other small regions where I was, and these counted more for being near by. On the whole, I don't think Canada ever excited any warm or patriotic feelings in me; perhaps it did once when I was a child, but the feelings died easily. In general it was just a thing that issued postage stamps and dollar bills, and set up customs offices next to American customs offices. Mind you, I have no rancour, I don't feel that Canada has cheated me of anything, I feel quite kindly disposed towards it. But I find that in the place where I am expected to have patriotic feelings there is a little void. This is an entirely personal deficiency, and has nothing to do with Canada: I have discovered many such little voids in myself as I have grown older, and I don't expect other people to have them as well. But when I go back to Canada, and I hear people waxing enthusiastic over the country (generally, when I am there, a little bit aggressively, with little glances out of the corners of their eyes challenging me to contradict them), the same kind of yawn comes over me as when someone tells me about his stamp collection. Then, on a purely practical level, the climate is atrocious, except for a few months of the year, and there is absolutely nothing one can do in Canada, except go fishing, that one can't do better, or more profitably, or more comfortably, or more easily, elsewhere.

Most people live in the country they were born in because it is much easier for them to do so. The problems of language and earning a living in a foreign country are generally insuperable for the great mass of people unless they are forced out by famine or wars, etc. Moreover, most people are conservative, and prefer their national customs, their national dishes – their culture, in a word. For my part, most of these difficulties of moving don't exist. I enjoy learning foreign languages and I have a personal predilection towards the exotic. And coming from a country which has no culture (ours is still a mixture of other cultures which hasn't fused into anything separate, and the elements of the mixture are principally Anglo-Saxon and Scotch, hence rather dreary) it is perhaps easier for me to find myself at home quickly in a new culture. And since the world is still reasonably large and reasonably various, it is obvious that a rootless person such as myself, if he looks about for a while, will find somewhere that suits his personal taste better than the place where, through no choice of his own, he was born.

Then there is another, purely personal reason (I guess there are a million more, of varying degrees of importance) why I don't seriously intend ever to live in Canada. It represents my childhood. And I can trace innumerable actions, likes and dislikes to a revulsion against my childhood.

SLAUGHTERHOUSE

Next morning I walked from the hotel to Portage and waited for a bus to take me to St Boniface. At the bus stop the man beside me kept repeating, 'It's a dirty wind. It's a dirty wind.' It was a cold wind that lifted the loose sand up from the sidewalk and the road and flung it into your face. I asked him how long it would take to get to the stockyards. He said about fifteen or twenty minutes.

'Going to work there?'
'No.'
'Where you from?'
'Ottawa.'

'I haven't been East for eighteen years. We've had a cold winter here. It began with a snowfall on Hallowe'en.'

The bus came and we got on. We crossed over two bridges with muddy water flowing underneath. 'There's going to be floods when they break up,' the man said. Then he kept repeating the French names of the streets in St Boniface. Had I heard of Louis Riel? I said I had. He was buried here. Then the bus came to flat open country. I saw a large chimney stack behind a railway siding. The man told me to get off here. I walked over the railway tracks towards the stack and the building beside it; the ground was frozen.

What I expected was a smell of some sort, but there wasn't any. A truck stood underneath a long chute that came from a brick building and a man was carefully packing hides. He stood on top of the pile in the back of the truck and carefully put them in their place as if he was packing into a suitcase clothes that he did not want creased.

I was supposed to meet my guide at ten o'clock in the staffhouse cafeteria but something had gone wrong with my watch during the night and when I entered the modern, well-lit, clean building, the clock in the wall said 9.15. There was a sign outside the cafeteria: CONDUCTED TOURS EVERY DAY AT 2 P.M. Inside the cafeteria a few men in white overalls were sitting by the small tables. There were silk-screen prints of Canadian landscapes on the wall. A couple of waitresses stood behind the chrome-and-glass counter.

My guide was a short stocky young man in his twenties with curly blond hair and glasses. He called me Norm from the start, I called him Gerry. This show of friendliness is odd until you realize it means nothing, it's a convention. He led me into a room where white coats were hanging. I put one on over my clothes. I asked him who came for these two o'clock conducted tours. 'Lots of all sorts. Mostly out of town. Some farmers who want to see what happens to their animals. And women's auxiliary, Kiwanis, Jaycees . . .'

We walked outside and around the building until we came to wooden pens. There were some pigs in one; in another, calves. I could hear the sound of cows bellowing from inside the building. 'These pigs will be killed at two this afternoon,' Gerry said. 'The pens are not cleaned during the winter, the shit's frozen solid. There's about five feet of shit out there now.' We walked through a large barn. Cows bellowed from the far end of the barn, calves huddled in wooden pens along one side. On the other side, in a large enclosure with bales of hay were two very clean and white goats with two kids. 'Wouldn't they make a good picture?' Gerry said. The scene belonged to something one remembered from a child's illustrated book. 'They lead the sheep up the ramp. The sheep will follow the goats without making a fuss. Then once up, we take the goats away and bring them back here, and they bring the next lot of sheep up the ramp.'

We walked up a steel ramp covered with dry manure. At the top there was a narrow pen with steel gates, room enough for the animal lengthwise. Four cows were goaded into this pen, pressed tight, their heads twisted back over the other cow's back. They were controlled by the jabs from an electric poker which a man used on their rumps. The steel gate behind them closed. Then the man with the electric poker got them into the killing block. A deep wooden rectangular box, enough to take two cows at a time. 'They're scared alright,' Gerry said. 'They can smell blood.' A man stood above them on a steel ramp. He swung a pole-axe above his head, stunned one, then the other. They fell down heavily. Then the floor the cows had been standing on was quickly lowered down to the concrete floor below. They tumbled out on their sides, their legs twitching. A man put a manacle around one of the back legs, pressed a button with his left hand, and hoisted the animal up to a rail near the ceiling, legs up, head hanging limply down. Then, with his right hand, he carefully, without splashing himself, cut the cow's throat.

Another man put a bucket under the throat to catch the blood. The animal began to move upside down as the small wheel to which its back leg was attached began to travel on the rail by the ceiling at a steady slow pace. As soon as that bucket was full he replaced it with another. And full buckets of blood, with the crimson froth on top like candy floss, were taken away slowly on another rail to another part of the building.

I'm certain one could make a surrealistic film in a slaughterhouse on the killing floor without resort to any trickery. Just recording.

A few inches from where I was standing, heads, like in a Cocteau film, severed at the neck, without horns, eyes bulging, tongues hanging out, were going around like the figures of some old medieval clock. Beside it the full buckets of blood were carried on their hooks. Along the walls of the building were the carcasses, spaced a few feet apart, in various stages of being reduced. Some had the hide still on, some without their heads, some with their legs off. Carcasses continually moving slowly to the pace of those small turning wheels on the rails by the ceiling. Away from the walls were separate turn-tables with their own rails and hooks hanging down. Each had either a carcass or a cow's head. Blood was like water on the concrete floor. The men were covered in it. They each had one job to do in dismembering the animal. A machine cut bone, another emptied the stomach, a machine like a saw pulled the hide off, another cut the horns, another cut the animal in two. It went on, around the room, the pulling, the tearing, the cutting, the cage dropping to the floor, the twitching feet, the slash with the knife, the frothy crimson buckets. . . . At the end of the room they put the carcasses in shrouds so that the bright yellow fat wouldn't harden and bubble.

Suddenly a pistol shot and everyone on the floor stopped working. The man with the pole-axe stood above us grinning. 'That mocky,' Gerry said. 'He's only supposed to hit the steel to let the men know when he's finished knocking. But he does it when he wants to scare us.' We stood and watched. To Gerry it was a kind of sport. 'Now, I'll show you murder,' he said.

He led me to the far side of the floor where a tall figure with a thick middle and stooped rounded shoulders, in rubber boots and glasses and wearing a hat, was sharpening a knife very conscientiously on a small stone. The knife was long and thin, and the man wiped it spotlessly clean with a piece of cloth. 'He's a Rabbi,' Gerry said. 'This is where they do the kosher killing. I call it murder.'

Six calves were hanging head down by a back leg from a pulley. They kicked with their remaining free legs. They swung. They bleated. Then the man with the knife stepped up to a small wooden platform and with one stroke cut the throats of each animal. As soon as the six were done another man moved the hanging animals behind a steel partition. The blood splashed down on the tin like rain on a tin roof in a thunderstorm. Some still kicked with their legs. Then the man with the glasses washed the knife and began to sharpen it again. Another six calves were hoisted up.

Gerry took me to another room on this floor. He had to unlock the door. On the floor lay about twenty or thirty skin-enclosed bundles. They looked like bundles of dirty laundry tied together or like huge ears blown up. Some had a small dark head hanging out of the skin, a small calf's head with its tongue fully out. One dark calf lay completely out of the skin bag, its wet fur standing up in tufts. They were the unborn calves taken out of the slaughtered cows. 'You realize, Norm, you're getting things we don't show to others, like this room. I've got two of their skins at home. Their hide is worth more than the whole hide of a cow.' They lay on the concrete floor, blown up skinbags, a soft green and white and the small dark head sticking out with its tongue. Many of the skin bags were unbroken and you could see the dark shadows where the dead calf lay inside.

In another room men and women were by tables cleaning the guts to be used for casings. Gerry stopped and became sentimental. 'If I have an hour or so free from my desk I usually go and play with the guts here. I like the feel of them. I worked in a mortuary before coming here and I always wanted to get hold of the guts, but I couldn't. I knew that here was a stiff lying just full of guts that I couldn't get hold of. Have you ever had guts go through your hands? It's a wonderful feeling.'

In another room girls were sitting on chairs by small tables in straight rows like a classroom by conveyor belts which carried sliced pieces of bacon. Their job was to put the bacon slices in cellophane-wrapped packages, in pound weights. A girl would take some bacon that came along the belt. On a clock beside her was a simple scale balance that showed if she was short or over. A snip of the scissors and a quick wrapping up. It was all done quickly and without concentration. They sat there, hands and eyes working mechanically while they talked.

'See them gas away,' Gerry said. 'You know what they're talking about? If they got shagged last night. All of them are easy as any-

thing. A bunch of dopes, doing it for free; they haven't even finished public school. Yesterday I pulled the pants off this one.' He
pointed to a young heavily-built girl with blonde close-cropped hair.
'She's got the biggest tits I've seen, but the smallest nipples. If you
like, come back to my room and you can see what's going on in the
cars in the car-park with my binoculars. I'm going with one in the
cafeteria and a friend of mine is going with one in the gut room.
They've asked us to take our holidays with them so we're using
their cars. We'll drive down to California.' He grinned. 'It's really
a shagging holiday.'

I saw lambs hanging upside down. The man had stopped knocking cows and was on the other floor sticking pigs and sheep. I came
down the ramp with the dry manure. The two kids were playing
on the bales of hay; a cow was being brought in by truck. . . . After
it was over Gerry said, 'Come on to the cafeteria; you're entitled to
a free cup of coffee on the company.' The waitress who served us
was in her late twenties, tall, stout, fat shapeless legs, a large
bosom, and a vacant expression in her face. She reminded me of a
docile cow. 'I'm getting into her for my holiday,' he said. She
waddled around us swishing her behind slowly and sensually and
with a certain contempt.

When I came out it was snowing and the wind was blowing the
snow hard. The truck was still underneath the chute, the man still
carefully packing the hides on top.

It was only later, back in Winnipeg, passing a butcher-shop and
seeing a woman inside haggling over the price for a piece of meat
that the entire morning clicked into place.

I cannot get sentimental over animals.* But I did not eat that
day. There was the physical revulsion in seeing the commercial side

* I remember that year in Brighton when we lived in a large house on the
side of a hill. Everyone else in the Close had a large car and a gardener. They
went with the place and with the kind of people who retired here. About
once a month there would be a knock at the front door and an elderly
woman, well preserved and well dressed, brought us a sack from a car. Could
we fill it up with our old things or anything that we didn't want? Then
they would sell it. To help look after some dogs. At the time of the Hun-
garian uprising we had two sacks left by the door. One was to collect for the
Hungarians; the other for dogs.

of killing, the mass slaughter, the horror, not at the cutting of the throat or the blood, but in the detachment, the way a particular cow was quickly lost sight of in the efficiency of those machines, as other cows kept following on. But though I didn't feel like eating that day, I knew by tomorrow I would get hungry, the stomach would demand to be filled, and on a hungry stomach sensitivity is a luxury one cannot afford. And part of the nausea belonged to something else: to Moo-cows, Baa-lambs, Chook-Chooks, that were part of one's childhood, that saw them only in the field, on a farm. And later bringing the chickens to have their throats cut; it made sense when the next day we had them for supper. It was this remoteness that allowed one to feel nauseated watching, and that allowed one to forget. There was no connexion that one could feel personally. The food that one eats seems so remote from the slaughterhouse. One hates to be reminded, that there is a connexion. One would rather not know how much of living is just feeding, for the only time you are reminded is when you are hungry.

The robin in the garden followed me, as I cut the lawn, and snapped up the insects and flies and the small worms. Only after it had its fill, did it fly on to the low branch of the apple tree and begin to sing.

In the late spring, in Mousehole, our landlord, a kind man with a beard who lived off the land and had geese and ducks, killed a drake for us to eat. He showed me the insides. So much was sex organs and intestines.

You forget why the killing goes on, how one animal lives by devouring another: when your stomach is filled, then you are tricked into all these moralizing sentimental judgements about the taking of life. I'm sure that if I had not eaten that morning, when Gerry offered me those hot dogs and slices of ham from the conveyor belt and those pieces of baloney as we were going through, not only would I have gladly eaten them but I would have stored some away in my pocket for later use. And if one has to kill, to be cruel, I would rather it was to animals than human beings.

Mordecai Richler

DINNER WITH ORMSBY-FLETCHER

From *St Urbain's Horseman, a novel-in-progress*

Bad day at court, but – no fear, Jake – soon Ormsby-Fletcher, his
consolation, would arrive, remark on the weather, and clap his black
bowler down on the monk's bench in the outer hall; then the two
of them would retire to the study to mull over the day's defeats and
plan tomorrow's campaign.

Ormsby-Fletcher.

When it became obvious, even to Jake, that there would be no
stopping the girl's complaint and that the case would actually go to
court, his first embarrassed thought was that he did not want a
Jewish lawyer; no twisting, eloquent point-scorer who would outwit
judge and prosecutor, eat witnesses, alienate the jury, shine so foxily
in court, in fact, as to ultimately lose him the case. No. Say what
you like about the *goyim*, they had their uses. For his defence Jake
required an upright plodding WASP; and in his mind's eye, swishing cognac around in his glass night after night, Jake methodically
fabricated his Identikit champion. He would be unaggressively
handsome, after the fashion of the British upper classes, that is to
say, somewhat wanting, like an underdeveloped photograph. Without salt. He would commute, Jake imagined, from a detached in an
unspoiled village in Surrey (nr. Guildford, 40 min. Waterloo), where
on weekends he tended to the rose bushes and fought off the en-
croaching crabgrass with his wife. (If it isn't too much to hope for,
Jake thought, fighting down the tears, we'll swop cuttings, my *goy*
and I.) *England worries him.* Raised on the King James Version,
lemon squash, *Tom Brown's Schooldays*, golliwogs, Daddy's Ceylon
tea shares, duty, debentures, and chocolate digestives, he would find
today's swingers perplexing. He would approve of the court's decision on *Lady Chatterley's Lover*, but would argue – Jake hoped –

that issuing the novel in paperback, thereby making it available to untutored minds, was going too far, like OBEs for the Beatles. He would have been to a good but minor public school, doing his national service with a decent regiment, going on from there to Pembroke, Cambridge (his father's college), and then to read law at Lincoln's Inn. He would not have crammed at university because his nagging parents had never had the chance oi and were doing without oi oi : he would have muddled through to a degree. He was a Tory, but no Blimp. While he felt, for instance, that black Africans were not quite ready for self-government, he could jolly well understand their point of view. His wife – 'the vicar's daughter', Jake decided aloud – bought a joint (tenderized) for Sunday and cleverly made it do (shepherd's pie, curry) until Tuesday. Waste not, want not. Instead of dinner on Wednesday they got by with high tea, cucumber and fish-paste sandwiches, bread and jam, while he helped his son with his Latin prep and she read *Mary Poppins* aloud to their little girl. Mmnnn . . . I know, Jake added, clapping his hands, there is no central heating because they both agreed it was unhealthful. When she was having her menstrual period he was not so boorishly selfish as to hint at alternative forms of gratification : instead he came home bearing boxes of chocolates.

My *goy's* wife, Jake thought, drives him to his commuters' train each morning, both of them fastened into their seat belts, and – Jake added – if he makes a telephone call from my house will offer me fourpence. If she has stunning breasts she would keep them decently bound and cashmered : similarly, if her bottom was ravishingly round it would be broadened with Yorkshire puddings and squared into a tweed skirt.

We'll chat about politics, Jake thought, my *goy* and I, agreeing that while Harold Wilson was too clever by half and George Brown wasn't the sort of chap you'd send to see the Queen, they were, after all, entitled to their innings. Jake's solicitor would no more fiddle the tax inspector than cheat his mother at bezique; and what about the *Times* crossword? Yes, yes, of course he does it. Faithfully.

Perfect !

But where, oh where, Jake wondered, consumed with ardour for his image, will I find such a limp prick? And then he remembered

Ormsby-Fletcher. Stiff-collared, cherub-mouthed Ormsby-Fletcher, whom he had met at one of Connell's parties, finding him as abandoned as an empty bottle in a corner of the living-room. 'I daresay,' Ormsby-Fletcher said, 'I'm the only one here not connected with the arts. I'm Adele's cousin, you see.'

So Jake located Ormsby-Fletcher and phoned him at his office. 'Mr Ormsby-Fletcher,' he said, 'I'm afraid you won't remember me. This is Jacob Hersh —'

'Indeed I do.'

'I'm in trouble.'

'I'm afraid I don't handle divorces myself, but I'd be glad to refer —'

'What about, um, criminal law?'

'I see,' Ormsby-Fletcher said, faltering, retreating, already contriving excuses, Jake thought.

'Couldn't we meet,' Jake cut in. 'Informally, if you like?'

They met at a pub, Jake arriving first, showily carrying a *Times* and *Punch*. 'I fancy a long drink myself,' Jake said, already tight. 'What about you?' A gin, he said; and then Jake suffered chitchat and fortified himself with uncounted doubles before he risked saying, 'This is probably not your cup of tea, Mr Ormsby-Fletcher. I shouldn't have troubled you. You see, it's a sex charge.'

The blood went from Ormsby-Fletcher's strawberry-coloured cheeks and he drew his long legs in from under the table, tight as he could to his chair.

'Hold on. I'm not a queer. It's —'

'Perhaps if you begin at the beginning.'

Brilliant. So Jake started to talk, circling close to repellent details, backpedalling furiously, hemming, hawing, hinting obliquely, retreating from the excruciating moment he would have to get down to concrete details, the crux, which would oblige him, just for openers, to use words such as penis and penetration. . . . Or, Jake wondered, hesitating again, was he expected to lapse into a gruffer idiom, something more colonial. And then Ormsby-Fletcher, permanently endearing himself to Jake, volunteered, 'I see. So then he led her into your room, and on her own initiative, she took hold of your roger . . .'

My roger, of course. 'Yes,' Jake said, igniting with drunken delight, 'then the bitch took my roger in her hand ...'

'But if that's the case, Mr Hersh –'

Jake clapped his hand on Ormsby-Fletcher's shoulder and locked him in a manful, heartfelt look. ' "Jake",' he said.

' "Eric",' Ormsby-Fletcher responded without hesitation. Unburdening himself now, Jake released the sewer gates. Careful not to incriminate Harry, he told all. Well, almost.

'I see.'

'Well, Eric?'

'Can't promise anything, you understand, but I'll see what I can do.'

'That's good enough for me,' Jake said, compromising him, he hoped.

'I suggest you come to our chambers first thing tomorrow morning,' Ormsby-Fletcher said, and he called for a round for the road.

'Sorry. No more for me,' Jake said, beaming. 'I'm driving, you see.'

It was, as it turned out, the first of a seemingly endless run of conferences at chambers, with ruinously expensive barristers, and at Jake's house.

Jake, doting on Ormsby-Fletcher, came to anticipate his needs. Five sugars and milk heated hot enough to make a fatty skin for his coffee. Brandy, yes, but not three fingersful ostentatiously sloshed into a snifter : rather, a splash, British-style, sufficient to dampen the bottom of the glass. Ormsby-Fletcher liked to relax with a cigar and natter about the present state of this island. 'I daresay, to your way of looking, we are hopelessly inefficient ...'

'But living here,' Jake protested, looking deep, 'is so much more civilized than it is in America. After all, man doesn't live by time-motion studies and computers alone, does he?'

Ormsby-Fletcher asked, 'Is it really true that corporations interview and grade executives' wives?'

'It's ghastly. Diabolical,' Jake said, shaking his head. 'I simply wouldn't know where to begin ...'

Ormsby-Fletcher enjoyed sucking Smarties as he pondered his brief. Hooked on glitter, he liked to think Jake was on intimate terms with the stars, and Jake, lying outrageously, cribbing gossip from *Variety*, more than obliged. 'Bloody Marlon,' Jake began one evening, unaware that Nancy had just entered the room, 'has done it again. He –'

'Marlon who?' Nancy asked.

'The baby's crying.'

Suddenly Ormsby-Fletcher said, 'If it doesn't sound too dreary, I wonder, well, Pamela thought if you had nothing better on, perhaps you'd both drive out to our place to dinner on Saturday night?'

'Why that would be absolutely super,' Jake said.

But he wakened ill-tempered, dubious, and he phoned Ormsby-Fletcher at his office. 'Eric, about Saturday night –'

'You needn't explain. Something's come up.'

'No. Not at all. It's, well – your wife – Pamela – does she know what I'm charged with?' Would I disgust her? he wanted to say.

'You mustn't even think like that, Jake. We'll expect you at eight.'

Wednesday morning a postcard came, written in the most ornate hand and signed Pamela Ormsby-Fletcher. Were there any foods that didn't agree with either of them? Now there's breeding for you, Jake thought, and he wrote back to say all foods agreed with them.

The next morning Ormsby-Fletcher phoned. 'It's just, ah, well, are there any dietary laws...?'

No, no, Jake said. Not to worry.

But swinging out on to the Kingston bypass on Saturday night, Nancy seated in the car beside him, he began to worry more than a little himself. She must remember, he warned, not to say shit or balls. 'And let's not have that smart-assed argument about pantos and homosexuality, the principal boy being a girl...'

The Ormsby-Fletcher's cottage, overlooking the common in an unspoiled village in Surrey, exceeded Jake's fondest fantasies. It was Georgian, painted white, with magnificent windows and climbing red roses. Pulling into the driveway, Jake braked immediately behind a black Humber with the licence plate EOF 1, grateful that Nancy hadn't noticed the plate, because he did not want to tell her that Eric's father, who had bought the original, had been called

Ernest, and that Eric was so-called because no other anything-OF 1
plate was available.

'Hullo, hullo,' Ormsby-Fletcher said, and he led them through the
house into the garden.

Floribunda roses. Immense pink hydrangeas. Luscious dahlias. . . .
Pamela, a streaky blonde and very nice to look at, wore a Mary
Quant sheath cut high above the knees, and white crocheted stockings. There was another guest, a plump, rumpled sybarite called
Desmond – something in the City he was – waiting on the terrace,
where drinks were served with cheese sticks and potato crisps. Suddenly a pale, stammering boy called Edward was thrusting a book
and pen at Jake. 'What?' Jake asked, startled.

'It's the guest book,' Nancy said. 'You sign your name and
birthdate.'

The *au pair* girl fetched Ormsby-Fletcher's other son, an unpleasant three-year-old called Eliot, to be kissed good night. This done,
Pamela began to chat about the theatre : she was mad keen.

'But how do actors do it,' Desmond asked Jake, 'going on night
after night, doing the same bloody thing . . .?'

'They're children, inspired children,' Jake said triumphantly.

Pamela jumped up. 'Would anybody like to wash their hands?'
she asked.

'What?'

Nancy kicked Jake in the ankle.

'Oh, yes. Sure.'

Pamela led Nancy to the downstairs toilet and Jake was directed
upstairs. Passing Eliot's bedroom, he discovered the boy squatting
on his potty, whining. The *au pair* girl was with him. 'Anything
wrong?' Jake asked.

The *au pair* girl looked up, alarmed. Obviously she had seen
Jake's picture in the newspapers. She knew the story. 'He won't go
to sleep without his golliwog,' she said, 'but he won't tell me where
he put it.'

Jake locked himself in the bathroom and immediately reached
into his jacket pocket for the salami on rye Nancy had thoughtfully
prepared for him. Munching his sandwich, he opened the medicine
cabinet, but it yielded no secrets. Next he tried the laundry hamper.

Shirts, socks, then at last, Pamela's smalls. Intricately laced black panties, no more than a peekaboo web. A spidery black bra, almost all filigree. You naughty thing, he thought.

Dinner commenced with hard-boiled eggs, sliced in half. Paprika had been sprinkled over the eggs and then they had been heated under the grill to suck out whatever moisture they still retained. Pamela flitted from place to place, proffering white toast to go with the eggs. 'You *are* a clever thing,' Desmond said, tucking in.

Jake washed down his egg with a glass of warm, sickeningly sweet, white Yugoslav wine, watching gloomily as Pamela brought in three platters. One contained a gluey substance in which toenail-size chunks of meat and walnuts and bloated onions floated; the next, a heap of dry lukewarm potatoes; and the third, frozen peas, the colour running. Pamela doled out the meat, with two ice-cream scoops of potatoes and an enormous spoonful of peas, and then passed around the toast again. Afterward the cheese board came out, a slab of British Railways cheddar, which looked uncannily like a cake of floor soap. There was dessert too. A runny pink blob called raspberry fool.

Desmond did most of the talking. The Tories, he admitted, seemed all played out at the moment, but one of these days another leader with fire in his belly would emerge and then we should see the last of that faceless little man in Number Ten.

'We'll leave the men to their port now, shall we?' Pamela said, and, to Jake's astonishment, she led Nancy out of the dining-room.

There actually was port. And cigars. Desmond apologized for the absence of his wife. She was in the hospital, he said, adding, 'It's nothing. Just a plumbing job.'

Ormsby-Fletcher recalled that when he had done his national service with the Guards on the Rhine he had occasionally gone to Hamburg on leave. 'A chance to dip the wick, don't you know?'

Jake leaned back in his chair, aghast; Ormsby-Fletcher, he thought, you saucy fellow, dipping the wick on the Reeperbahn; and just as he was searching himself for an appropriate off-colour story, Desmond rode to the rescue with the one about the Duchess of Devonshire. 'On her wedding night,' he said, 'the Duke naturally decided to have a bash. The Duchess, it turned out, couldn't get enough. "Is this what they call fucking?" she asked at last. "Yes," the Duke said. "Well then," she said, "it's too good for the working classes." '

Ho ho ho. Time to join the ladies. Jake excused himself, going to the upstairs toilet, ruminating there, but when he finally rose to pull the chain nothing happened. This didn't surprise him at first, knowing British plumbing as well as he did, but again and again he pulled, and still nothing happened. Oh my God, Jake thought, a big fat stool staring him in the face. What to do? Ah, he thought, opening the toilet door softly. There was nobody in the hall. Jake slipped into the adjoining bathroom, found a plastic pail, filled it with water, tiptoed back to the toilet, and poured it into the bowl. Now the stool floated level with the toilet seat. Flood tide. Pig, Jake thought. Sensualist. Hirsute Jew.

Don't panic, Jake thought, easing the toilet window open a crack. It's yours, your very own bodily waste, and disgust for it is bourgeois. Yes, yes, Jake agreed, *but how do I pick it up?* Sunshine soldier! Middlebrow! Unable to face life fully. Everything is holy, Jake. *Yes, but how do I pick it up?* Open the window wide, wrap it quickly in your underwear, lean back, and heave it into the rose bushes. The Hersh garbage ball, remember? Inimitable, unhittable. In an instant Jake stood resolutely over his stool, underwear in hand, counting down: ten-nine-eight-seven-six-five-four ... three ... two ... one and a half ... one and a quarter ... one! ... seven-eights – *whoa! Voices in the garden.* Jake tottered backward, relieved. Another second, he thought, and I would have done it: I'm no chicken.

Jake lit a cigarillo. So, he thought, they're all outside on the terrace again. Good, good, he thought, stepping into his underwear, sneaking out of the toilet, swiftly down the stairs, and then into the downstairs toilet. *Boruch atoh Adonoi*, he said twice, before he pulled the chain. It flushed. Should I go upstairs again, fetch the stool, and ...? No. Exhilarated, Jake flushed it again noisily, and then he began to pound on the door. Finally Ormsby-Fletcher came. 'I seem to be locked in,' Jake shouted.

'Oh, dear.' Ormsby-Fletcher told Jake how to unlock the door and then he led him into the garden, where Pamela was exhibiting paintings. A landscape, a boat in the harbour, a portrait, all reminiscent of the jigsaw puzzles of Jake's childhood. He made loud appreciative noises.

'Now nobody tell him.' Then Pamela, brimming with mischief, turned to Jake. 'Would you say these pictures showed talent?'

'Absolutely,' Jake said.

'But amateur?' she asked enticingly.

Jake glanced imploringly at Nancy but her face showed nothing. He stepped closer to the picture on display. 'Mmnnn,' he said, gratefully accepting a brandy from Ormsby-Fletcher. 'Professional. The brushwork,' he added. 'Oh, yes. Professional, I'd say.'

Desmond clapped a pink hand to his mouth, stifling a laugh.

They're hers, Jake thought. Afternoons, wearing her spidery black bra and nearly-nothing panties, she –

'Oh, for heaven's sake,' Ormsby-Fletcher said. 'Tell him.'

Pamela waited, savouring the expectant silence. Finally, breathlessly, she said, 'All these pictures were executed by mouth and foot painting artists !'

Jake gasped.

'You didn't guess?' Pamela said.

'Um, no.'

Ormsby-Fletcher explained that Pamela was a director of the Society for Mouth and Foot Painting Artists.

'And still finds time to make such sumptuous meals,' Desmond said. 'Oh, you are clever.'

'This picture,' Pamela said, holding up a seascape, 'was done by a boy of seventeen, *holding the brush between his teeth.*'

With trembling hand, Jake held out his brandy glass to Ormsby-Fletcher.

'He has been paralysed for eight years.'

'Amazing,' Jake said despairingly.

Desmond felt the group's work should be publicized in America. Swinging London, decadence, and all that tosh. Here was a bunch of disabled people who refused to cadge on the welfare state. An example to us all.

'This one,' Pamela said, holding up a portrait of General Montgomery, 'is a foot painting. It's one of a series done by a veteran of

El Alamein.' Next she showed another mouth painting, a still life, done by a street accident victim.

Holding out his glass for yet another brandy, Jake shouted, 'I'll buy it.'

Pamela's mouth formed an enormous reproachful O. 'Now you'll go away thinking I'm frightful,' she said.

'But it's for a very good cause,' Jake protested.

Pamela's enthusiasm ebbed. 'You may only buy one if you really, really think it's good. You mustn't condescend to disabled people.'

Jake pleaded, and Pamela, all forgiveness now, allowed him to have the Montgomery portrait for twenty-five guineas. Then she started into what Jake figured must be her set piece for women's club luncheons.

'If a man has the talent and urge to paint,' she said, 'he will paint. He will still paint even if it means living in a back street garret on a near starvation diet. If he has no arms he will paint with the canvas on the floor and a brush between his toes. If both arms and feet are lost he will grip the brush with his teeth.'

The upstairs toilet light went on. Jake gripped his brandy glass tighter and hastily lit a cigarillo.

'Speaking as a creative person, wouldn't you say Jake,' Pamela asked heatedly, 'that art thrives on difficulty?'

Another upstairs light was turned on. 'You're goddam right,' Jake said.

The *au pair* girl raised her voice, a pause, then Eliot began to shriek. Ormsby-Fletcher leaped to his feet. 'I'll see what it is, darling.'

'It seems to me,' Pamela said, 'the sterner the trials of creation the finer that which is created.'

'My wife isn't feeling well,' Jake said, shooting Nancy a fierce look.

'Pardon?'

'I must take Nancy home immediately.'

In the house again, they ran into a flushed, ill-tempered Ormsby-Fletcher; he was coming from the kitchen, carrying a pump.

'What is it?' Pamela asked.

Eliot sat at the top of the stairs. 'Didn't do it,' he wailed. 'Didn't do it.'

'He's been naughty,' Ormsby-Fletcher said tightly.

'Don't be too hard on him,' Jake pleaded compulsively.

Ormsby-Fletcher seemed to notice Jake for the first time. 'Not going so soon, are you?'

'It's Nancy,' Jake said. 'She's unwell.'

'Just an upset stomach,' Nancy said, trying to be helpful.

'No, *not a* –' Jake stopped himself. 'What I mean is . . . she's being brave. Good night everybody.' He assured the Ormsby-Fletchers that they had had an absolutely super evening, and clutching his Montgomery portrait, he hurried Nancy into the car. Eliot's howling pursued him.

'What in the hell's got into you?' Nancy asked.

But Jake wouldn't talk until they reached the highway. 'I've got a splitting headache, that's all.'

'What do you think the child did?'

'Stuffed his bloody golliwog down the toilet, that's what.'

Daryl Hine

THE WASP

It was a wasp or an imprudent bee
Against my skin, underneath my shirt,
That stung as I was trying to set it free.
Art is perhaps too long, or life too short.

Ignorant of entomology
I watched it at the crumbs of my dessert,
Numbered its stripes, curious what sort
Of wasp it was, of what tribe of bee,

While bored, aware that it was watched, maybe,
Buzzing, it appeared to pay me court,
And darted in where I could not see
It, against my skin, underneath my shirt,

There in the sweaty twilight next to me
Its amorous antennae to disport,
But always armed. The minute, golden flirt
Stung as I was trying to set it free.

So it escaped, but died eventually,
An event exceeding its desert,
While I, stung as I deserved to be –
But art is perhaps too long, or life too short.

Trivial, scarce worthy of report,
Wonderful the wounds of love should be
Occasion, none the less, for poetry.
Thus deaths, that is the deaths of others, hurt.
                                    It was a wasp.

John Metcalf

KEYS AND WATERCRESS

David, with great concentration, worked the tip of his thumbnail under the fat scab on his knee. He carefully lifted the edges of the scab enjoying the tingling sensation as it tore free. His rod was propped against his other leg and he could just see the red blur of his float from the corner of his eye. He started to probe the centre of the crust.

'Had any luck?' a voice behind him said suddenly.

Startled, his thumbnail jumped, ripping the scab away. A bright bead of blood welled into the pit. The sun, breaking from behind the clouds, swept the meadow into a brighter green and made the bead of blood glisten like the bezel of a ring.

'Had any luck?' the old man said again. David twisted round to look at him. He wasn't in uniform and he wasn't wearing a badge and anyway he was far too old to be a bailiff. Unless he was a Club Member – and they could report you too. And break your fishing-rod.

David glanced down the river towards the bridge and the forbidding white sign. 'I'm only fishing for eels,' he said. 'With a sea-hook.'

'Slippery fellows, eels,' said the old man. 'Difficult to catch.'

'I haven't caught any yet,' said David, hoping the old man wouldn't notice the grey eel-slime on the bank and the smeared fishing-bag.

The old man started to sit down. Wheezing harshly with the effort, he lowered himself until he was kneeling, and then, supporting himself on his hands, laboriously stretched out each leg like a dying insect in a jam jar. His anguished breathing eased slowly away into a throaty mutter. David felt more confident because he knew he could run nearly to the bridge by the time the old man had struggled to his feet.

Taking a blue silk handkerchief from the top pocket of his linen jacket, the old man dabbed at his forehead. 'My word, yes!' he said. 'Extremely slippery fellows.' He took off his straw hat and rubbed his bald head with the blue handkerchief.

'They're a nuisance,' said David. 'The Club Members don't like catching them.'

'And why is that?'

'Because they swallow the hook right down and you can't get it out,' said David.

'You've hurt your knee,' said the old man. The bead of blood had grown too large and toppled over, trickling down his knee to run into the top of his stocking.

'Oh, that's nothing,' said David. 'Only a scab.'

'Yes,' said the old man reflectively, 'it's a pleasant day. A beautiful sky – beautiful afternoon clouds.'

They sat silently staring across the flow of the river. Near the far bank in the shallows under the elderberry bushes the huge roach and chub basked in the sunshine, rising every now and then to nose soft circles in the water.

'Do you know the name of clouds like those?' asked the old man suddenly. 'The *proper* name, I mean.'

'No,' said David.

'Well, the correct name is cumulus. Cumulus. You say it yourself.'

'Cumulus,' said David.

'Good! You won't forget, will you? Promise me you won't forget.' There was a silence while the old man put on his spectacles from a tin case. Then, taking a fountain-pen and a small black book from his inside pocket, he said, 'But boys forget things. It's no use denying it – boys forget. So I'm going to write it down.' He tore a page from the notebook and printed on it 'CUMULUS (CLOUDS)'.

As David tucked the paper into his shirt-pocket, he looked across at the old man who was staring into the water, a vague and absent look in his eyes. David watched him for a moment and then turned back to his float watching the current break and flow past it in a constant flurry. He tried to follow the invisible nylon line down into the depths where it ended in a ledger-weight and a turning, twisting worm.

'Every evening,' said the old man, speaking slowly and more to himself than David, 'when the light begins to fail, the cattle come down here to drink. Just as the night closes in.'

'They've trampled the bank down further up-stream,' said David.

'And I watch them coming across the fields,' said the old man as though he hadn't heard. 'I see them from my window.'

The old man's voice died away into silence but suddenly, without warning, he belched loudly – long, rumbling, unforced belches of which he seemed quite unaware. David looked away. To cover his embarrassment, he started reeling in his line to check the bait and the clack of the ratchet seemed to arouse the old man. He groped inside his jacket and pulled out a large flat watch. With a click the lid sprang open. 'Have you ever seen such a watch before?' he asked. 'Such a beautiful watch?' He held it out on the palm of his hand.

'Do you know what watches like these are called?'

'No,' said David. 'I've never seen one before.'

'They're called Hunters. And numbers like these are called roman numerals.'

As the old man counted off the numbers on the watch-face, David stared at the old man's hand. The mottled flesh was puffy and gorged with fat blue veins which stood beneath the skin. He tried to take the watch without touching the hand which held it.

'What time does the watch say?' asked the old man.

'Half past four,' said David.

'Well then, it's time we had our tea,' said the old man. 'And you shall come and have tea with me.'

'Thank you,' said David, 'but I've got to go home.'

'But tea's prepared,' said the old man and as he spoke he started to struggle to his feet. 'Tea's prepared. In the house across the bridge – in the house with the big garden.'

'But I really have to go,' said David. 'My mother'll be angry if I'm late.'

'Nonsense!' said the old man loudly. 'Quite untrue.'

'Really. I do have to. . .'

'We won't be long,' said the old man. 'You like my watch, don't you? You *do* like my watch.'

'Oh, yes.'

'Well, there you are then. What more proof do you need? *And*,' said the old man, 'I have many treasures in my house.' He stared at David angrily. 'You would be a rude boy to refuse.'

'Well . . .' said David. 'I really mustn't be long.'

'Do you go to school?' the old man asked suddenly.

'Parkview Junior,' said David.

'Yes,' said the old man. 'I went to school when I was a boy.'

As David was sliding the rod-sections into the cloth case, the old man gripped his arm and said, 'You may keep the watch in your pocket until we reach the bridge. Or you could hold it in your hand. Whichever you like.' Then stopping David again he said, 'And such a watch is called a . . .?'

'A Hunter,' said David.

The old man relaxed his hold on David's arm and said, 'Excellent! Quite excellent! Always be attentive. Always accumulate *facts*.' He seemed very pleased and as they walked slowly along the river-path towards the bridge made little chuckling sounds inside his throat.

His breath labouring again after the incline from the bridge, the old man rested for a few moments with his hand on the garden gate. Then, pushing the gate open, he said, 'Come along, boy. Come along. Raspberry canes everywhere, just as I told you.'

David followed the old man along the path and into the cool hall. His eyes were bewildered at first after the strong sunlight, and he stumbled against the dark shape of the hall-stand.

'Just leave your things here,' said the old man, 'and we'll go straight in to tea.'

David dropped his fishing-bag behind the door and stood his rod in the umbrella-stand. The old man went ahead down the passage and ushered him into the sitting-room.

The room was long and, in spite of the french windows at the far end, rather dark. It was stuffy and smelled like his grandma.

In the centre of the room stood a table covered with green baize, but tea was laid out on a small cardtable at the far end of the room in front of the french windows.

Bookshelves lined the walls and books ran from ceiling to floor. The floor too was covered with piles of books and papers; old books with leather covers, musty and smelling of damp and dust, and perilous stacks of yellow *National Geographic* magazines.

A vast mirror, the biggest he'd ever seen, bigger even than the one in the barber's, stood above the fireplace, carved and golden with golden statues on each side.

David stared and stared about him, but his eyes kept returning to the lion which stood in front of the fireplace.

'Do you like it?' asked the old man. 'It's stuffed.'

'Oh, yes!' exclaimed David. 'Can I touch it?'

'I've often wondered,' said the old man, 'if it's in good taste.'

'Where did it come from?'

'Oh, Africa. Undoubtedly Africa. They all do, you know.'

'I think it's terrific,' said David.

'You may stay here, then, and I will go and put the kettle on,' said the old man. As soon as the door had closed, David went and stuck his hand into the lion's snarling mouth and stroked the dusty orbs of its eyes with his finger-tips. When he heard the old man's footsteps shuffling back down the passage, he moved away from the lion and pretended to be looking at a book.

'Do you take sugar?' asked the old man as they sat down at the cardtable in front of the french windows.

'No thank you,' said David. 'Just milk.'

'No? Most interesting! Most interesting. In my experience, boys like sweet things. A deplorable taste, of course. Youth and inexperience.'

He passed the teacup across the table and said sternly, 'The palate must be educated.' David didn't know what to say and because the old man was staring at him looked away and moved the teaspoon in his saucer. Putting down the silver teapot, the old man wrote in his notebook, 'The love of sweetness is an uneducated love.' Handing the note across the table he said, 'Facts, eh? *Facts.*' He chuckled again inside his throat.

'And now,' he continued – but then broke off again as he saw

David staring out of the window into the orchard. 'If you're quite ready? We have brown bread. Wholemeal. Thin-cut. And with Cornish butter.' He ticked off each point on his fingers. 'To be eaten with fresh watercress. Do you think that will please you?'

'Very nice, thank you,' said David politely.

'But it's not simply a matter of *taste*, you see,' said the old man fixing David with his eye. He shook his head slowly.

'Not simple at all.'

'What isn't?' asked David.

'Not at all simple. Taste, yes, I grant you,' said the old man, 'but what about texture? Umm? Umm? What about vision?'

'What isn't simple?' David asked again.

The old man clicked his tongue in annoyance and said, 'Come along, boy!' He glared across the table. 'Your attention is lax. Always be attentive.' He leaned across the cardtable and held up his finger. 'Observe!' he said. 'Observe the tablecloth. Cotton? Dear me, no! Irish linen. And this.' His finger-tips rubbed slowly over the facets of the bowl. 'Waterford glass – brilliant. Can you see the colours? The green of the cress and the drops of water like diamonds? Brilliant. A question of the lead-content, you see. You *do* see, don't you. You do understand what I'm telling you.'

'Well . . . please,' said David, 'what's a texture?'

And once again the old man took out his notebook and his fountain-pen.

When tea was finished, the old man wiped his lips with a linen napkin and said eagerly, 'Well? Do you think you're ready? Shall you see them?'

'Please,' said David, 'I'd like to very much.'

The old man pulled on a thick, tasselled rope which hung by the side of the window and slowly closed the red velvet curtains. 'We don't want to be overlooked,' he whispered.

'But there's no one there,' said David. The old man was excitedly brushing the green baize and didn't seem to hear. With the red curtains closed, the room smelled even more stuffy, hot and stifling, as if the air itself were thick and red. And in the warm gloom the lion lost its colour and turned into a dark shape, a pinpoint of light glinting off its dusty eye. As David crossed over to the table he saw himself moving in the mysterious depths of the mirror.

'Come along, boy!' said the old man impatiently. 'We'll start with the yellow box. There. Under the table.'

The old man lifted the lid of the box and took out three small leather sacks. They were like the pictures in pirate books and as he laid them on the baize they chinked and jangled. Slowly, while David watched, very slowly, the old fingers trembled at the knots, and then suddenly the old man tipped the first sack spreading keys across the table-top.

There were hundreds of keys; long rusted keys, flat keys, keys with little round numbers tied to them, keys bunched together on rings, here and there sparkling new Yale keys, keys to fit clocks and keys for clock-work toys. The old man's fingers played greedily among them, spreading them, separating large and small.

'Well?' he said, looking up suddenly.

'I've never seen so many,' said David.

'Few people have,' said the old man. 'Few people have.' His eyes turned back to the table, and he moved one or two of the keys as though they were not in their proper place. And then, as if remembering his manners, he said, 'You may touch them. I don't mind if you do.'

David picked up a few keys and looked at them. His hands became red with rust, and he dropped them back on the table, stirring them about idly with his finger-tip.

'Not like that!' snapped the old man suddenly. 'Do it properly! You have to heap them up and scatter them. If you're going to do it do it properly.'

He pulled at the strings on the other bags and cascaded a stream of keys on to the table. The air swam with red dust. David sneezed loudly and the old man said, 'Pay attention!'

He raked the keys together into a large heap and burrowed his hands deep into them. When they were quite buried, he stopped, his eyes gleaming with a tense excitement. His breathing was loud and shallow. He looked up at David, and his eyes widened. 'Now!' he shouted, and heaved his hands into the air.

Keys rained and rattled about the room, clicking against the mirror, breaking a cup on the cardtable, slapping against the leather-covered books, and falling loudly on the floor-boards. A small key hit David on the forehead. The old man remained bent across the table as if the excitement had exhausted him. The silence deepened.

Suddenly, a key which had landed on the edge of the mantelpiece overbalanced and fell, rattling loudly on the tiles of the hearth. Still the old man did not move. David shifted his weight restlessly and said into the silence, 'I think I'll have to be getting home now. My mother's expecting me.'

The old man gave no sign that he had heard. David said again, 'I'll have to be going now.' His voice sounded flat and awkward in the silent room.

The old man pushed himself up from the table. Deep lines of irritation scored the sides of his mouth. David began to blush under the fierceness of the old man's eyes. 'I can't quite make up my mind about you,' the old man said slowly. He did not take his eyes from David's face.

'Sometimes I think you're a polite boy and sometimes I think you're a rude boy.' He paused. 'It's unsettling.' David looked down and fiddled with one of the buttons on his shirt.

'Lift up another box of keys,' said the old man suddenly.

'But I have to go home,' said David.

'Quite untrue,' said the old man.

'Really I do.'

'A lie!' shouted the old man. 'You are lying. You are telling lies!' He pounded on the table with his fist so that the keys jumped. 'I will not tolerate the telling of lies!'

'Please,' said David, 'can I open the curtains?'

'I'm beginning to suspect,' said the old man slowly, 'that you don't really like my keys. I'm beginning to think that I was mistaken in you.'

'Please. Honest. I have to,' said David desperately, his voice high and tight with fear of the old man's anger.

'Very well,' said the old man curtly. 'But you are a rude boy with very little appreciation. I want you to know that.' Reaching inside his jacket, leaving brown rustmarks on the lapel, he took out his notebook and wrote in it. He passed the piece of paper across the table. David read, '*You have very little appreciation.*'

The old man turned away, presenting his silent and offended back. David didn't know what to do. Hesitantly he said, 'I do like the keys. Really I do. And the lion. And thank you for the tea.'

'So you're going now, are you?' asked the old man without turning round.

'Well I have to,' said David.

'It's a great pity because I don't show it to many people,' said the old man.

'Show what?'

'It would only take a moment,' said the old man turning round, 'but you're in too much of a hurry.'

'What is it?'

'Can you really spare me two minutes? Could you bear to stay with me that long?' Suddenly he chuckled. 'Of *course* you want to,' he said. 'Go and sit on the settee over there and I'll bring it to you.'

'Can I open the curtains now?' asked David. 'I don't ... I mean, it's hot with them closed.'

'Don't touch them! No. You mustn't!' said the old man urgently. He was struggling to take something from one of the bookshelves. He came and stood over David and then stooped so that David could see the black leather case in his hands. It was so stuffy in the room that it was difficult to breathe properly, and when the old man was so close to him David became aware of a strong smell of urine. He tried to move away.

Almost reverently, the old man opened the leather case and lying on the red silk lining was a small grey ball. They looked at it in silence.

'There!' breathed the old man. 'Do you know what it is?'

'No,' said David.

'Go on! Go on!' urged the old man.

'I don't know,' said David.

'Try.'

'A marble?'

'A marble!' shouted the old man. 'Why would I keep a marble

in a leather case ! Of course it isn't a marble ! That's one of the most stupid remarks I've ever heard.'

'I'm sorry,' said David, frightened again by the anger in the old man's glaring face.

'You're an extremely silly boy. A brainless boy. A stupid boy.' He slammed shut the leather case. 'Stupid ! Silly !' shouted the old man.

'I want to go home now,' said David, beginning to get up from the settee. The old man pushed him back. 'A marble !' he muttered.

'Please . . .' said David.

'It's a bullet !' shouted the old man. 'A rifle bullet.'

'I didn't know,' said David. He tried to get up again, but he was hemmed in by an occasional table and the crowding presence of the old man. The dim light in the room seemed to be failing into darkness. David's throat was dry and aching.

'This bullet,' said the old man, 'was cut out of my leg in 1899. December 1899. Next I suppose you'll tell me that you've never heard of the Boer War !'

David said nothing, and the old man's black shape loomed over him.

'*Have* you heard of the Boer War?'

David began to cry.

'*Have* you?'

'I want to go home,' said David in a small and uncertain voice.

'Quite untrue,' said the old man. 'I will not tolerate liars. You told me you went to school, and yet you claim not to have heard of the Boer War.' He gripped David by the shoulder. 'Why? Why are you lying to me?'

'Please,' said David. 'I'm not telling lies. Please let me go.'

'Oh, very well,' said the old man. 'Maybe you aren't. But stop crying. It irritates me. Here. You may touch the bullet.' He opened and held out the leather case.

'There's no need to cry.'

'I want to go home,' snuffled David.

'I know !' said the old man. 'I know what you'd like. I'll show you my leg. The bullet smashed the bone, you know. You *would* like that, wouldn't you?'

'No,' said David.

'Of course you would.'

The old man moved even nearer to the settee, and leaning forward over David, lifting with his hands, slowly raised his leg until his foot was resting on the cushion. The harsh wheezing of his breath seemed to fill the silent room. The smell of stale urine was strong on the still air. Slowly he began to tug at his trouser-leg, inching it upwards. The calf of his leg was white and hairless. The flesh sank deep, seamed and puckered, shiny, livid white and purple, towards a central pit.

'If you press hard,' said the old man, 'it sinks right in.'

David shrank further away from the white leg. The old man reached down and grasped David's hand. 'Give me your finger,' he said.

David tore his hand free and, kicking over the coffee-table, rolled off the settee. At first, in his panic, he wrenched the doorknob the wrong way. As he ran out of the darkened room, he heard the old man saying, 'I've tried to teach you. I've tried to teach you. But you have *no appreciation*.'

Réjean Ducharme

FROM *THE SWALLOWER SWALLOWED*

II

Four sparrows hop from bread-crumb to bread-crumb outside the door of the gardener's cottage. An icy gust blows them back under the eaves. Last year at the first frost, I put my tongue on the handle of the gate and it stuck, stuck so hard that I took the skin off when I pulled it away. I pull off my warm mittens and stand in front of the gate, stretching my clammy hands out towards the iron knob, which bristles with a white down of frost. I'm afraid. But the iron knob is irresistible. After drawing back and hesitating I don't know how many times, I make up my mind. I shut my eyes and let out a little cry and seize it in both hands. Ouch ! It's worse than getting hold of a red-hot coal. It's as if the metal were boiling with cold. I can feel my palms sticking and the skin dissolving. My courage fails. My mouth opens. Don't scream. Choke back those disgusting screams, Bernice Einberg ! I try to pull my hands off. The skin tears away from the flesh. Suffer but don't scream ! Think of Father Brébeuf. He didn't scream when the Indians put a white-hot collar round his neck. The savage warriors, amazed at the frail paleface's courage, fought over who should have his heart. Don't lose your head, Bernice Einberg ! Pain only hurts your flesh. To scream like a hen that's picked up by the legs hurts your soul. The Indians knew that Father Brébeuf was in pain, but that wasn't enough for them. They wanted him to scream and thrash about and lose control of himself; they wanted his pride to fail. Don't lose control. Hold your soul safe in your arms, Bernice Einberg. It's always possible to take courage and not scream like a hen that's picked up by the legs. After last year's experience I learned that in such a situation there's a way of getting out of it without flaying yourself alive. What you have to do is put up with the pain and wait for the metal to get warm.

My hands are burning, it can't be long before they pass some heat on to something else. I'm suffering more than Father Brébeuf. And I haven't cried out. I've revenged myself on the knob. I've conquered. I smile at myself. I approve of myself. Last year. . . . Alas, as she did last year, the Grand Duchess of Mingrélie has come to spend our winter holidays with us. She arrived yesterday from Dniepropetrovsk in all her glory.

It hasn't snowed yet. It was very cold last night. When I came out of the house early this morning there was a thick rime sifted all over the ground and the stony tracks; coating the bare poplars and the still reeds; veiling the gardener's cottage, the elm and the mine-hoist.

At first we only try with our toes the thin jet paving that formed over the stream a few hours ago in the dead of night. It bears the weight without creaking or giving, and we venture trembling farther from the edge. We slide our feet along carefully, leaning against one another. Old folk who live on the mainland say the channel is bottomless this side of the causeway. If there is a bottom it's a long way down. Once, ages ago, some engineers came to measure how deep it was. The plumbline they brought was so long the weight of it nearly sank their boat. The lead still hadn't touched bottom when all the line was paid out. Last year, when we were trying the ice as we were today, a rumble like thunder started up below us. As we stood petrified with fright, a wide crack ran quick as lightning between our feet, then branched out and disappeared among the reeds by each bank, leaving behind on the black surface a track like a big white tree. Today the ice doesn't crack, doesn't give any sign of weakness. We advance more boldly. We take longer and firmer steps, and soon it's a mad rush, a wild quadrille, fits of laughter. We're still not quite sure though. We need more conclusive proof. We fall down on the dark mirror and put it to a last test, hammering at it as hard as we can with our steel-tipped boots. The ice chips but doesn't split. Victory ! The ice is sound ! We tear back to the house and announce the news to Dead Cat. She frowns and asks the gardener what he thinks.

He confirms that the ice is sound.

I clap my hands and jump up and down.

'Don't make so much noise,' hisses Dead Cat. 'Mingrélie's still asleep.'

We put our skates on sitting on the mat in the porch so as not to spoil the parquet flooring. Dead Cat helps Christian tie his laces. She has to press hard on the last cross-over while he threads the laces through the next eye-holes. She presses with the tip of her beautiful finger, her tapering finger with its ring set with a pointed pink jewel. He blushes like a bride. Not that I've ever seen any brides. And the boot has to be tight round the ankle so that you feel firm on your skates. I had to insist that Dead Cat shouldn't help me with my laces. I do it myself, as best I can, and that's that. Dead Cat winds a woollen scarf round my forehead and neck. Her fine large hand brushes against my face, supple, delicate and sweet-smelling as a flower. She's bound me up like a mummy. I'm suffocating.

'Christian !' she calls, opening the door. 'Mind you take good care of your little sister !'

He takes me by the hand. One day it will be me that takes care and takes Christian by the hand. Stars and diamonds shoot from under Christian's skates. He's off ! He's found the current, it's seized him, he glides along like a cutter. He poises himself now and then as if at the end of a waltz. I don't know what's the matter with my feet : I've never been able to learn to skate. I long to catch up with Christian, to enter into the game, to be carried along with him as if downhill, to be initiated into the spell that gives him so much grace and pleasure. After all it can't be so difficult. I watch him closely. You let yourself slide along, first on one skate, then on the other, then you're carried along. Let's have another try ! I slide my foot forward. It glides so fast I lose control, skid, collapse. Up I get. I have another go. Again I get carried away and find myself flat on my face. I resign myself to walking, until I lose patience and start to run. My skates turn over, my legs shoot in opposite directions, and I lose my balance. I re-bash my head and re-shatter my spine. I ask Christian to help me. He gets hold of me by the shoulders and I manage to go ten feet or so without falling. He says I skate like a champion and lets go of me. He goes off and I fall down. But I don't give up. It'll come in time. I try again, pretending that Christian's still holding me up. I really try. No one's ever put their bottom through it with the remorselessness and enthusiasm I do. But the time I gave myself to become master of the art has run out and I'm no further forward. I haven't either the strength or the desire to get up again. I roll about in despair. Sometimes on my face, sometimes on my back, I kick with my heels and hammer with my fists, cursing fate and my helplessness and everything else I can think of. I ask Christian to help me again. Excited by the ice and the open air, he amuses himself by showing off how good he is, making fun of me, turning the knife in the wound. He skates round me as fast as a comet, sometimes on one foot, sometimes backwards. He jumps over me. He brakes right under my nose, sending up a spray of powdered ice. To crown all the Grand Duchess of Mingrélie comes and joins us. She takes her skating seriously. She's got up in a short skirt and tights. First she does a few entrechats, then she goes off to spin round and round, moving along all the time. She looks like a real ballerina, a butterfly gathering honey. I get even more furious. I bang my head on the ice, I try to bite it. Then I trample on my pride and start to crawl after her on all fours. Christian won't teach me to skate! Will you?

Translated by Barbara Bray

Northrop Frye

CONCLUSION

From *Literary History of Canada*

After the Northwest passage failed to materialize, Canada became a colony in the mercantilist sense, treated by others less like a society than as a place to look for things. French, English, Americans plunged into it to carry off its supplies of furs, minerals, and pulpwood, aware only of their immediate objectives. From time to time recruiting officers searched the farms and villages to carry young men off to death in a European dynastic quarrel. The travellers reviewed by Mrs Waterston visit Canada much as they would visit a zoo : even when their eyes momentarily focus on the natives they are still thinking primarily of how their own sensibility is going to react to what it sees. Mrs Waterston speaks of a feature of Canadian life that has been noted by writers from Susanna Moodie onward : 'the paradox of vast empty spaces plus lack of privacy', without defences against the prying or avaricious eye. The resentment expressed against this in Canada seems to have taken political rather than literary forms : this may be partly because Canadians have learned from their imaginative experience to look at each other in much the same way : 'as objects, even as obstacles', to quote Miss Macpherson on a Canadian autobiography.

It is not much wonder if Canada developed with the bewilderment of a neglected child, preoccupied with trying to define its own identity, alternately bumptious and diffident about its own achievements. Adolescent dreams of glory haunt the Canadian consciousness (and unconsciousness), some naïve and some sophisticated. In the naïve area are the predictions that the twentieth century belongs to Canada, that our cities will become much bigger than they ought to be, or, like Edmonton and Vancouver, 'gateways' to somewhere else, reconstructed Northwest passages. The more sophisticated usually take the form of a Messianic complex about Canadian culture, for Canadian culture, no less than Alberta, has always been 'next year country'. The myth of the hero brought up in the forest retreat, awaiting the moment when his giant strength will be fully grown and he can emerge into the world, informs a good deal of Canadian criticism down to our own time.

Certain features of life in a new country that are bound to handicap its writers are obvious enough. The difficulties of drama, which depends on a theatre and consequently on a highly organized urban life, are set out by Mr Tait. Here the foreshortening of historical development has been particularly cruel, as drama was strangled by the movie just as it was getting started as a popular medium. Other literary genres have similar difficulties. Culture is born in leisure and an awareness of standards, and pioneer conditions tend to make energetic and uncritical work an end in itself, to preach a gospel of social unconsciousness, which lingers long after the pioneer conditions have disappeared. The impressive achievements of such a society are likely to be technological. It is in the inarticulate part of communication, railways and bridges and canals and highways, that Canada, one of whose symbols is the taciturn beaver, has shown its real strength. Again, Canadian culture, and literature in particular, has felt the force of what may be called Emerson's law. Emerson remarks in his journals that in a provincial society it is extremely easy to reach the highest level of cultivation, extremely difficult to take one step beyond that. In surveying Canadian poetry and fiction, we feel constantly that all the energy has been absorbed in meeting a standard, a self-defeating enterprise because real standards can only be established, not met. Such writing is academic in the pejorative sense of that term, an imitation of a prescribed model, second-rate in conception, not merely in execution. It is natural that academic writing of this kind should develop where literature is a social prestige symbol, as Mr Cogswell says. However, it is not the handicaps of Canadian writers but the distinctive features that appear in spite of them which are the main concern of this book, and so of its conclusion.

II

The sense of probing into the distance, of fixing the eyes on the skyline, is something that Canadian sensibility has inherited from the *voyageurs*. It comes into Canadian painting a good deal, in Thomson whose focus is so often farthest back in the picture, where a river or a gorge in the hills twists elusively out of sight, in Emily Carr whose vision is always, in the title of a compatriot's book of poems, 'deeper into the forest'. Even in the Maritimes, where the feeling of linear distance is less urgent, Roberts contemplates the Tantramar marshes in the same way, the refrain of 'miles and miles' having clearly some incantatory power for him. It would be interesting to know how many Canadian novels associate nobility of character with a faraway look, or base their perorations on a long-range perspective. This might be only a cliché, except that it is often found in sharply observed and distinctively written books. Here, as a random example, is the last sentence of W. O. Mitchell's *Who Has Seen the Wind*: 'The wind turns in silent frenzy upon itself, whirling into a smoking funnel, breathing up top soil and tumble-weed skeletons to carry them on its spinning way over the prairie, out and out to the far line of the sky.' Mr Pacey quotes the similarly long-sighted conclusion of *Such is My Beloved*.

A vast country sparsely inhabited naturally depends on its modes of transportation, whether canoe, railway, or the driving and riding 'circuits' of the judge, the Methodist preacher, or the Yankee peddler. The feeling of nomadic movement over great distances persists even into the age of the aeroplane, in a country where writers can hardly meet one another without a social organization that provides travel grants. Pratt's poetry is full of his fascination with means of communication, not simply the physical means of great ships and locomotives, though he is one of the best of all poets on such subjects, but with communication as message, with radar and asdic and wireless signals, and in his war poems, with the power of rhetoric over fighting men. What is perhaps the most comprehensive structure of ideas yet made by a Canadian thinker, the structure embodied in Innis's *Bias of Communication*, is concerned with the same theme, and a disciple of Innis, Marshall McLuhan, continues to emphasize the unity of communication, as a complex containing both verbal and non-verbal factors, and warns us against making unreal divisions within it. Perhaps it is not too fanciful to see this need for continuity in the Canadian attitude to time as well as space, in its preoccupation with its own history (the motto of the Province of Quebec is *je me souviens*) and its relentless cultural stock-takings and self-inventories. The Burke sense of society as a continuum – consistent with the pragmatic and conservative outlook of Canadians – is strong and begins early. Mr Irving quotes an expression of it in McCulloch, and another quotation shows that it was one of the most deeply held ideas of Brett. As I write, the centennial of Confederation in 1967 looms up before the country with the moral urgency of a Day of Atonement : I use a Jewish metaphor because there is something Hebraic about the Canadian tendency to read its conquest of a promised land, its Maccabean victories of 1812, its struggle for the central fortress on the hill at Quebec, as oracles of a future. It is doubtless only an accident that the theme of one of the most passionate and intense of all Canadian novels, A. M. Klein's *The Second Scroll*, is Zionism.

Civilization in Canada, as elsewhere, has advanced geometrically across the country, throwing down the long parallel lines of the railways, dividing up the farm lands into chessboards of square-mile sections and concession-line roads. There is little adaptation to nature : in both architecture and arrangement, Canadian cities and villages express rather an arrogant abstraction, the conquest of nature by an intelligence that does not love it. The word conquest suggests something military, as it should – one thinks of General Braddock, preferring to have his army annihilated rather than fight the natural man on his own asymmetrical ground. There are some features of this generally North American phenomenon that have a particular emphasis in Canada. It has been remarked – Mr Kilbourn quotes Creighton on the subject – that Canadian expansion westward had a tight grip of authority over it that American expansion, with its outlaws and sheriffs and vigilantes and the like, did not have in the same measure. America moved from the back country to the wild west; Canada moved from a New France held down by British military occupation to a northwest patrolled by mounted police. Canada has not had, strictly speaking, an Indian war : there has been much less of the 'another redskin bit the dust' feeling in our historical imagination, and only Riel remains to haunt the later period of it, though he is a formidable figure enough, rather like what a combination of John Brown and Vanzetti would be in the American conscience. Otherwise, the conquest, for the last two centuries, has been mainly of the unconscious forces of nature, personified by the dragon of the Lake Superior rocks in Pratt's *Towards the Last Spike* :

> On the North Shore a reptile lay asleep –
> A hybrid that the myths might have conceived,
> But not delivered.

Yet the conquest of nature has its own perils for the imagination, in a country where the winters are so cold and where conditions of life have so often been blank and comfortless, where even the mosquitoes have been described, Mr Klinck tells us, as 'mementoes of the fall'. I have long been impressed in Canadian poetry by a tone of deep terror in regard to nature, a theme to which we shall return. It is not a terror of the dangers or discomforts or even the mysteries of nature, but a terror of the soul at something that these things manifest. The human mind has nothing but human and moral values to cling to if it is to preserve its integrity or even its sanity, yet the vast unconsciousness of nature in front of it seems an unanswerable denial of those values. I notice that a sharp-witted Methodist preacher quoted by Mr Cogswell speaks of the 'shutting out of the whole moral creation' in the loneliness of the forests.

If we put together a few of these impressions, we may get some approach in characterizing the way in which the Canadian imagination has developed in its literature. Small and isolated communities surrounded with a physical or psychological 'frontier', separated from one another and from their American and British cultural sources : communities that provide all that their members have in the way of distinctively human values, and that are compelled to feel a great respect for the law and order that holds them together, yet confronted with a huge, unthinking, menacing, and formidable physical setting – such communities are bound to develop what we may provisionally call a garrison mentality. In the earliest maps of the country the only inhabited centres are forts, and that remains true of the cultural maps for a much later time. Frances Brooke, in her eighteenth-century *Emily Montague*, wrote of what was literally a garrison; novelists of our day studying the impact of Montreal on Westmount write of a psychological one.

A garrison is a closely knit and beleaguered society, and its moral and social values are unquestionable. In a perilous enterprise one does not discuss causes or motives: one is either a fighter or a deserter. Here again we may turn to Pratt, with his infallible instinct for what is central in the Canadian imagination. The societies in Pratt's poems are always tense and tight groups engaged in war, rescue, martyrdom, or crisis, and the moral values expressed are simply those of that group. In such a society the terror is not for the common enemy, even when the enemy is or seems victorious, as in the extermination of the Jesuit missionaries or the crew of Franklin (a great Canadian theme, well described in this book by Mr Hopwood, that Pratt pondered but never completed). The real terror comes when the individual feels himself becoming an individual, pulling away from the group, losing the sense of driving power that the group gives him, aware of a conflict within himself far subtler than the struggle of morality against evil. It is much easier to multiply garrisons, and when that happens, something anti-cultural comes into Canadian life, a dominating herd-mind in which nothing original can grow. The intensity of the sectarian divisiveness in Canadian towns, both religious and political, is an example: what such groups represent, of course, vis-à-vis one another, is 'two solitudes', the death of communication and dialogue. Separatism, whether English or French, is culturally the most sterile of all creeds. But at present I am concerned rather with a more creative side of the garrison mentality, one that has had positive effects on our intellectual life.

They were so certain of their moral values, says Mr Cogswell, a little sadly, speaking of the early Maritime writers. Right was white, wrong black, and nothing else counted or even existed. He goes on to point out that such certainty invariably produces a sub-literary rhetoric. Or, as Yeats would say, we make rhetoric out of quarrels with one another, poetry out of the quarrel with ourselves. To use words, for any other purpose than straight description or command, is a form of play, a manifestation of *homo ludens*. But there are two forms of play, the contest and the construct. The editorial writer attacking the Family Compact, the preacher demolishing imaginary atheists with the argument of design, are using words aggressively, in theses that imply antitheses. Ideas are weapons; one seeks the verbal *coup de grâce*, the irrefutable refutation. Such a use of words is congenial enough to the earlier Canadian community : all the evidence, including the evidence of this book, points to a highly articulate and argumentative society in nineteenth-century Canada. Mr MacLure remarks on the fact that scholarship in Canada has so often been written with more conviction and authority, and has attracted wider recognition, than the literature itself. There are historical reasons for this, apart from the fact, which will become clearer as we go on, that scholarly writing is more easily attached to its central tradition.

Leacock has a story which I often turn to because the particular aspect of Canadian culture it reflects has never been more accurately caught. He tells us of the rivalry in an Ontario town between two preachers, one Anglican and the other Presbyterian. The latter taught ethics in the local college on weekdays – without salary – and preached on Sundays. He gave his students, says Leacock, three parts Hegel and two parts St Paul, and on Sunday he reversed the dose and gave his parishioners three parts St Paul and two parts Hegel. Religion has been a major – perhaps the major – cultural force in Canada, at least down to the last generation or two. The names of two Methodist publishers, William Briggs and Lorne Pierce, recur more than once in this book, and illustrate the fact that the churches not only influenced the cultural climate but took an active part in the production of poetry and fiction, as the popularity of Ralph Connor reminds us. But the effective religious factors in Canada were doctrinal and evangelical, those that stressed the arguments of religion at the expense of its imagery.

Such a reliance on the arguing intellect was encouraged by the philosophers, who in the nineteenth century, as Mr Irving shows, were invariably idealists with a strong religious bias. Mr Irving quotes George as saying that civilization consists 'in the conscience and intellect' of a cultivated people, and Watson as asserting that 'we are capable of knowing Reality as it actually is . . . . Reality when so known is absolutely rational.' An even higher point may have been reached by that triumphant theologian cited by Mr Thomson, whose book I have not read but whose title I greatly admire : *The Riddle of the Universe Solved*. Naturally sophisticated intelligence of this kind was the normal means of contact with literature. Mr MacLure tells us that James Cappon judged poetry according to whether it had a 'rationalized concept' or not – this would have been a very common critical assumption. Sara Jeanette Duncan shows us a clergyman borrowing a copy of Browning's *Sordello*, no easy reading, and returning it with original suggestions for interpretation. Such an interest in ideas is not merely cultivated but exuberant.

But using language as one would use an axe, formulating arguments with sharp cutting edges that will help to clarify one's view of the landscape, remains a rhetorical and not a poetic achievement. To quote Yeats again, one can refute Hegel (perhaps even St Paul) but not the *Song of Sixpence*. To create a disinterested structure of words, in poetry or in fiction, is a very different achievement, and it is clear that an intelligent and able rhetorician finds it particularly hard to understand how different it is. A rhetorician practising poetry is apt to express himself in spectral arguments, generalizations that escape the feeling of possible refutation only by being vast enough to contain it, or vaporous enough to elude it. The mystique of Canadianism was accompanied by an intellectual tendency of this kind, as Mr Daniells indicates. World-views that avoided dialectic, of a theosophical or transcendentalist cast, became popular among the Canadian poets of that time, Roberts and Carman particularly, and later among painters, as the reminiscences of the Group of Seven make clear. Bucke's *Cosmic Consciousness*, though not mentioned by any of our authors so far as I remember, is an influential Canadian book in this area. When minor rhetorically-minded poets sought what Samuel Johnson calls, though in a very different context, the 'grandeur of generality', the result is what is so well described by Mr Beattie as 'jejune chatter about infinity', and the like.

Mr Watt's very important chapter on the literature of protest isolates another rhetorical tradition. In the nineteenth century the common assumption that nature had revealed the truth of progress, and that it was the duty of reason to accommodate that truth to mankind, could be either a conservative or a radical view. But in either case it was a revolutionary doctrine, introducing the conception of change as the key to the social process. In those whom Mr Watt calls proletarian social Darwinists, and who represented 'the unholy fusion of secularism, science and social discontent', there was a strong tendency to regard literature as a product and a symbol of a ruling-class mentality, with, as we have tried to indicate, some justification. Hence radicals tended either to hope that 'the literature of the future will be the powerful ally of Democracy and Labour Reform', or to assume that serious thought and action would bypass the creative writer entirely, building a scientific socialism and leaving him to his Utopian dreams.

The radicalism of the period up to the Russian Revolution was, from a later point of view, largely undifferentiated. A labour magazine could regard Ignatius Donnelly, with his anti-Semitic and other crank views, as an advanced thinker equally with William Morris and Edward Bellamy. Similarly, even today, in Western Canadian elections, a protest vote may go Social Credit or N.D.P. without much regard to the difference in political philosophy between these parties. The depression introduced a dialectic into Canadian social thought which profoundly affected its literature. In Mr Watt's striking phrase, 'the Depression was like an intense magnetic field that deflected the courses of all the poets who went through it.' In this period there were, of course, the inevitable manifestoes, assuring the writer that only social significance, as understood by Marxism, would bring vitality to his work. The *New Frontier*, a far-left journal of that period referred to several times in this book, shows an uneasy sense on the part of its contributors that this literary elixir of youth might have to be mixed with various other potions, not all favourable to the creative process: attending endless meetings, organizing, agitating, marching, demonstrating, or joining the Spanish Loyalists. It is easy for the critic to point out the fallacy of judging the merit of literature by its subject-matter, but these arguments over the role of 'propaganda' were genuine and serious moral conflicts. Besides helping to shape the argument of such novels as Grove's *The Master of the Mill* and Callaghan's *They Shall Inherit the Earth*, they raised the fundamental issue of the role of the creative mind in society, and by doing so helped to give a maturity and depth to Canadian writing which is a permanent part of its heritage.

It is not surprising, given this background, that the belief in the inspiration of literature by social significance continued to be an active force long after it had ceased to be attached to any specifically Marxist or other political programmes. It is still strong in the *Preview* group in the forties, and in their immediate successors, though the best of them have developed in different directions. The theme of social realism is at its most attractive, and least theoretical, in the poetry of Souster. The existentialist movement, with its emphasis on the self-determination of social attitudes, seems to have had very little direct influence in Canada : Mr Beattie's comment on the absence of the existential in Pratt suggests that this lack of influence may be significant.

During the last decade or so a kind of social Freudianism has been taking shape, mainly in the United States, as a democratic counterpart of Marxism. Here society is seen as controlled by certain anxieties, real or imaginary, which are designed to repress or sublimate human impulses toward a greater freedom. These impulses include the creative and the sexual, which are closely linked. The enemy of the poet is not the capitalist but the 'square', or representative of repressive morality. The advantage of this attitude is that it preserves the position of rebellion against society for the poet, without imposing on him any specific social obligations. This movement has had a rather limited development in Canada, somewhat surprisingly considering how easy a target the square is in Canada: it has influenced Layton and many younger Montreal poets, but has not affected fiction to any great degree, though there may be something of it in Richler. It ignores the old political alignments : the Communists are usually regarded as Puritanic and repressive equally with the bourgeoisie, and a recent poem of Layton's contrasts the social hypocrisy in Canada with contemporary Spain. Thus it represents to some extent a return to the undifferentiated radicalism of a century before, though no longer in a political context.

As the centre of Canadian life moves from the fortress to the metropolis, the garrison mentality changes correspondingly. It begins as an expression of the moral values generally accepted in the group as a whole, and then, as society gets more complicated and more in control of its environment, it becomes more of a revolutionary garrison within a metropolitan society. But though it changes from a defence of to an attack on what society accepts as conventional standards, the literature it produces, at every stage, tends to be rhetorical, an illustration or allegory of certain social attitudes. These attitudes help to unify the mind of the writer by externalizing his enemy, the enemy being the anti-creative elements in life as he sees life. To approach these elements in a less rhetorical way would introduce the theme of self-conflict, a more perilous but ultimately more rewarding theme. The conflict involved is between the poetic impulse to construct and the rhetorical impulse to assert, and the victory of the former is the sign of the maturing of the writer.

Notes on Authors

HUBERT AQUIN: a leading Separatist, was born in Montreal and received his *licence en philosophie* from the University of Montreal. He spent three years at the Institut d'Études Politiques of the University of Paris, and then returned to the University of Montreal where he studied for one year at the Institut d'Histoire. He has worked as a radio and T.V. producer with the Canadian Broadcasting Company and won many awards for films directed for the National Film Board. His first novel, *Prochain épisode*, was published in 1965. He is about to publish his third novel, *L'Antiphonaire*.

MARGARET ATWOOD was born in Ottawa in 1939, and has lived in the Quebec northland, Toronto, Vancouver, Boston and Montreal. She is now living in Edmonton, Alberta. Her first collection of poetry, *The Circle Game*, won the Governor-General's Award, and her second, *The Animals In That Country*, won first prize in the Centennial Commission's poetry competition. Her novel, *The Edible Woman*, was published in England in 1969.

EARLE BIRNEY is the author of nine books of poetry and two novels. His awards include the Stephen Leacock medal for humour, and the Canada Council medal for outstanding achievement in the arts. He has been associated with various universities in Canada and the U.S.A., both as a Chaucerian scholar and as a writer in residence. He has made extensive reading tours in North and South America and recently in Australia and New Zealand.

MARIE-CLAIRE BLAIS was born in Quebec in 1939 and educated at Laval University. She then studied for a year in France and now lives in Wellfleet, Massachusetts. Her first novel, *La Belle tête* (*Mad Shadows*), was followed by *Tête blanche* and *A Season in the Life of Emmanuel*.

GEORGE BOWERING teaches at Sir George Williams University in Montreal. He has published a novel, *Mirror on the Floor* (1967), and seven books of poetry, of which the last two, *Rocky Mountain Foot* and *The Gangs of Kosmos*, appeared in 1968 and 1969.

AUSTIN C. CLARKE was born in Barbados, studied at the University of Toronto, and then taught for a while at a West Indian school. In 1955 he emigrated to Canada and now lives in Toronto. He is a visiting professor at Yale and a Jacob Ziskind lecturer at Brandies University. His novels include *The Survivors of the Crossing, Amongst Thistles and Thorns* and *The Meeting Point*.

LEONARD COHEN was born in Montreal in 1934 and educated at McGill and Columbia Universities. His first collection of poems, *Let Us Compare Mythologies*, was followed by *Spice-box of Earth, Flowers for Hitler, Parasites of Heaven* and *Selected Poems 1956–68*. He has also written two novels: *The Favorite Game* and *Beautiful Losers*. He divides his time between Montreal and New York, and has recently begun composing songs which he has recorded himself.

JOHN ROBERT COLOMBO lives in Toronto, where he is one of the editors of *Tamarack Review*. He has published four books of poetry, the last two entitled *Abracadabra* and *John Toronto*.

NEIL COMPTON was born in Montreal, served on loan to the British Army during the Second World War, and studied at McGill, the London School of Economics and Pembroke College, Cambridge. He is Professor of English at Sir George Williams University, Montreal, and contributes regularly to *Commentary, New American Review*, and a number of Canadian magazines. Married, he lives with his wife and children in Montreal.

RÉJEAN DUCHARME was born in 1941 at Saint-Félix de Valois, Quebec. He has worked in various jobs: cinema attendant, workman, shoe salesman, office boy. He has travelled in the United States and Mexico, and now lives on an island in Saint-Ignace de Loyola, Berthier, Quebec. He has published two novels, *L'Avalée des avalés* and *Le Nez qui voque*.

NORTHROP FRYE was born in Sherbrooke, Quebec, in 1912, and educated at Moncton, New Brunswick, and at Victoria College and Emmanuel College, University of Toronto. He completed his studies at Oxford and was principal of Victoria College, University of Toronto, from 1959 to 1966, when he became University Professor. His books include *Fearful Symmetry: A Study of William Blake, Anatomy of Criticism, By Liberal Things* and *The Modern Century*.

ROBERT FULFORD: a leading Canadian literary critic, is at present editing *Saturday Night Magazine* in Toronto. His books include *This was Expo* and *Crisis at the Victory Burlesk*, a collection of his essays. He is currently working on a book-length study of a major Canadian writer.

J. K. GALBRAITH was born in 1908 at Iona Station, Ontario, and educated at Toronto, California and Cambridge universities. He has taught at the universities of California and Princeton and is now Paul M. Warburg professor of Economics at Harvard. From 1961–3 he was American ambassador to India. He is married, with three sons. J. K. Galbraith is a well-known contributor to leading American journals and to the *Financial Times*. His books include *A Theory of Price Control, American Capitalism, The Affluent Society, The Great Crash 1929,* and *The Liberal Hour.*

MAVIS GALLANT was born in Montreal and came to live in Europe in 1950. Her books include *The Other Paris, Green Water, Green Sky* and *An Unmarried Man's Summer.* Her short stories appear regularly in the *New Yorker.*

ROLAND GIGUÈRE was born in Montreal in 1929 and educated at the École des Arts Graphiques and the École Estienne, in Paris. He conducts a studio in Montreal where he produces 'Éditions Erta', booklets of poems. His first collection of poems, *Faire naître* was followed by *Les Armes blanches* and *Le Défaut des ruines est d'avoir des habitants.*

JOHN GLASSCO, poet and translator of French-Canadian poetry into English, divides his time between Montreal and a farm in Foster, Quebec. His most recent collection of poems, *A Point of Sky*, was published in 1964, and the Oxford University Press will shortly publish a memoir about his years as a young writer in Paris in the late 1920s.

JACQUES GODBOUT was born in Montreal in 1933 and was educated at the University of Montreal. He has travelled widely in Mexico, Africa, Europe and the West Indies. He published four books of poetry and three novels, *L'Aquarium, Le Couteau sur la table,* and *Salut Galarneau.* With the National Film Board, he has produced six short films and one feature, which have won awards in Venice, Chicago, and Paris.

ANNE HÉBERT was born in 1916 in Montreal. An invalid for many years owing to illness as a child, she was educated by her parents. Her collections of poems include *Le Tombeau des rois* and *Poèmes*. She has also published a surrealistic novel, *Les Chambres de bois*, and a collection of stories, *Le Torrent*.

GILLES HÉNAULT was born in Saint-Majorique, Quebec, in 1920. His collections of poems include *Totems*, *Voyage au pays de mémoire*, and *Sémaphore*.

JOHN HERBERT is the pseudonym of John Brundage, who was born in Toronto and has worked for a dozen years in the theatre. He has supported himself at many assorted jobs and is currently a waiter in a men's club. *Fortune and Men's Eyes* was first produced at the Actors' Playhouse, New York, in 1967, and has recently been produced in London. The play has been published by Grove Press.

DARYL HINE was born in 1936 in Burbary, British Columbia, and educated at McGill University. He worked for three years on the staff of the Canadian Legation in Paris, and now lives in the United States. His collections of poetry include *Five Poems* and *The Devil's Picture Book*. He has also published a novel, *The Prince of Darkness & Co.*, and an account of his experiences in Poland, *Polish sub-titles: Impressions of a Journey*.

HUGH HOOD: born in Toronto in 1928, studied at the university of Toronto, and afterwards lived for several years in Connecticut. He is married with four children, and now lives in Montreal, where he teaches at the University of Montreal. His novels include *White Figure, White Ground* and *The Camera Always Lies*, and he has published two collections of stories, *Flying A Red Kite* and *Around the Mountain*.

NAIM KATTAN was born in Iraq in 1928, and studied law in Baghdad and French literature at the Sorbonne. In 1962–3 he lectured in Social Sciences at Laval University, Quebec. He is a member of the editorial board of *Les Lettres Nouvelles* (for which he has edited a special edition on Canadian Literature), and is a correspondent for *La Quinzaine Littéraire*, and a regular contributor to *Le Devoir, Canadian Literature, Liberté*, and *Preuves* (Paris). He is at present in charge of the literary section of the Canada Council.

WILLIAM KILBOURN was educated at Toronto, Oxford and Harvard Universities. Married, with five children, he is Professor of Humanities at York University, Toronto, and an editor of *Tamarack Review* and *The Canadian Forum*. His books include *The Firebrand, The Elements Combined*, and *The Making of a Nation*.

MARGARET LAURENCE was born in Neepawa, Manitoba, in 1926, and educated at the University of Manitoba. Married, with two children, she has lived in Somaliland and Ghana, and for the past few years in England. Her novels include *This Side Jordan, The Stone Angel*, and *A Jest of God*. She has also published a collection of stories, *The Tomorrow-Tamer*, and a travel book, *The Prophet's Camel Bell*.

IRVING LAYTON was born in Romania in 1912, and came to Montreal at the age of one. He was educated at Macdonald College and McGill University. Married, with three children, he teaches at York University. His poetry collections include *Here and Now, The Black Huntsmen, The Improved Binoculars*, and *A Red Carpet for the Sun*, which won him a Governor-General's Award. His *Collected Poems* were published in 1965.

NORMAN LEVINE was born in 1924 and educated at McGill University. He left Canada in 1949 for England, and has lived there since, except for 1965–6 when he was resident writer at the University of New Brunswick. His books include *Canada Made Me*, and *One Way Ticket*, a collection of short stories. He is one of the writers due to appear in the Penguin Modern Stories Series. Married, he lives in St Ives, Cornwall, with his wife and three daughters. He has a new novel, *From a Seaside Town*, coming out in the summer.

JACK LUDWIG was born in Winnipeg in 1922 and educated at the University of Manitoba and U.C.L.A. One of his numerous short stories was awarded an *Atlantic* 'First' and others have been included in two O. Henry Prize collections. He has published two novels: *Confusions* and *Above Ground*. Married, with two children, he works in the English Department of the State University, New York.

CLAIRE MARTIN lives in Ottawa. She has published two novels, *Douxamer* (1960) and *Quand j'aurai payé ton visage* (1962), and a volume of short stories, *Avec ou sans amour*, winner of the Prix du Cercle Livre de France (1958). In 1965 the first volume of her autobiography, *Dans un gant de fer*, received the Prix France-Quebec and the Prix de la Province de Quebec. The second volume was given the Governor-General's Award.

JOHN METCALF was born in England in 1938 and studied at Bristol University. He came to Canada in 1962 and taught high school in Montreal, where he still lives. His stories have appeared in *Canadian Forum*, *Prism*, and *Tamarack Review*. A collection of short stories, *The Lady Who Sold Furniture*, will appear early in 1970. He was awarded a Canada Council grant in 1968.

BRIAN MOORE was born in Belfast in 1921. After the war he went to Poland as a member of the U.N.R.R.A. mission, and in 1948 he became a Canadian citizen. His first novel, *The Lonely Passion of Judith Hearne*, was followed by *The Feast of Lupercal*, *The Luck of Ginger Coffey*, *An Answer from Limbo*, *The Emperor of Ice-Cream* and *I Am Mary Dunne*. He has held a Guggenheim Fellowship and has won the Governor-General's Award for Fiction. At present he lives in Malibu, California, with his wife.

ALICE MUNRO was educated at the University of Western Ontario, and now lives in Victoria, British Columbia, where she runs a bookshop with her husband. Her short stories have appeared in *Tamarack* and have been broadcast on the C.B.C. She won the Governor-General's Award for her first collection of stories, *Dance of the Happy Shades*, which was published in 1968.

JOHN NEWLOVE was born in Regina in 1938 and is now settled in British Columbia. He has worked as a teacher, radio announcer and labourer. His poetry has appeared in American, Mexican, and European magazines, and his first commercially published collection of poems, *Black Night Window*, was published in 1968.

ALDEN NOWLAN is thirty-four years old. He was born in Windsor, Nova Scotia, and left school early, working as a farm labourer and a sawmill worker and managing a hillbilly orchestra. Eventually he became a newspaperman and is now news editor of the *Telegraph-Journal* in Saint-John, New Brunswick. He has won a Guggenheim Fellowship and has twice received Canada Council grants. He has published six volumes of poetry, the most recent being *Bread, Wine and Salt*.

JEAN-GUY PILON was born in 1930 at Saint-Polycarpe, Quebec, and studied law at the University of Montreal. He lives in Montreal, where he works for the Canadian Broadcasting Company and is also literary director of the review *Liberté*. His collections of poetry include *La Fiancée du matin* and *Recours au pays*.

ALFRED PURDY was born near Wooler, Ontario, in 1918, and served in the R.C.A.F. during the Second World War. He is the author of ten collections of poems, including *The Cariboo Horses*, which won the Governor-General's Award in 1965. His poems have appeared in almost every literary magazine in Canada, and at least fourteen of his radio and T.V. plays have been produced by the Canadian Broadcasting Company. His volume of poems, *North of Summer*, was published after he had spent a summer on Baffin Island, and his most recent book is *Wild Grape Wine*. He now lives with his wife in south-eastern Ontario.

JAMES REANEY was born in 1926 near Stratford, Ontario, and was educated at the University of Toronto. He teaches at the University of Western Ontario and is founder of *Alphabet: a semi-annual devoted to the iconography of the imagination*. His books include *The Red Heart*, *A Suit of Nettles* and *The Killdeer and Other Plays*. *The Killdeer* has been produced in Toronto and Glasgow; *Colours in the Dark*, a two-act play, at the Festival Theatre, Stratford, Ontario, and at the Playhouse Theatre, Vancouver.

MORDECAI RICHLER, born in Montreal in 1931, has been living in London for the past twelve years with his wife and five children. His novels include *The Apprenticeship of Duddy Kravitz* and *Cocksure*. His stories and essays appear in *Encounter*, *Commentary*, *New American Review*, the *New Statesman*, and the *New York Review of Books*. He was awarded a Guggenheim Fellowship in 1962 and a Canada Council Senior Arts Fellowship in 1966.

FRANKLIN RUSSELL was born in New Zealand in 1926 and came to Canada in 1954, settling in Toronto. His books include *Watchers at the Pond*, *Argen the Gull*, and *The Secret Islands*. He was awarded a Guggenheim Fellowship in 1964 and a Canada Council grant in 1967. At present, he lives on a farm in Frenchtown, New Jersey, with his wife and two sons.

HECTOR DE SAINT-DENYS-GARNEAU (1912–43), was born in Montreal and educated at Collège Saint-Marie and the École des Beaux Arts. An attack of rheumatic fever in 1928 left him with a damaged heart, and

330 Notes on Authors

a serious illness in 1933 put an end to his studies. He was one of the founders of *La Relève*, a literary review founded in sympathy with the Christian revival movement in France. Before he died in self-imposed exile in 1943, he published a single collection of poems, *Regards et jeux dans l'espace* (1937), which initiated the whole modern movement in French-Canadian poetry. A second collection, *Les Solitudes*, and his *Journal*, were published posthumously.

PIERRE ELLIOTT TRUDEAU was born in 1920 in Montreal. He was educated at Collège Jean-de-Brébeuf, the University of Montreal, Harvard, the University of Paris and the London School of Economics. He was, for a time, a contributing editor of *Cité Libre* and was elected to parliament in 1965. In April 1967 he was appointed Minister of Justice and he has been Prime Minister since April 1968.

WILLIAM WEINTRAUB was born in Montreal in 1926 and educated at McGill University. He now writes and produces documentaries for the National Film Board of Canada. His novel, *Why Rock the Boat*, was published in 1961.

DAVID WEVILL was born in Japan in 1935, moved to Canada as a child and grew up in Ottawa. He came to England in 1954 to read History and English at Cambridge and, apart from two years which he spent teaching English at Mandalay University, he has lived in England ever since. He has published two collections of poems: *Birth of a Shark* and *A Christ of the Ice-Floes*, and is one of three poets represented in Penguin Modern Poets 4. He won the Richard Hillary Prize in 1965.

GEORGE WHALLEY was born in Kingston, Ontario, in 1915, and was educated at Bishop's University, at Oxford as a Rhodes scholar, and at King's College, London. He served in the navy during the Second World War and is now Professor of English at Queen's University, Kingston, Ontario. He was elected to the Royal Society of Canada in 1959. His books include *Poetic Process: An Essay in Poetics*, *Coleridge and Sara Hutchinson and the Asra Poems* and *The Legend of John Hornby*.

ADÈLE WISEMAN was born and educated in Winnipeg, Manitoba. She has travelled fairly extensively, and held a variety of jobs, including the teaching of English Literature at Macdonald College of McGill University. Besides the recently completed novel *Crackpot*, she has written another novel, *The Sacrifice*, and a play, *The Lovebound*.

GEORGE WOODCOCK was born in 1912 in Winnipeg, but left Canada at an early age and spent most of his childhood and youth in England, where he edited the little magazine NOW from 1940–47. Since 1959 he has edited *Canadian Literature*, a quarterly which he founded. He has published travel books, biography, criticism, poetry, political commentary, and art criticism. His own favourites among his books are *Incas and Other Men*, *Anarchism*, and *The Crystal Spirit* (a study of George Orwell). He is married and lives in Vancouver.

More About Penguins

Penguinews, which appears every month, contains details of all the new books issued by Penguins as they are published. From time to time it is supplemented by *Penguins in Print*, which is a complete list of all books published by Penguins which are in print. (There are well over three thousand of these.)

A specimen copy of *Penguinews* will be sent to you free on request, and you can become a subscriber for the price of the postage. For a year's issues (including the complete lists) please send 4s. if you live in the United Kingdom, or 8s. if you live elsewhere. Just write to Dept EP, Penguin Books Ltd, Harmondsworth, Middlesex, enclosing a cheque or postal order, and your name will be added to the mailing list.

Some other books in the same series are described on the following pages.

Note: *Penguinews* and *Penguins in Print* are not available in the U.S.A. or Canada

lso in the same series

Ezekiel Mphahlele

AFRICAN WRITING TODAY

African Writing Today provides a cross-section (in translation,
where necessary) of recent African work in English, French, and
Portuguese from the following countries:

Angola, Cameroun, Congo, Dahomey, Gambia, Ghana, Guinea,
Ivory Coast, Kenya, Moçambique, Nigeria, Ruanda, Senegal, Sierra
Leone, South Africa

The Writing Today Series

An interesting venture by Penguins which aims to inform the English-speaking reader of new developments in the literature of other countries.

The foll

Date Due

Australian Writing Today
Writers in the New Cuba
England Today : The Last Fifteen Years
New Writing in Czechoslovakia
Italian Writing Today
French Writing Today
South African Writing Today
Polish Writing Today
Latin American Writing Today
South African Writing Today
German Writing Today